FALLEN ANGEL™

HEROINE ADDICTION

FALLEN ANGEL™

HEROINE ADDICTION

IDW Publishing is:
Ted Adams, President
Robbie Robbins, EVP/Sr. Graphic Artist
Chris Ryall, Publisher/Editor-in-Chief
Clifford Meth, EVP of Strategies/Editorial
Alan Payne, VP of Sales
Neil Uyetake, Art Director
Tom Waltz, Editor
Andrew Steven Harris, Editor
Chris Mowry, Graphic Artist
Amauri Osorio, Graphic Artist
Dene Nee, Graphic Artist/Editor
Matthew Ruzicka, CPA, Controller
Alonzo Simon, Shipping Manager
Kris Oprisko, Editor/Foreign Lic. Rep.

Fallen Angel created by Peter David and David Lopez
Shi created by William Elliott Tucci

ISBN 978-1-60010-156-4
10 09 08 07 1 2 3 4 5

www.idwpublishing.com

Table of Contents

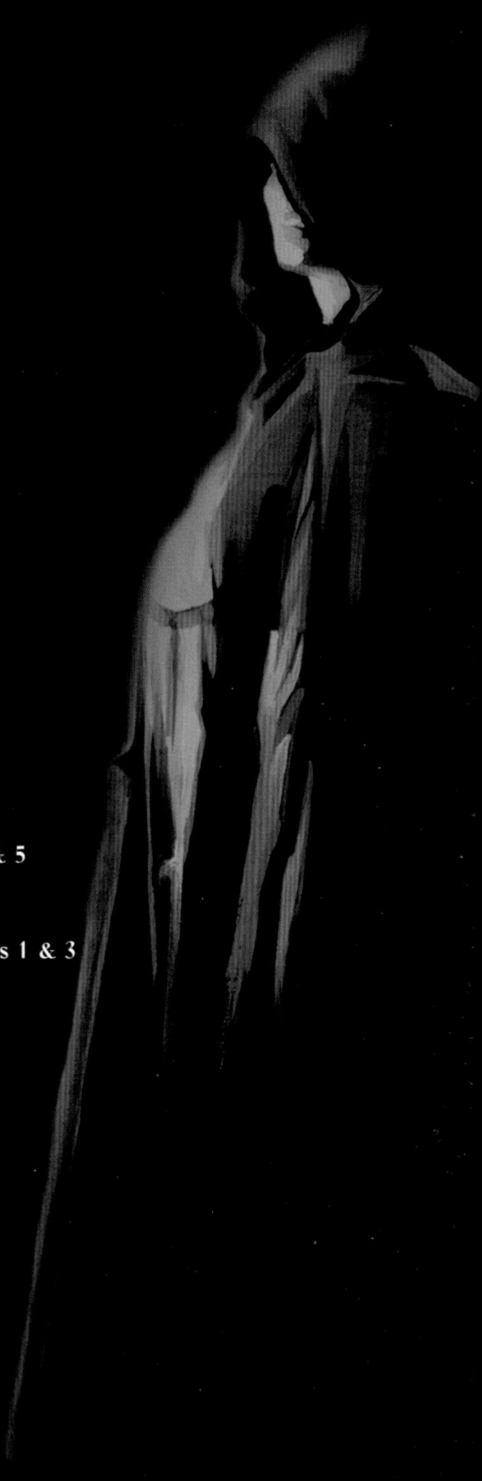

Written by Peter David
Cover & Art by Joe Corroney Chapter 1
Colors by Dave Bryant Chapter 1
Colors by George Kambadais Chapter 1
Art & Colors by J.K. Woodward, Chapters 2, 3, & 5
Covers by J.K. Woodward Chapters 1-5
Additional Cover Art Billy Tucci Chapters 1 & 3
Additional Color Covers Mark Sparacio Chapters 1 & 3
Art & Colors Dennis Calero Chapter 4

Letters by: Chris Mowry
Robbie Robbins
Neil Uyetake
Original Series Edited by: Chris Ryall
Andrew Steven Harris
Collection Edited by: Dene Nee
Book Design by: Chris Mowry & Neil Uyetake

Chapter 1

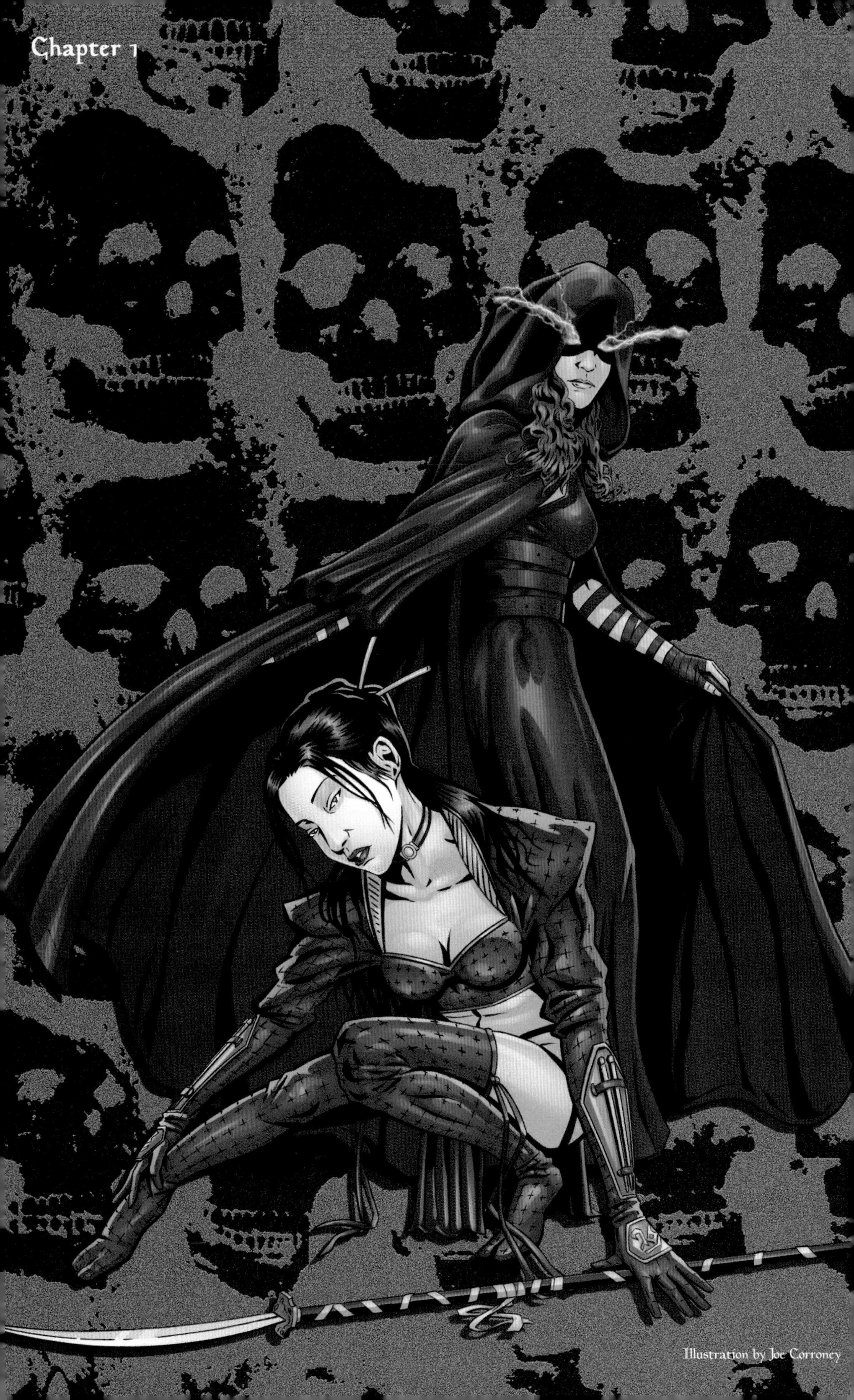

Illustration by Joe Corroney

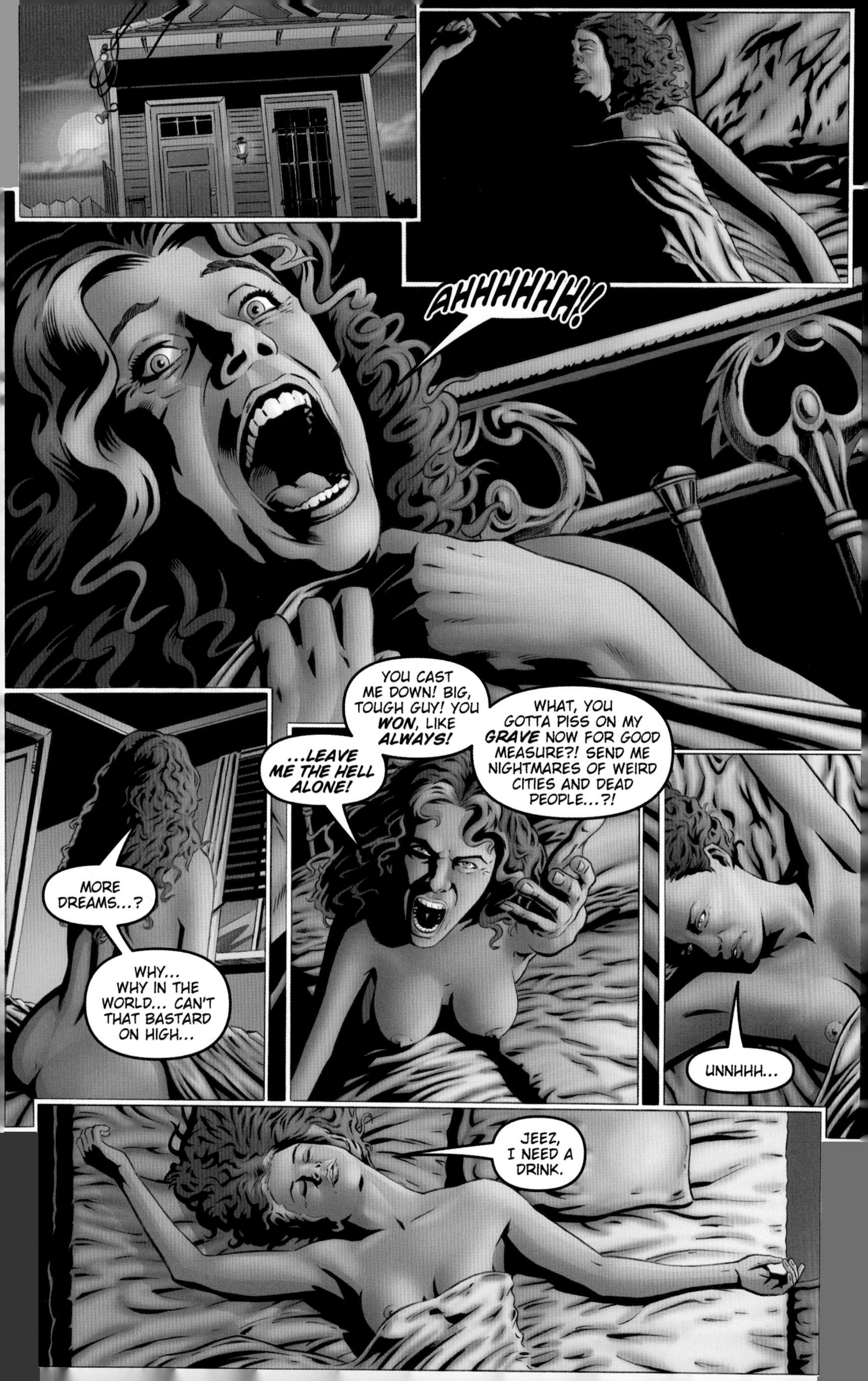
AHHHHHH!
MORE DREAMS...?
WHY... WHY IN THE WORLD... CAN'T THAT BASTARD ON HIGH...
...LEAVE ME THE HELL ALONE!
YOU CAST ME DOWN! BIG, TOUGH GUY! YOU WON, LIKE ALWAYS!
WHAT, YOU GOTTA PISS ON MY GRAVE NOW FOR GOOD MEASURE?! SEND ME NIGHTMARES OF WEIRD CITIES AND DEAD PEOPLE...?!
UNNHHH...
JEEZ, I NEED A DRINK.

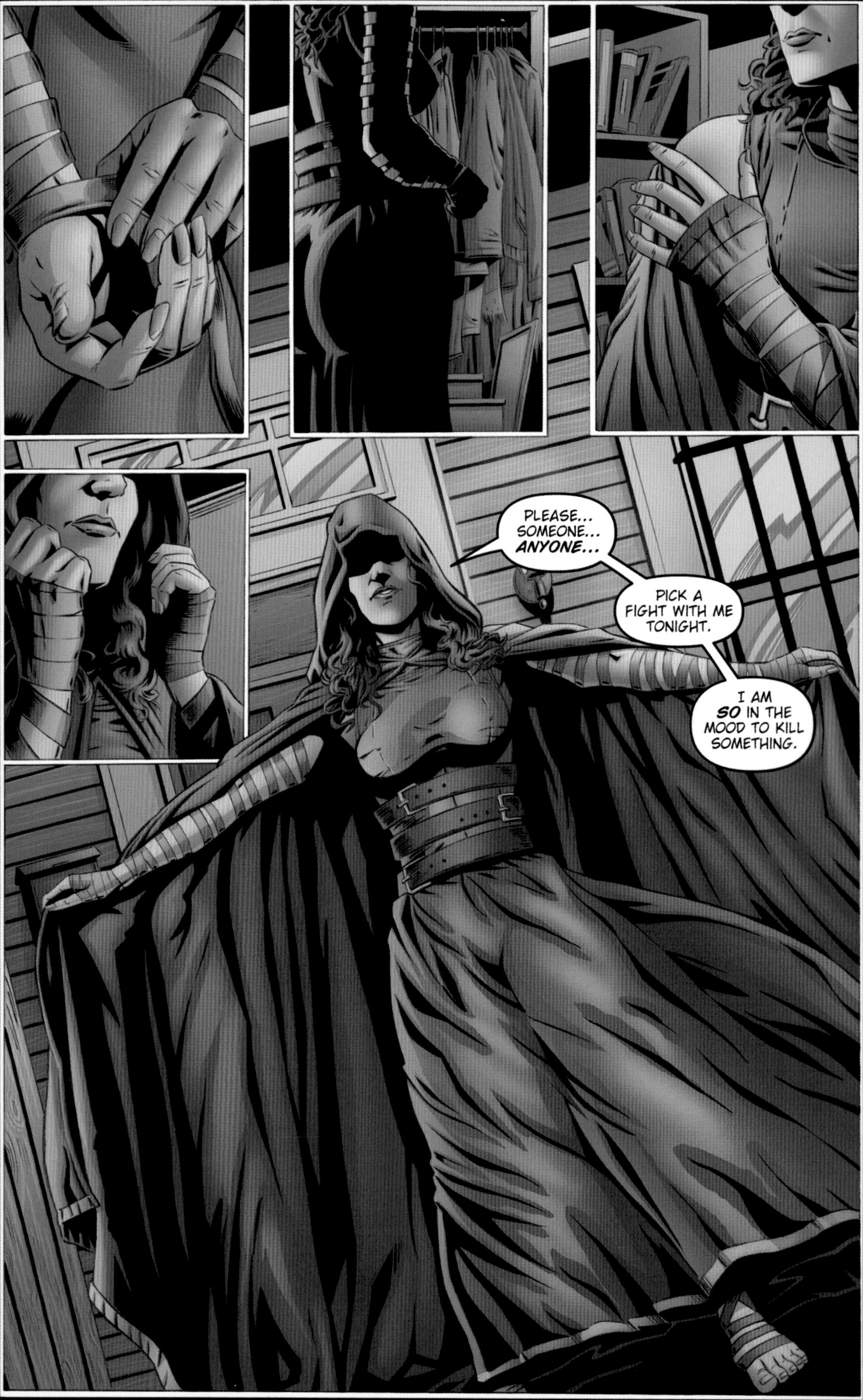
PLEASE... SOMEONE... *ANYONE...*
PICK A FIGHT WITH ME TONIGHT.
I AM *SO* IN THE MOOD TO KILL SOMETHING.

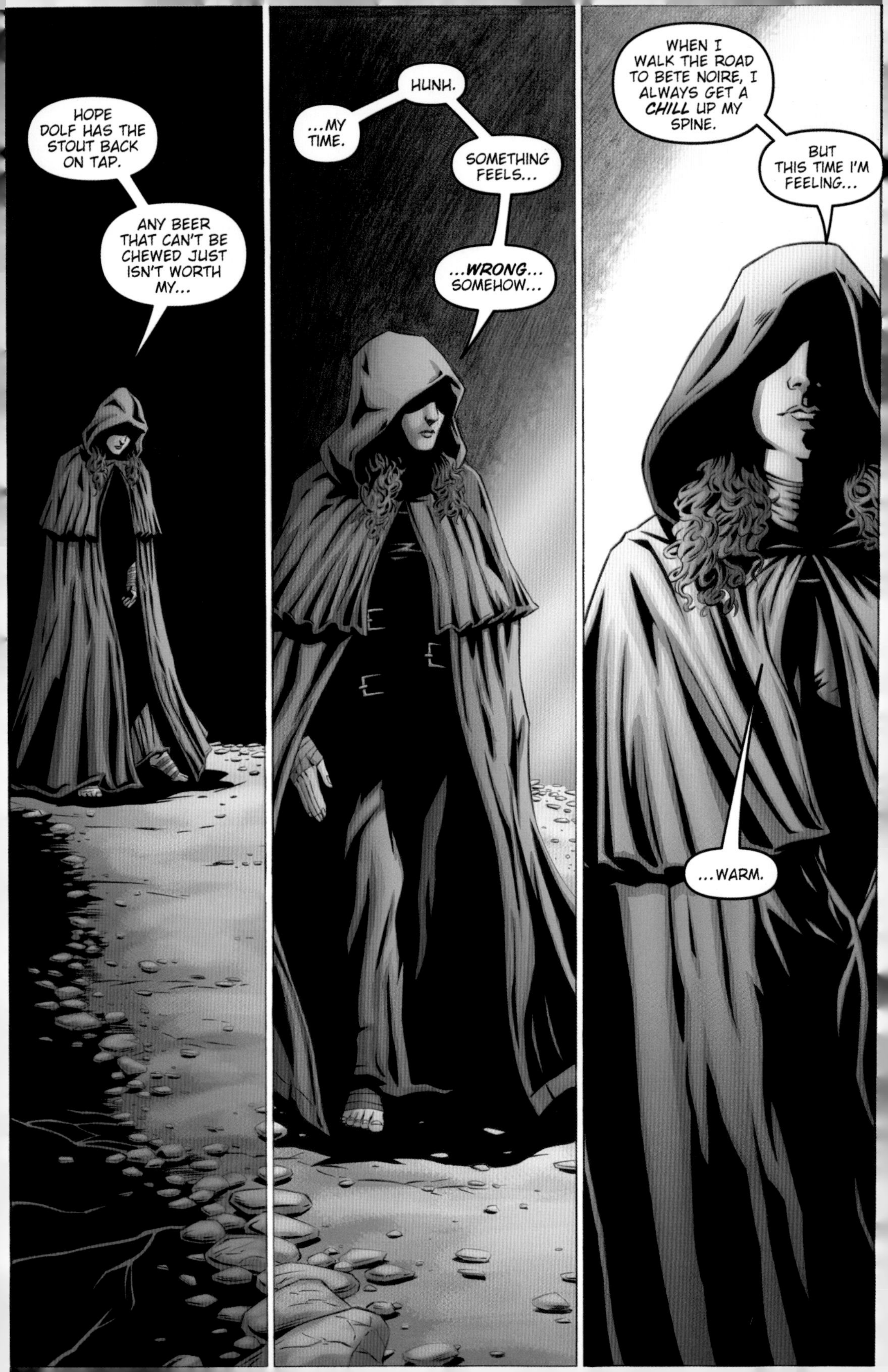
HOPE DOLF HAS THE STOUT BACK ON TAP.
ANY BEER THAT CAN'T BE CHEWED JUST ISN'T WORTH MY...
...MY TIME.
HUNH.
SOMETHING FEELS...
...WRONG... SOMEHOW...
WHEN I WALK THE ROAD TO BETE NOIRE, I ALWAYS GET A CHILL UP MY SPINE.
BUT THIS TIME I'M FEELING...
...WARM.

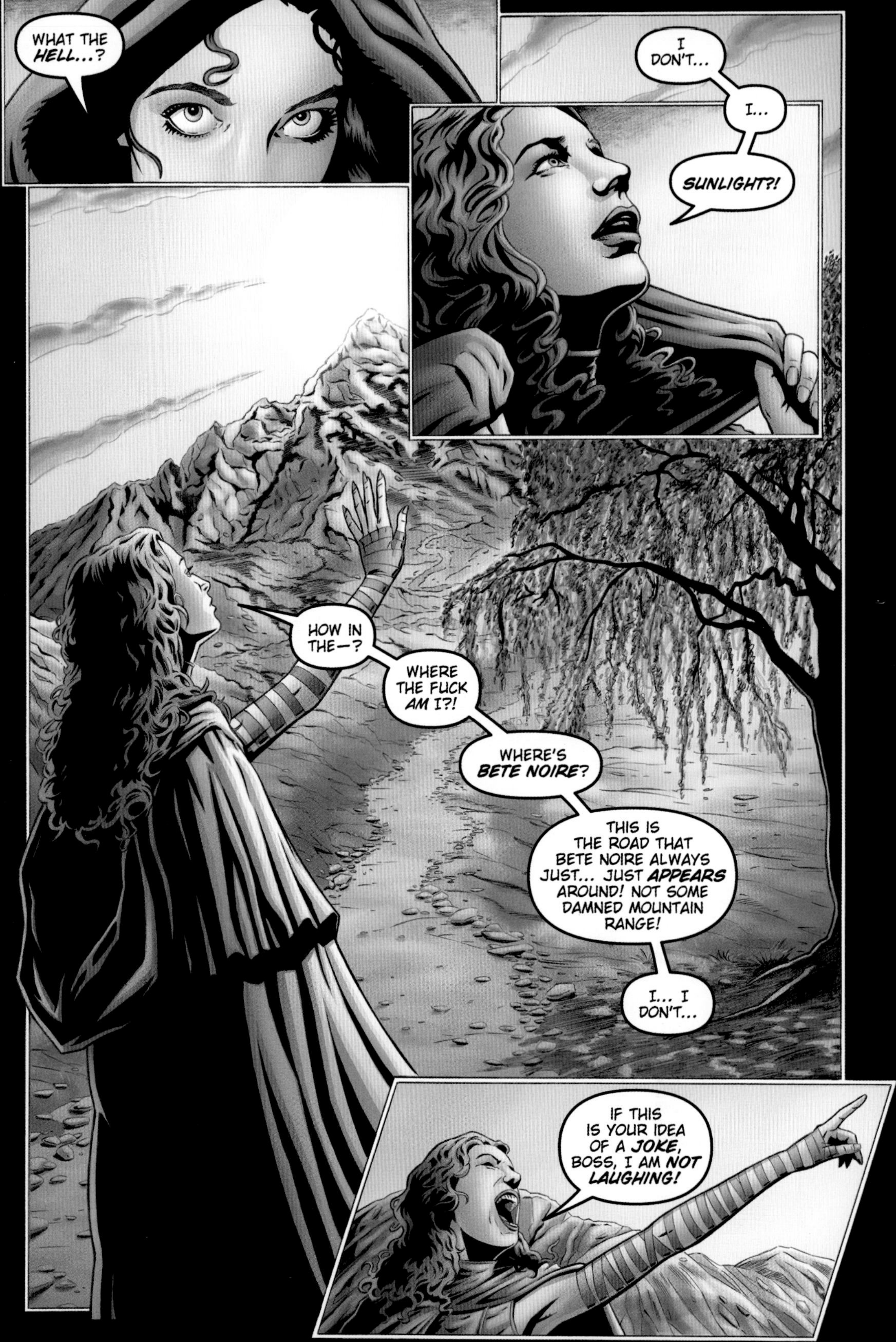

WHAT THE HELL...?
I DON'T...
I...
SUNLIGHT?!
HOW IN THE—?
WHERE THE FUCK AM I?!
WHERE'S BETE NOIRE?
THIS IS THE ROAD THAT BETE NOIRE ALWAYS JUST... JUST APPEARS AROUND! NOT SOME DAMNED MOUNTAIN RANGE!
I... I DON'T...
IF THIS IS YOUR IDEA OF A JOKE, BOSS, I AM NOT LAUGHING!

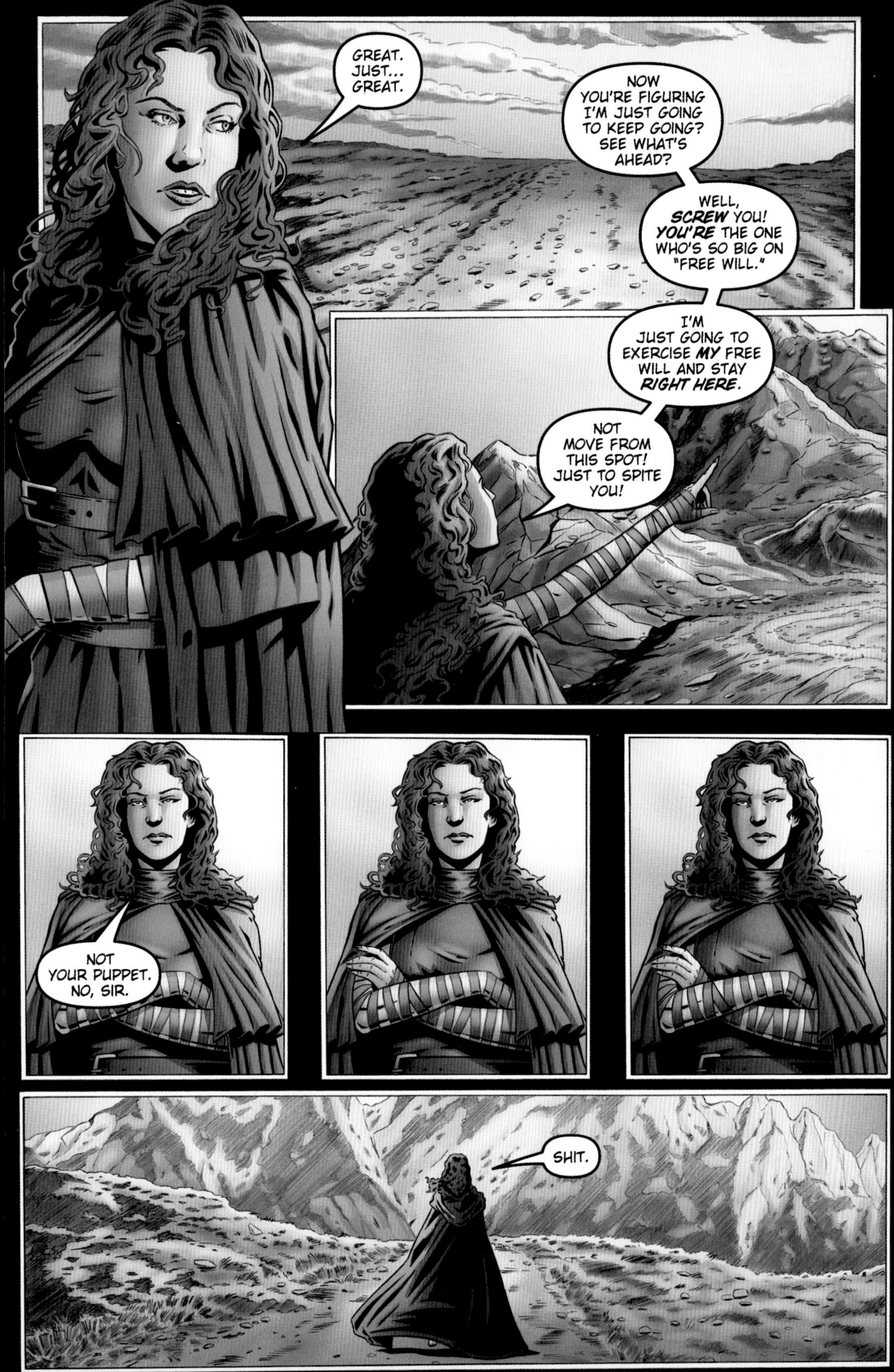
GREAT. JUST... GREAT.
NOW YOU'RE FIGURING I'M JUST GOING TO KEEP GOING? SEE WHAT'S AHEAD?
WELL, **SCREW** YOU! ***YOU'RE*** THE ONE WHO'S SO BIG ON "FREE WILL."
I'M JUST GOING TO EXERCISE ***MY*** FREE WILL AND STAY ***RIGHT HERE***.
NOT MOVE FROM THIS SPOT! JUST TO SPITE YOU!
NOT YOUR PUPPET. NO, SIR.
SHIT.

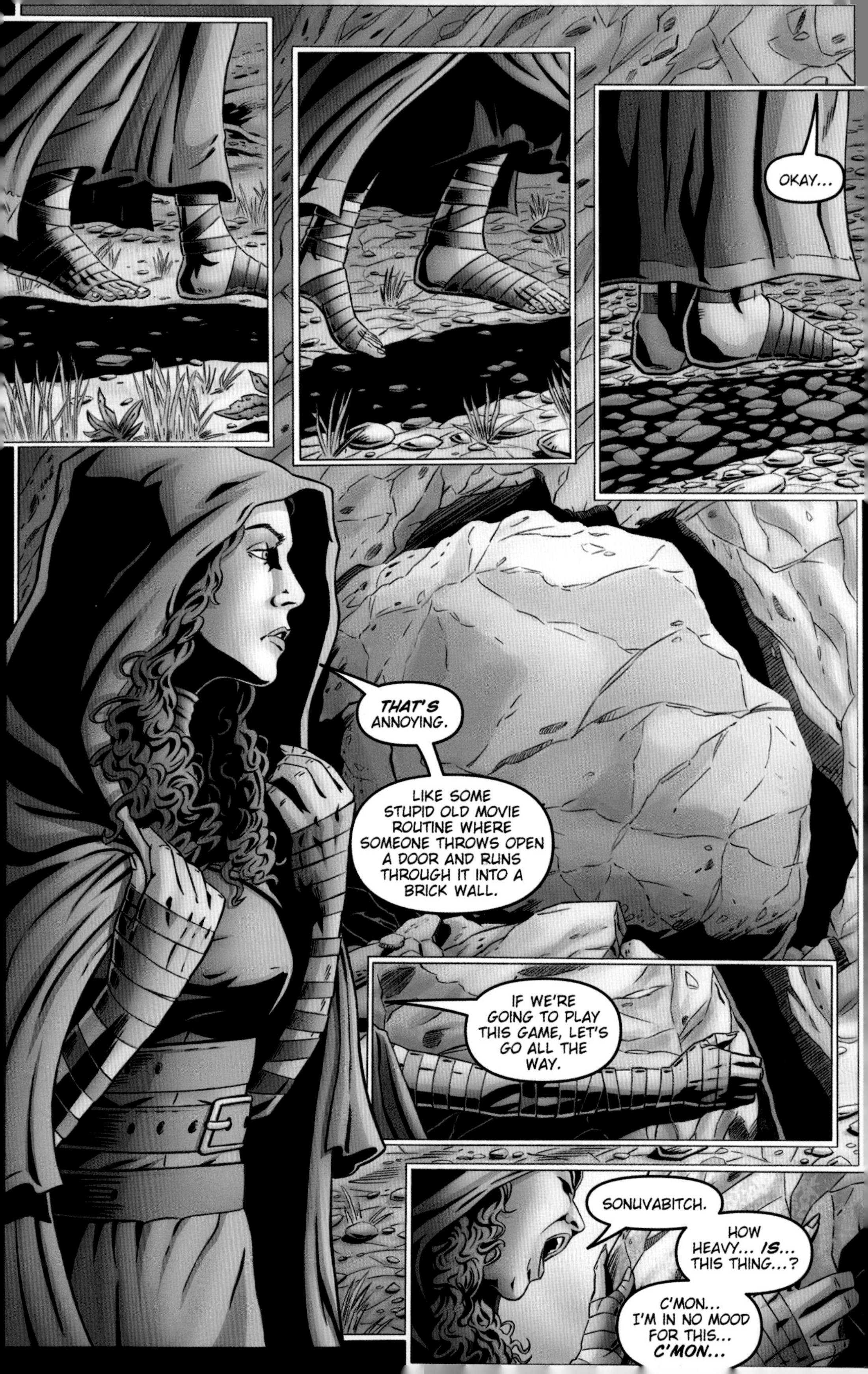
OKAY...
THAT'S ANNOYING.
LIKE SOME STUPID OLD MOVIE ROUTINE WHERE SOMEONE THROWS OPEN A DOOR AND RUNS THROUGH IT INTO A BRICK WALL.
IF WE'RE GOING TO PLAY THIS GAME, LET'S GO ALL THE WAY.
SONUVABITCH.
HOW HEAVY... *IS*... THIS THING...?
C'MON... I'M IN NO MOOD FOR THIS... ***C'MON...***

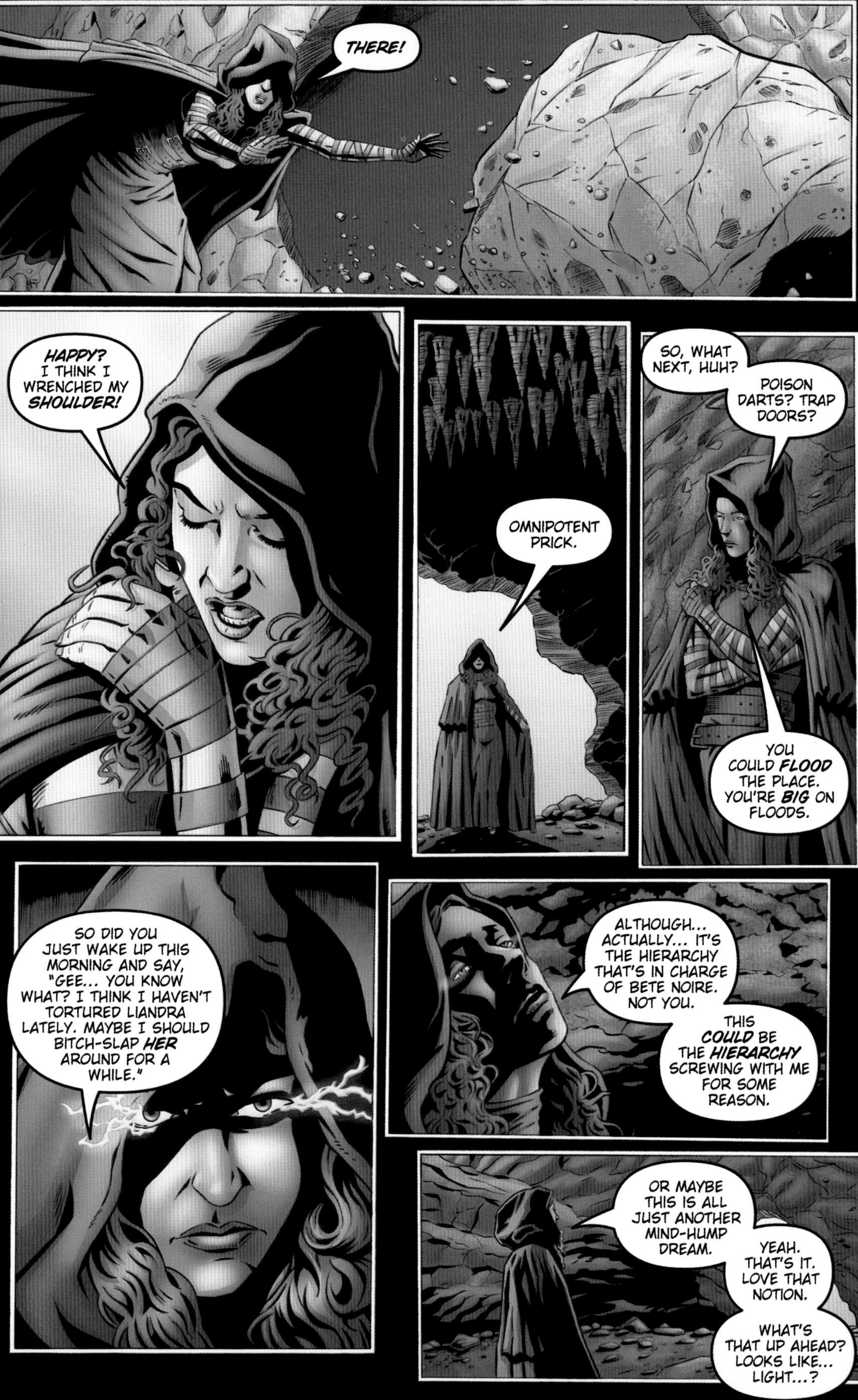
THERE!
HAPPY? I THINK I WRENCHED MY SHOULDER!
OMNIPOTENT PRICK.
SO, WHAT NEXT, HUH?
POISON DARTS? TRAP DOORS?
YOU COULD FLOOD THE PLACE. YOU'RE BIG ON FLOODS.
SO DID YOU JUST WAKE UP THIS MORNING AND SAY, "GEE... YOU KNOW WHAT? I THINK I HAVEN'T TORTURED LIANDRA LATELY. MAYBE I SHOULD BITCH-SLAP HER AROUND FOR A WHILE."
ALTHOUGH... ACTUALLY... IT'S THE HIERARCHY THAT'S IN CHARGE OF BETE NOIRE. NOT YOU.
THIS COULD BE THE HIERARCHY SCREWING WITH ME FOR SOME REASON.
OR MAYBE THIS IS ALL JUST ANOTHER MIND-HUMP DREAM.
YEAH. THAT'S IT. LOVE THAT NOTION.
WHAT'S THAT UP AHEAD? LOOKS LIKE... LIGHT...?

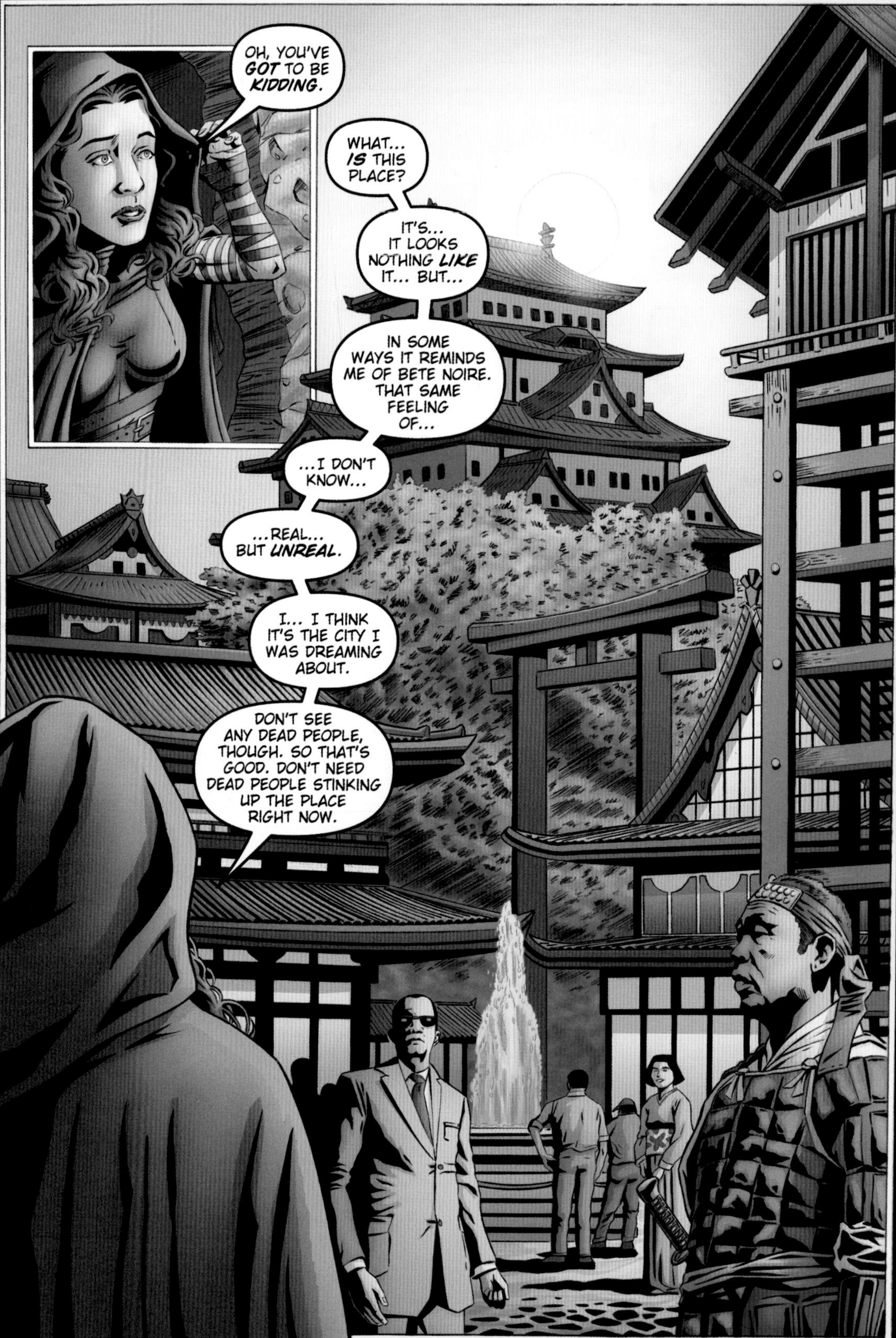
OH, YOU'VE *GOT* TO BE *KIDDING*.
WHAT... *IS* THIS PLACE?
IT'S... IT LOOKS NOTHING *LIKE* IT... BUT...
IN SOME WAYS IT REMINDS ME OF BETE NOIRE. THAT SAME FEELING OF...
...I DON'T KNOW...
...REAL... BUT *UNREAL*.
I... I THINK IT'S THE CITY I WAS DREAMING ABOUT.
DON'T SEE ANY DEAD PEOPLE, THOUGH. SO THAT'S GOOD. DON'T NEED DEAD PEOPLE STINKING UP THE PLACE RIGHT NOW.

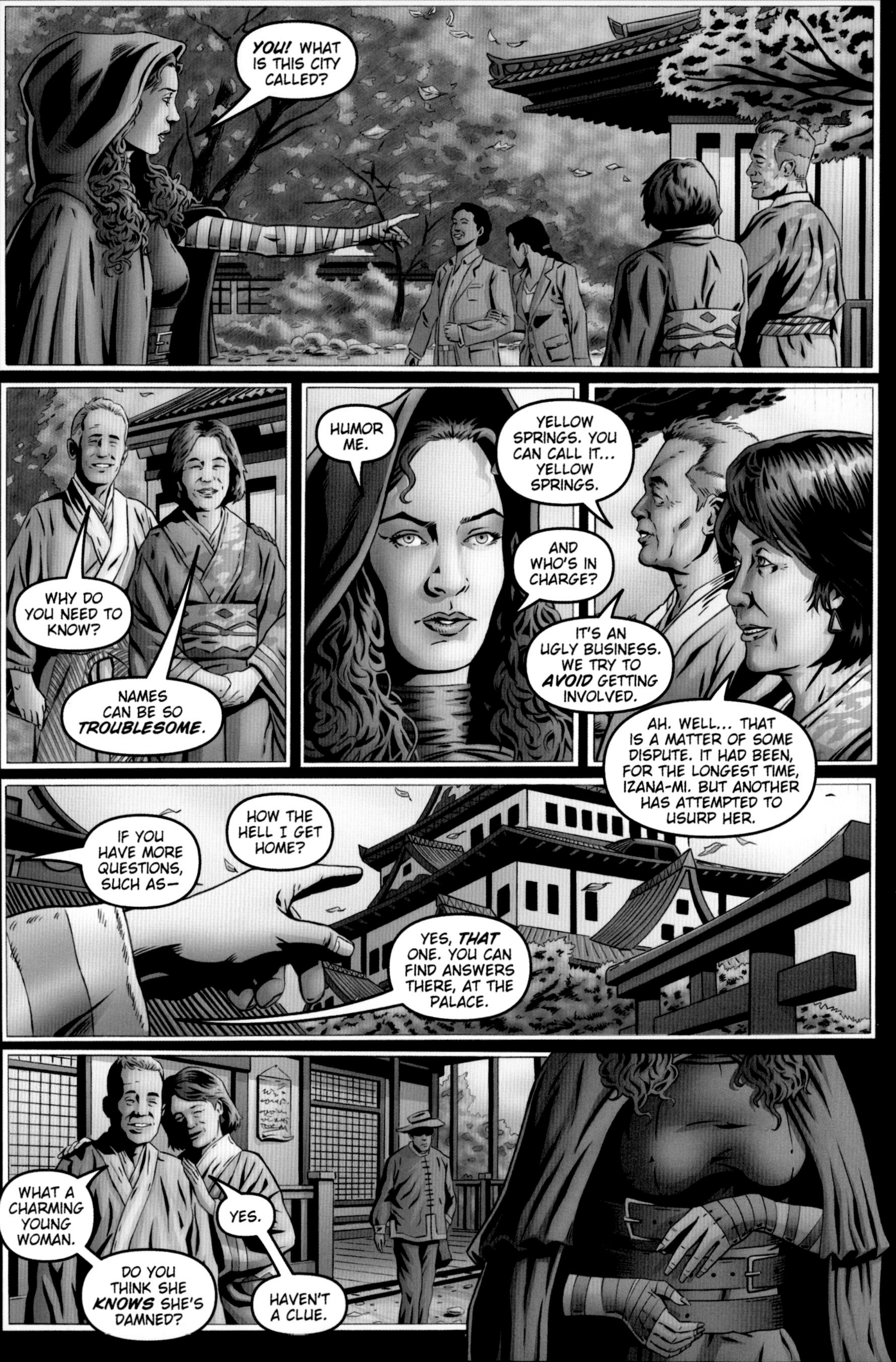
YOU! WHAT IS THIS CITY CALLED?
WHY DO YOU NEED TO KNOW?
NAMES CAN BE SO TROUBLESOME.
HUMOR ME.
YELLOW SPRINGS. YOU CAN CALL IT... YELLOW SPRINGS.
AND WHO'S IN CHARGE?
IT'S AN UGLY BUSINESS. WE TRY TO AVOID GETTING INVOLVED.
AH. WELL... THAT IS A MATTER OF SOME DISPUTE. IT HAD BEEN, FOR THE LONGEST TIME, IZANA-MI. BUT ANOTHER HAS ATTEMPTED TO USURP HER.
IF YOU HAVE MORE QUESTIONS, SUCH AS—
HOW THE HELL I GET HOME?
YES, THAT ONE. YOU CAN FIND ANSWERS THERE, AT THE PALACE.
WHAT A CHARMING YOUNG WOMAN.
YES.
DO YOU THINK SHE KNOWS SHE'S DAMNED?
HAVEN'T A CLUE.

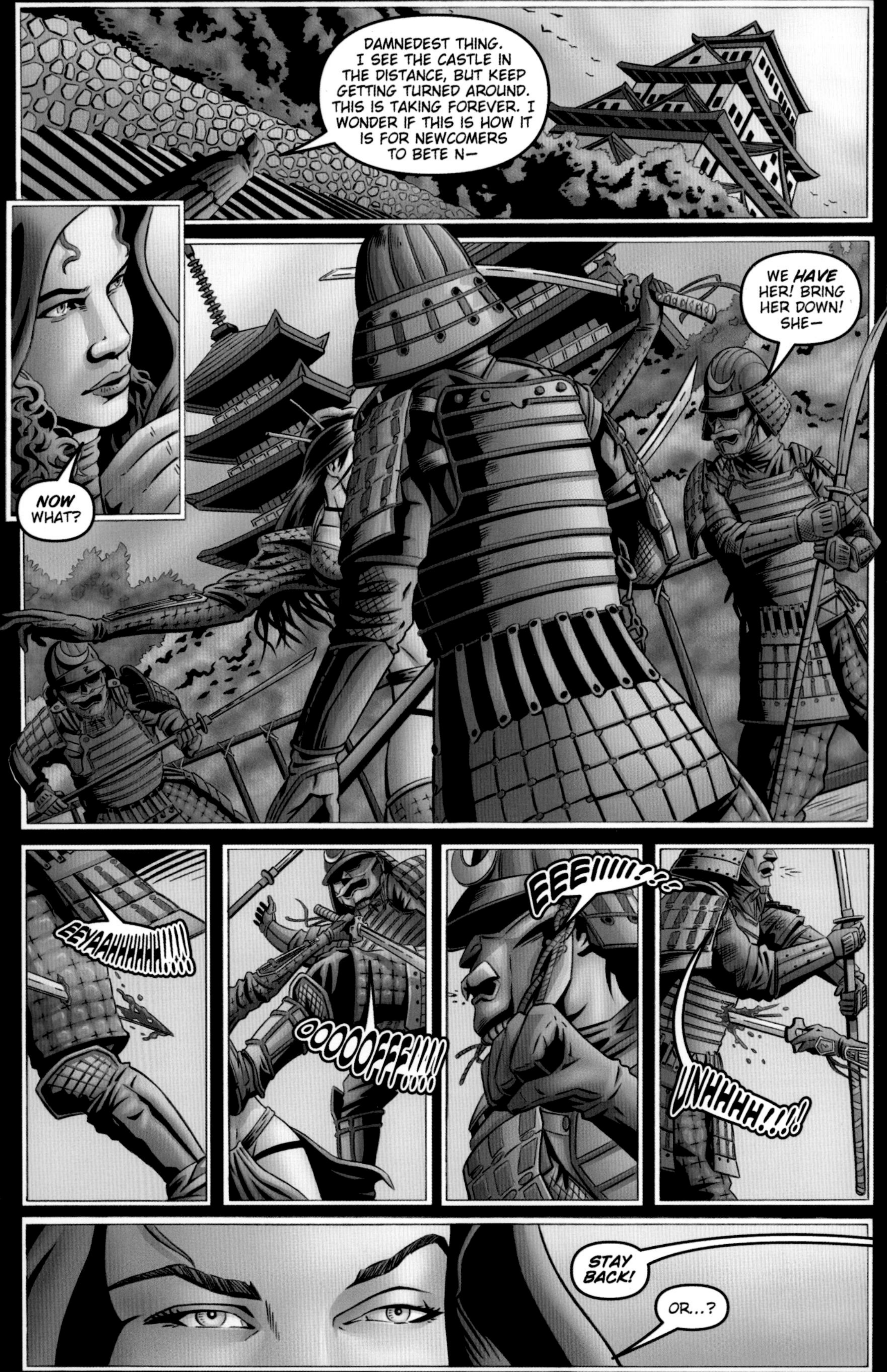
DAMNEDEST THING. I SEE THE CASTLE IN THE DISTANCE, BUT KEEP GETTING TURNED AROUND. THIS IS TAKING FOREVER. I WONDER IF THIS IS HOW IT IS FOR NEWCOMERS TO BETE N—
NOW WHAT?
WE HAVE HER! BRING HER DOWN! SHE—
EEYAAHHHHHH!!!!
OOOOOFFF!!!!
EEE!!!!!!
UNHHHH!!!!
STAY BACK!
OR...?

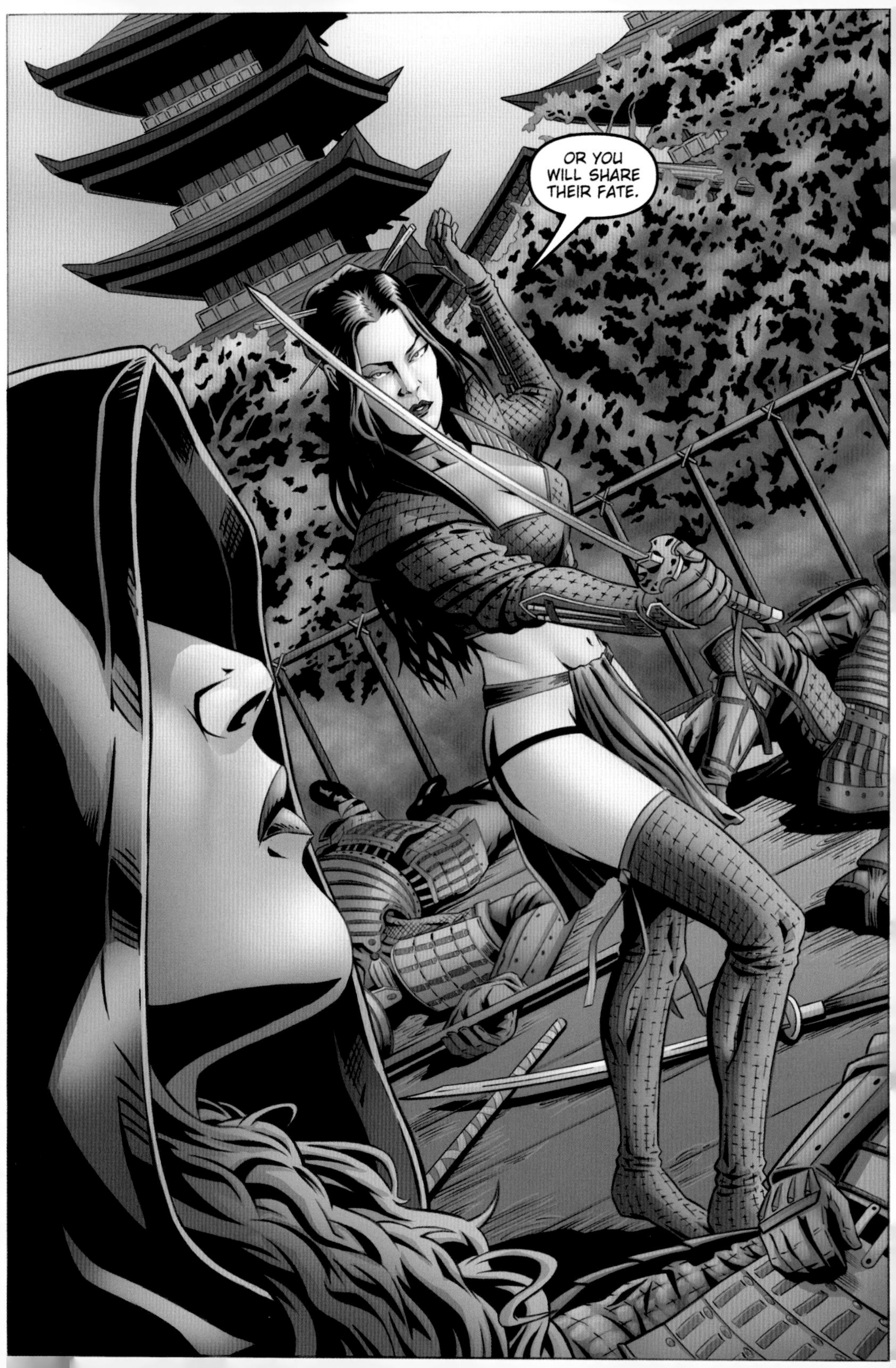
OR YOU WILL SHARE THEIR FATE.

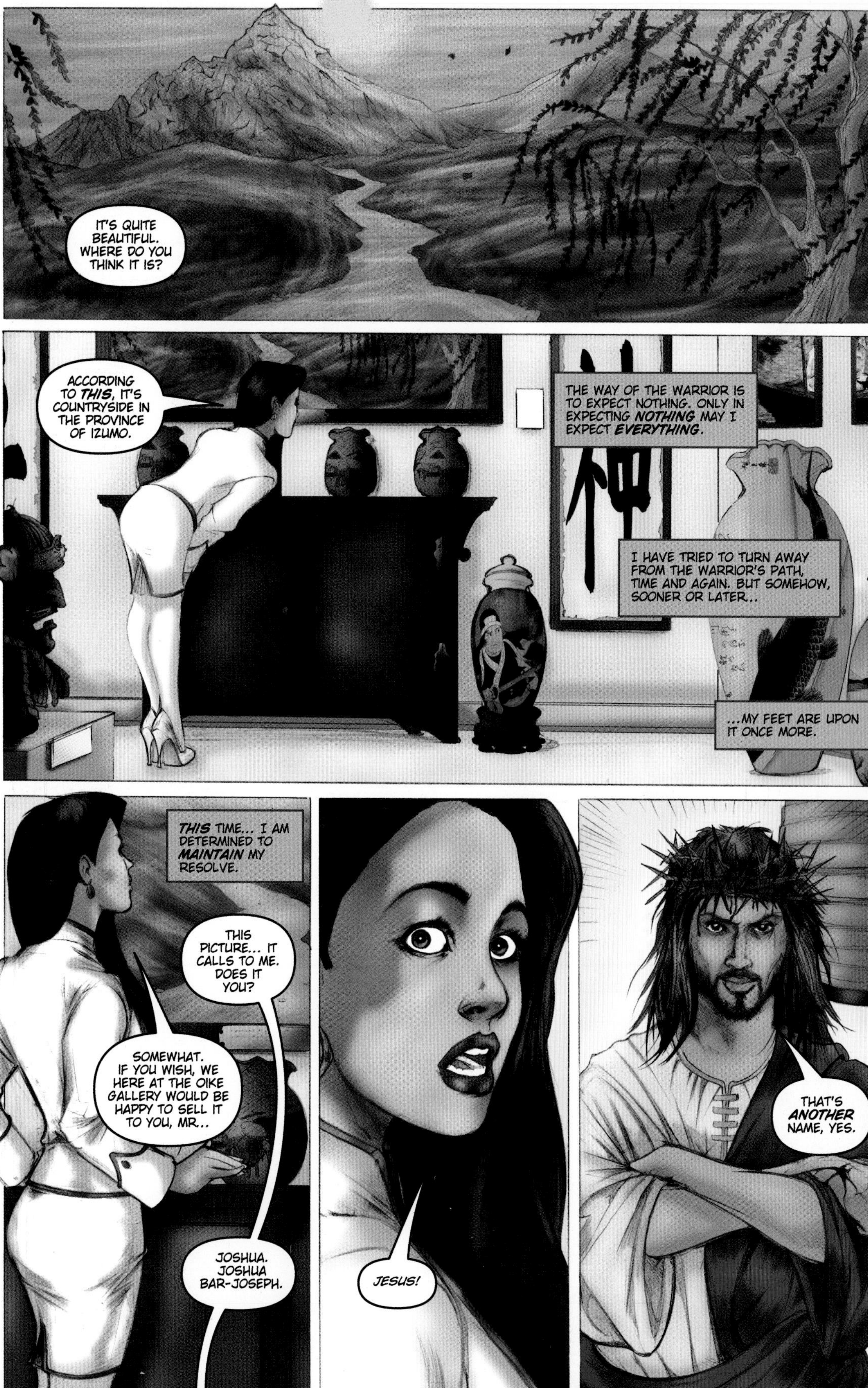
IT'S QUITE BEAUTIFUL. WHERE DO YOU THINK IT IS?
ACCORDING TO THIS, IT'S COUNTRYSIDE IN THE PROVINCE OF IZUMO.
THE WAY OF THE WARRIOR IS TO EXPECT NOTHING. ONLY IN EXPECTING NOTHING MAY I EXPECT EVERYTHING.
I HAVE TRIED TO TURN AWAY FROM THE WARRIOR'S PATH, TIME AND AGAIN. BUT SOMEHOW, SOONER OR LATER...
...MY FEET ARE UPON IT ONCE MORE.
THIS TIME... I AM DETERMINED TO MAINTAIN MY RESOLVE.
THIS PICTURE... IT CALLS TO ME. DOES IT YOU?
SOMEWHAT. IF YOU WISH, WE HERE AT THE OIKE GALLERY WOULD BE HAPPY TO SELL IT TO YOU, MR...
JOSHUA. JOSHUA BAR-JOSEPH.
JESUS!
THAT'S ANOTHER NAME, YES.

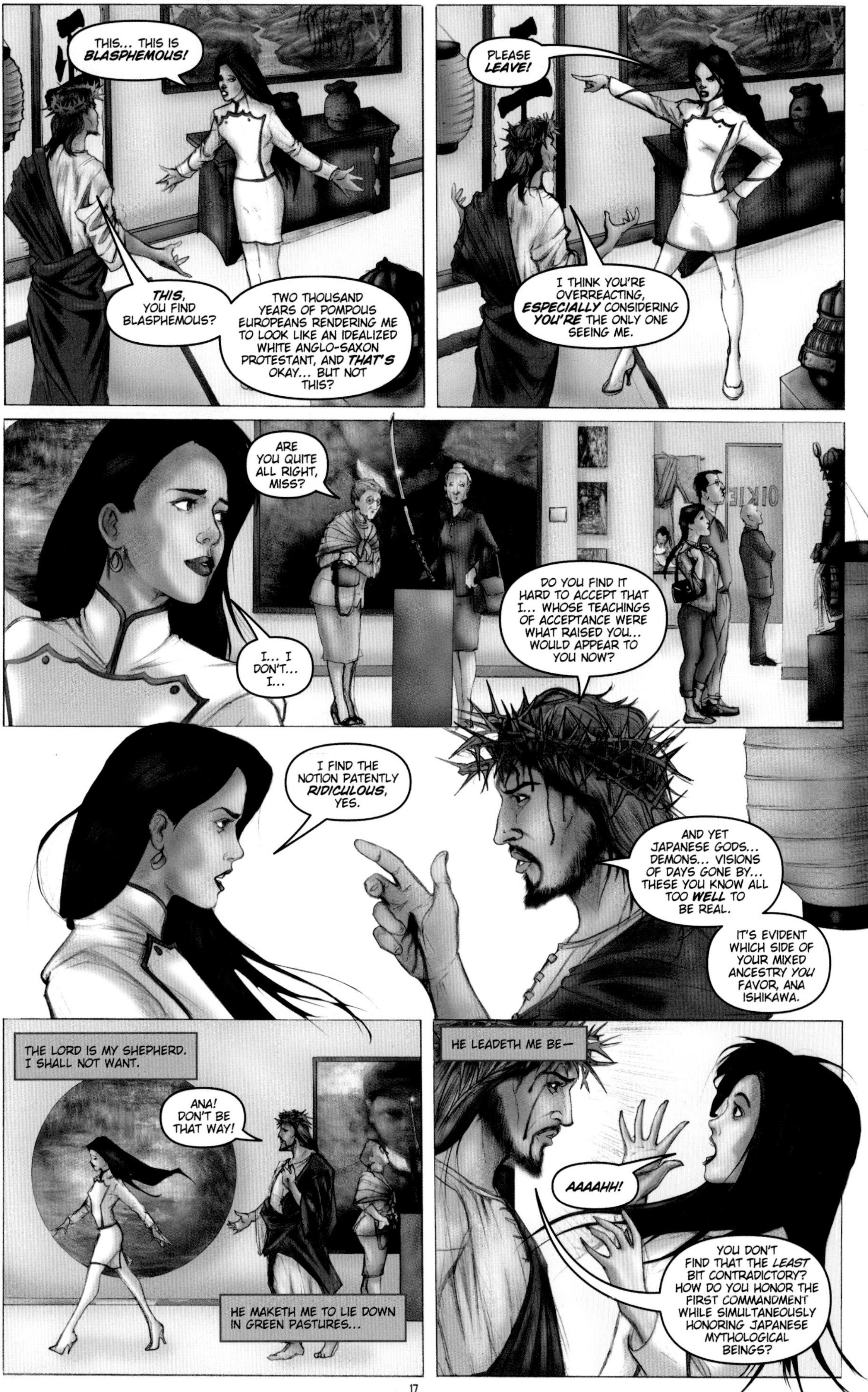
THIS... THIS IS BLASPHEMOUS!
THIS, YOU FIND BLASPHEMOUS?
TWO THOUSAND YEARS OF POMPOUS EUROPEANS RENDERING ME TO LOOK LIKE AN IDEALIZED WHITE ANGLO-SAXON PROTESTANT, AND THAT'S OKAY... BUT NOT THIS?
PLEASE LEAVE!
I THINK YOU'RE OVERREACTING, ESPECIALLY CONSIDERING YOU'RE THE ONLY ONE SEEING ME.
ARE YOU QUITE ALL RIGHT, MISS?
I... I DON'T... I...
DO YOU FIND IT HARD TO ACCEPT THAT I... WHOSE TEACHINGS OF ACCEPTANCE WERE WHAT RAISED YOU... WOULD APPEAR TO YOU NOW?
I FIND THE NOTION PATENTLY RIDICULOUS, YES.
AND YET JAPANESE GODS... DEMONS... VISIONS OF DAYS GONE BY... THESE YOU KNOW ALL TOO WELL TO BE REAL.
IT'S EVIDENT WHICH SIDE OF YOUR MIXED ANCESTRY YOU FAVOR, ANA ISHIKAWA.
THE LORD IS MY SHEPHERD. I SHALL NOT WANT.
ANA! DON'T BE THAT WAY!
HE MAKETH ME TO LIE DOWN IN GREEN PASTURES...
HE LEADETH ME BE—
AAAAHH!
YOU DON'T FIND THAT THE LEAST BIT CONTRADICTORY? HOW DO YOU HONOR THE FIRST COMMANDMENT WHILE SIMULTANEOUSLY HONORING JAPANESE MYTHOLOGICAL BEINGS?

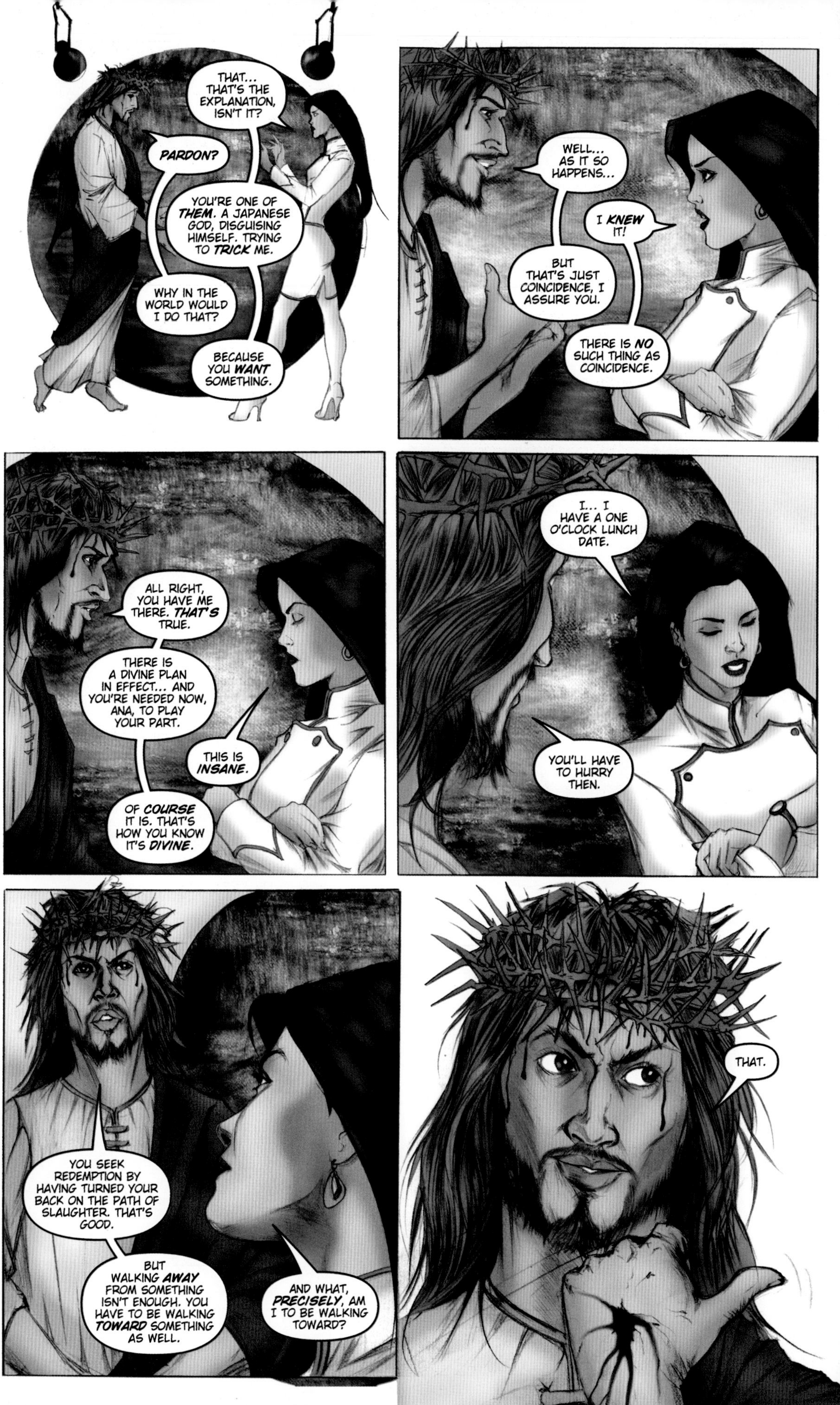
THAT... THAT'S THE EXPLANATION, ISN'T IT?
PARDON?
YOU'RE ONE OF *THEM*. A JAPANESE GOD, DISGUISING HIMSELF. TRYING TO *TRICK* ME.
WHY IN THE WORLD WOULD I DO THAT?
BECAUSE YOU *WANT* SOMETHING.
WELL... AS IT SO HAPPENS...
I *KNEW* IT!
BUT THAT'S JUST COINCIDENCE, I ASSURE YOU.
THERE IS *NO* SUCH THING AS COINCIDENCE.
ALL RIGHT, YOU HAVE ME THERE. *THAT'S* TRUE.
THERE IS A DIVINE PLAN IN EFFECT... AND YOU'RE NEEDED NOW, ANA, TO PLAY YOUR PART.
THIS IS *INSANE*.
OF *COURSE* IT IS. THAT'S HOW YOU KNOW IT'S *DIVINE*.
I... I HAVE A ONE O'CLOCK LUNCH DATE.
YOU'LL HAVE TO HURRY THEN.
YOU SEEK REDEMPTION BY HAVING TURNED YOUR BACK ON THE PATH OF SLAUGHTER. THAT'S GOOD.
BUT WALKING *AWAY* FROM SOMETHING ISN'T ENOUGH. YOU HAVE TO BE WALKING *TOWARD* SOMETHING AS WELL.
AND WHAT, *PRECISELY*, AM I TO BE WALKING TOWARD?
THAT.

THAT IS THE PATH THAT YOU MUST WALK. THAT *SHI* MUST WALK.

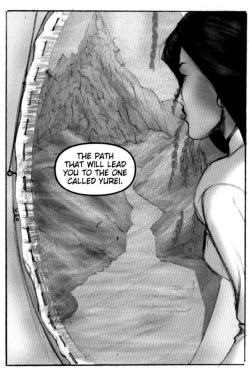

THE PATH THAT WILL LEAD YOU TO THE ONE CALLED YUREI.

YOU MUST *EXCISE* HIM... AS ONE WOULD A CANCER.

DO THIS AND HELP TO EARN YOUR SALVATION. DO THIS, DAUGHTER OF JESUS...

...AND SHOW YOURSELF *WORTHY* OF THE LOVE I GIVE YOU *FREELY.*

IF IT'S *FREELY GIVEN,* I SHOULDN'T HAVE TO PROVE MYSELF *WORTHY* OF IT!

MARVELOUS.

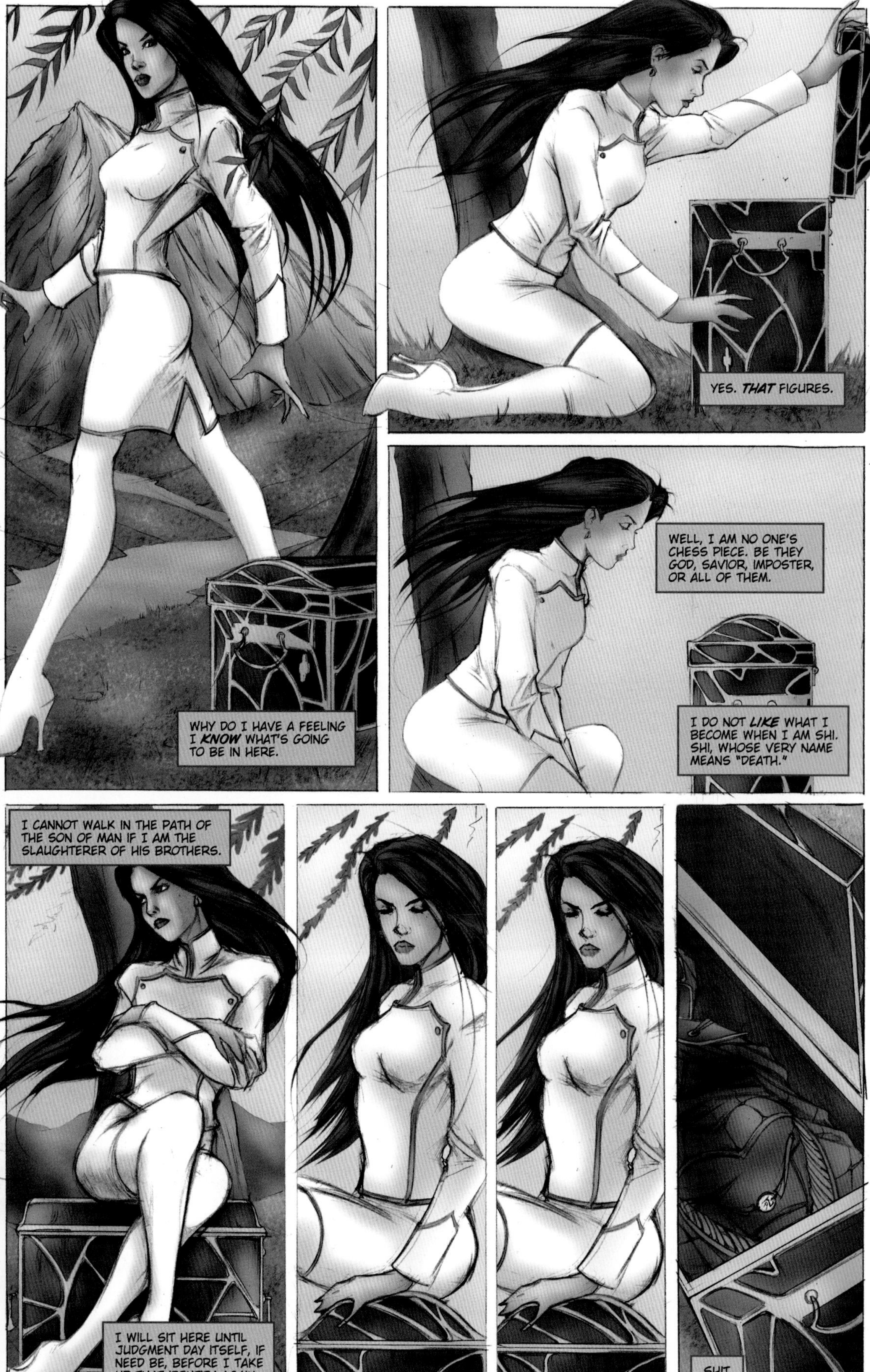
WHY DO I HAVE A FEELING I KNOW WHAT'S GOING TO BE IN HERE.
YES. THAT FIGURES.
WELL, I AM NO ONE'S CHESS PIECE. BE THEY GOD, SAVIOR, IMPOSTER, OR ALL OF THEM.
I DO NOT LIKE WHAT I BECOME WHEN I AM SHI. SHI, WHOSE VERY NAME MEANS "DEATH."
I CANNOT WALK IN THE PATH OF THE SON OF MAN IF I AM THE SLAUGHTERER OF HIS BROTHERS.
I WILL SIT HERE UNTIL JUDGMENT DAY ITSELF, IF NEED BE, BEFORE I TAKE UP THAT IDENTITY AGAIN.
SHIT.

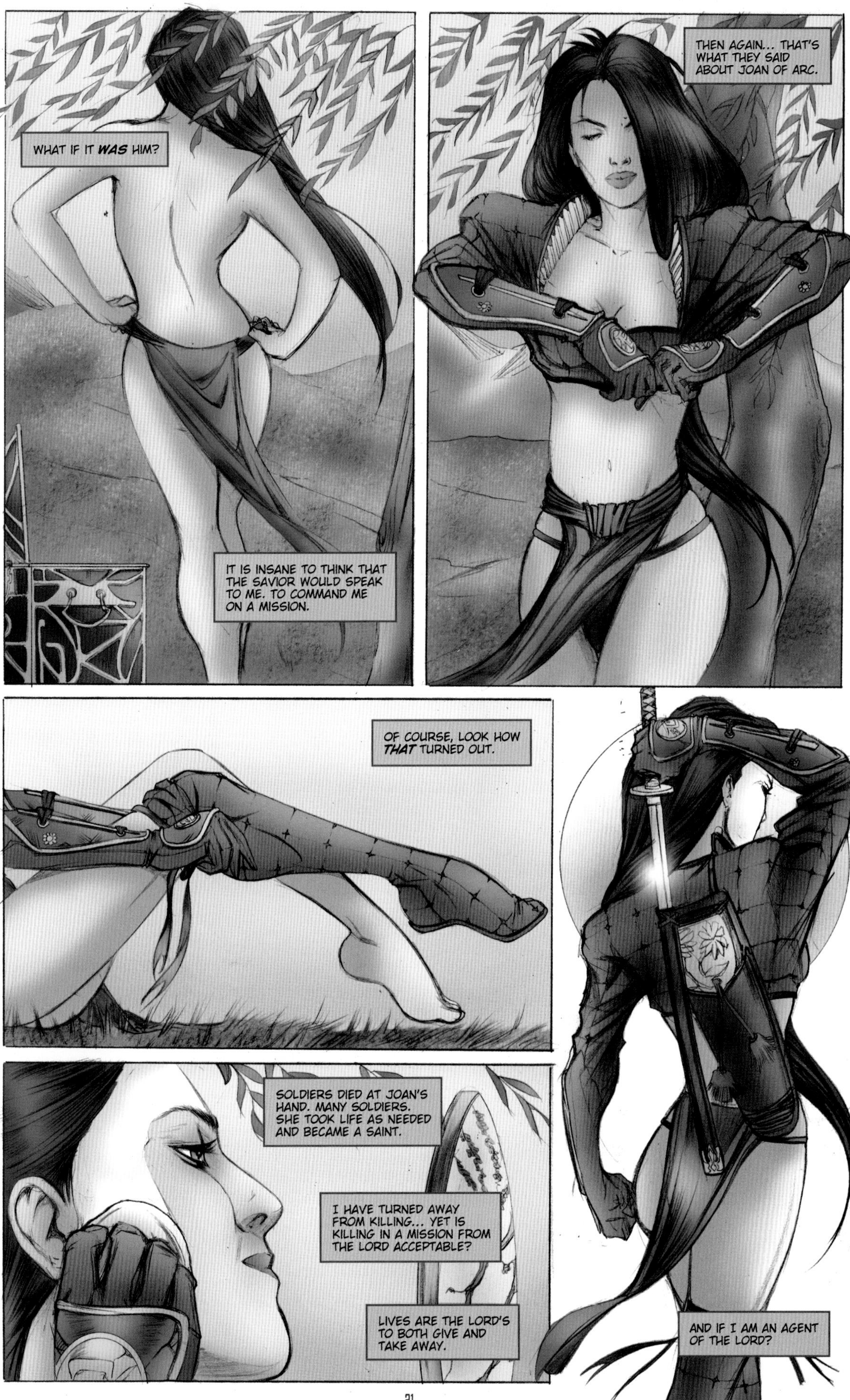
WHAT IF IT ***WAS*** HIM?
IT IS INSANE TO THINK THAT THE SAVIOR WOULD SPEAK TO ME. TO COMMAND ME ON A MISSION.
THEN AGAIN... THAT'S WHAT THEY SAID ABOUT JOAN OF ARC.
OF COURSE, LOOK HOW ***THAT*** TURNED OUT.
SOLDIERS DIED AT JOAN'S HAND. MANY SOLDIERS. SHE TOOK LIFE AS NEEDED AND BECAME A SAINT.
I HAVE TURNED AWAY FROM KILLING... YET IS KILLING IN A MISSION FROM THE LORD ACCEPTABLE?
LIVES ARE THE LORD'S TO BOTH GIVE AND TAKE AWAY.
AND IF I AM AN AGENT OF THE LORD?

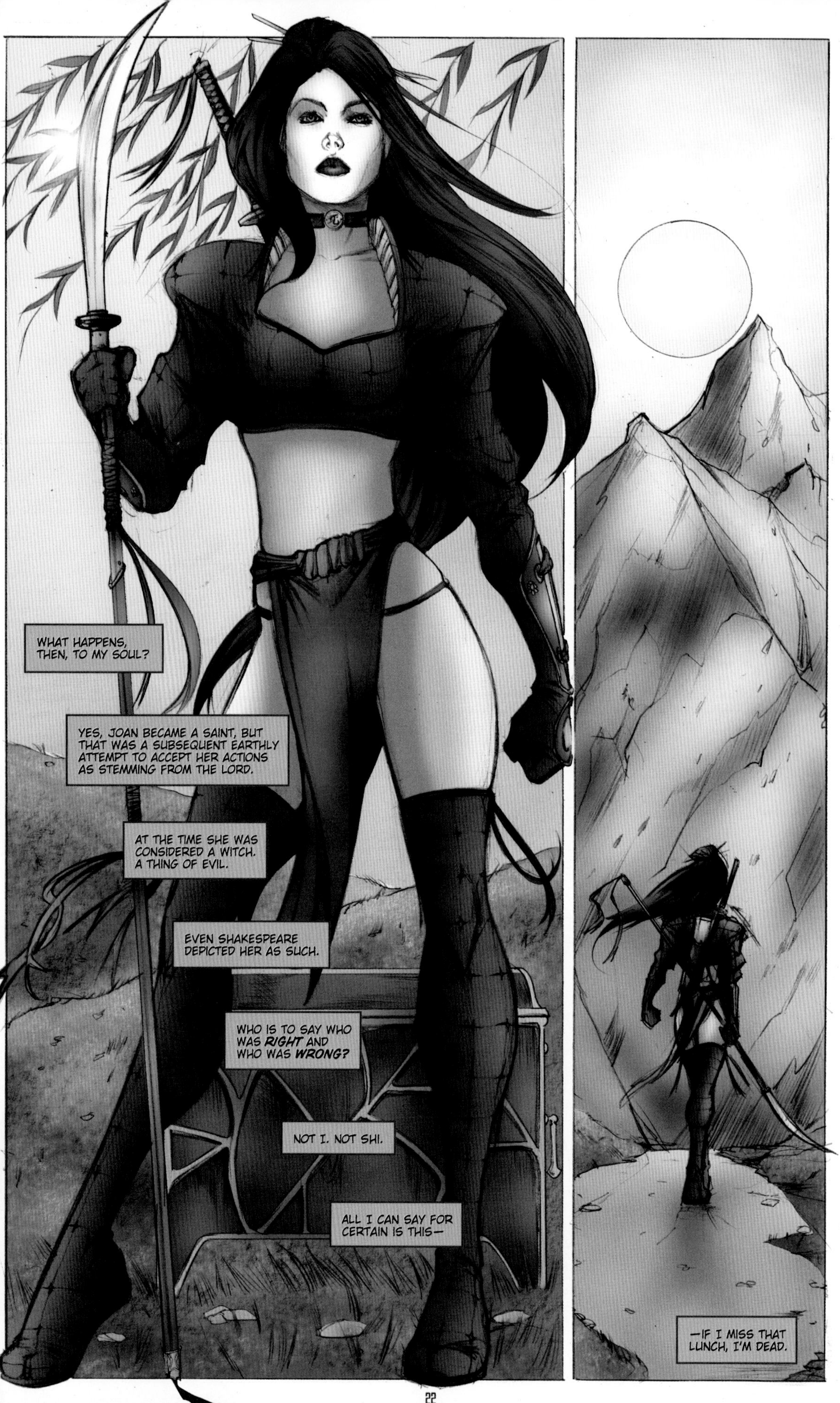
WHAT HAPPENS, THEN, TO MY SOUL?
YES, JOAN BECAME A SAINT, BUT THAT WAS A SUBSEQUENT EARTHLY ATTEMPT TO ACCEPT HER ACTIONS AS STEMMING FROM THE LORD.
AT THE TIME SHE WAS CONSIDERED A WITCH. A THING OF EVIL.
EVEN SHAKESPEARE DEPICTED HER AS SUCH.
WHO IS TO SAY WHO WAS RIGHT AND WHO WAS WRONG?
NOT I. NOT SHI.
ALL I CAN SAY FOR CERTAIN IS THIS—
—IF I MISS THAT LUNCH, I'M DEAD.

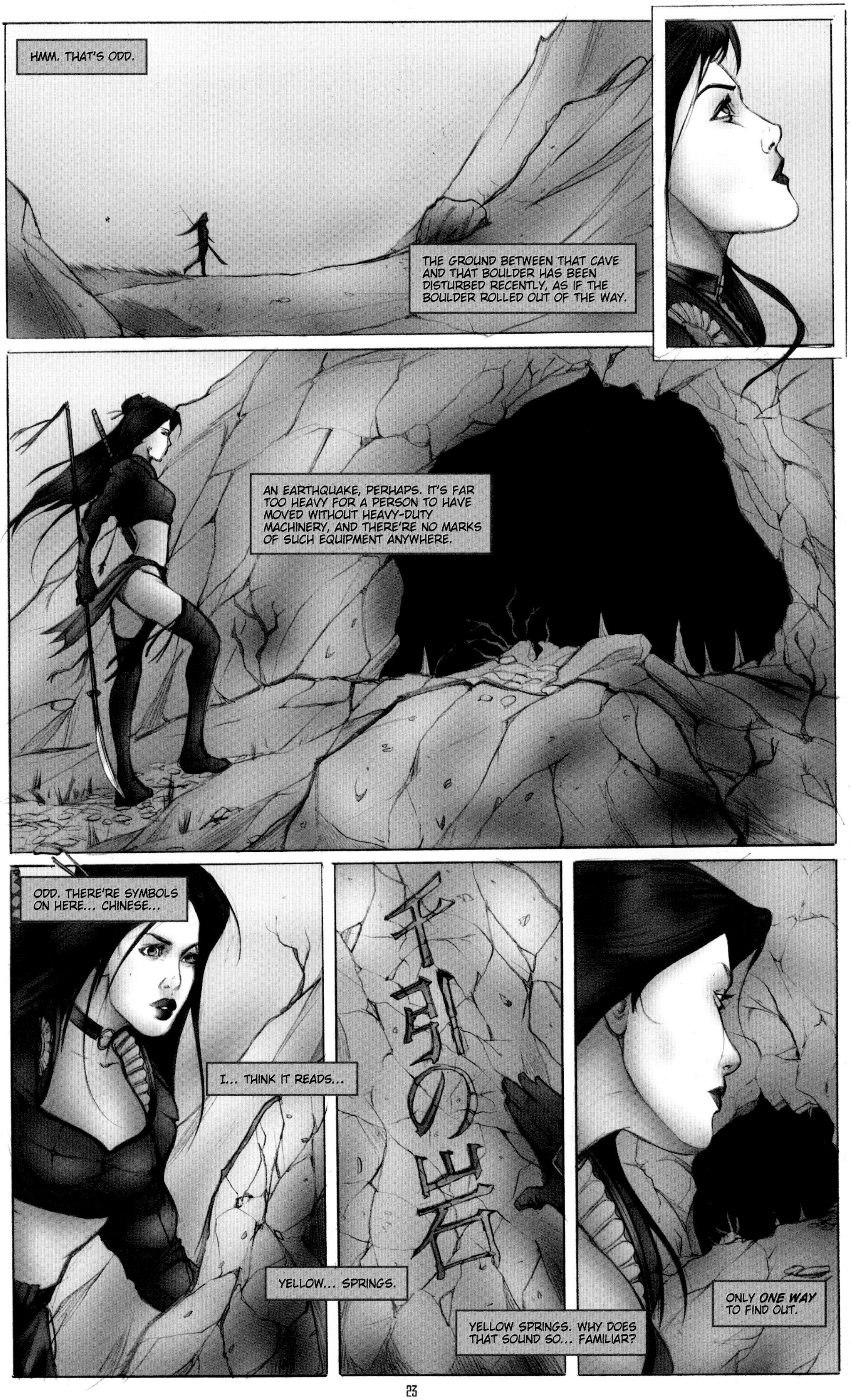
HMM. THAT'S ODD.
THE GROUND BETWEEN THAT CAVE AND THAT BOULDER HAS BEEN DISTURBED RECENTLY, AS IF THE BOULDER ROLLED OUT OF THE WAY.
AN EARTHQUAKE, PERHAPS. IT'S FAR TOO HEAVY FOR A PERSON TO HAVE MOVED WITHOUT HEAVY-DUTY MACHINERY, AND THERE'RE NO MARKS OF SUCH EQUIPMENT ANYWHERE.
ODD. THERE'RE SYMBOLS ON HERE... CHINESE...
I... THINK IT READS...
YELLOW... SPRINGS.
YELLOW SPRINGS. WHY DOES THAT SOUND SO... FAMILIAR?
ONLY *ONE WAY* TO FIND OUT.

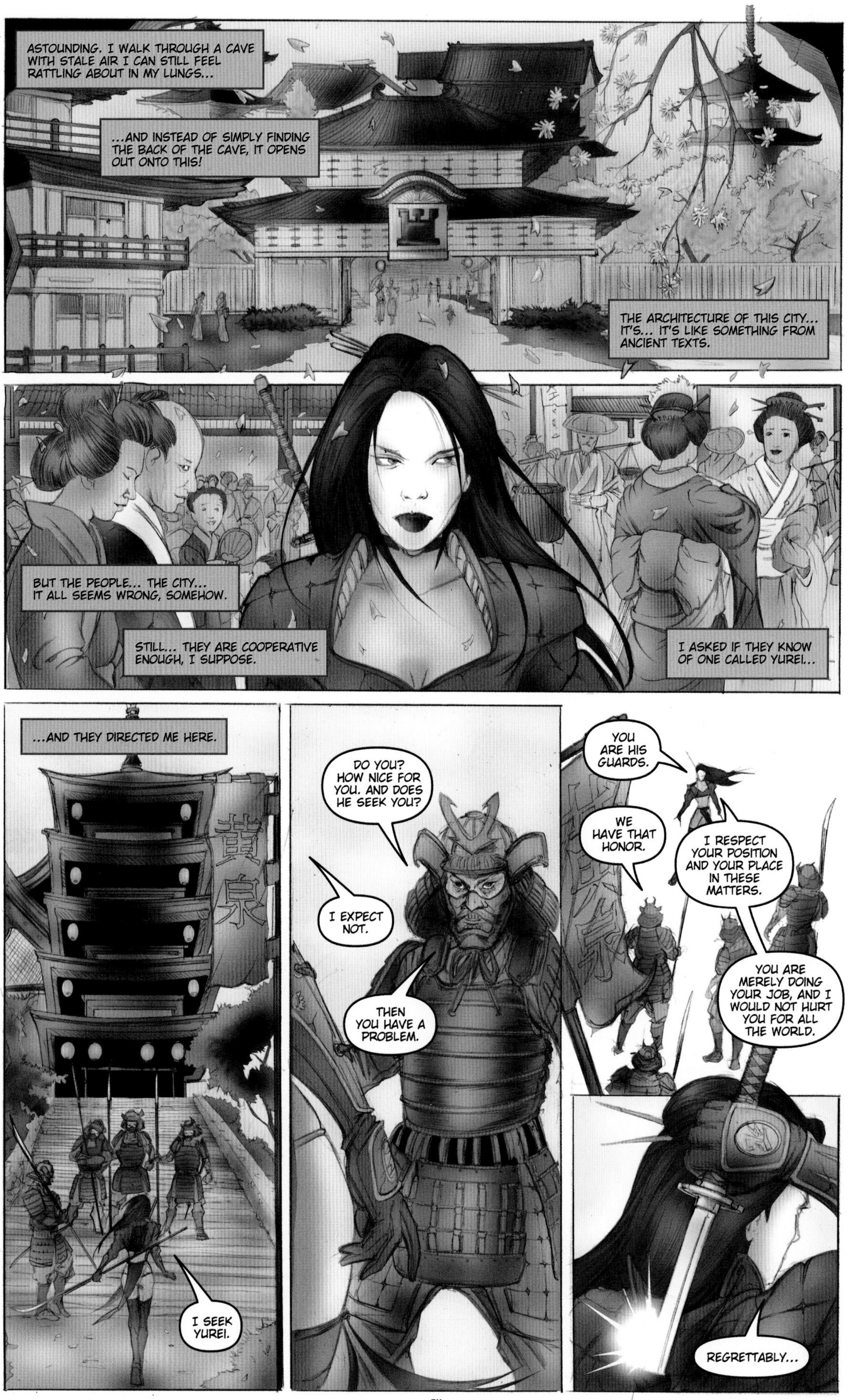

ASTOUNDING. I WALK THROUGH A CAVE WITH STALE AIR I CAN STILL FEEL RATTLING ABOUT IN MY LUNGS...
...AND INSTEAD OF SIMPLY FINDING THE BACK OF THE CAVE, IT OPENS OUT ONTO THIS!
THE ARCHITECTURE OF THIS CITY... IT'S... IT'S LIKE SOMETHING FROM ANCIENT TEXTS.
BUT THE PEOPLE... THE CITY... IT ALL SEEMS WRONG, SOMEHOW.
STILL... THEY ARE COOPERATIVE ENOUGH, I SUPPOSE.
I ASKED IF THEY KNOW OF ONE CALLED YUREI...
...AND THEY DIRECTED ME HERE.
I SEEK YUREI.
DO YOU? HOW NICE FOR YOU. AND DOES HE SEEK YOU?
I EXPECT NOT.
THEN YOU HAVE A PROBLEM.
YOU ARE HIS GUARDS.
WE HAVE THAT HONOR.
I RESPECT YOUR POSITION AND YOUR PLACE IN THESE MATTERS.
YOU ARE MERELY DOING YOUR JOB, AND I WOULD NOT HURT YOU FOR ALL THE WORLD.
REGRETTABLY...

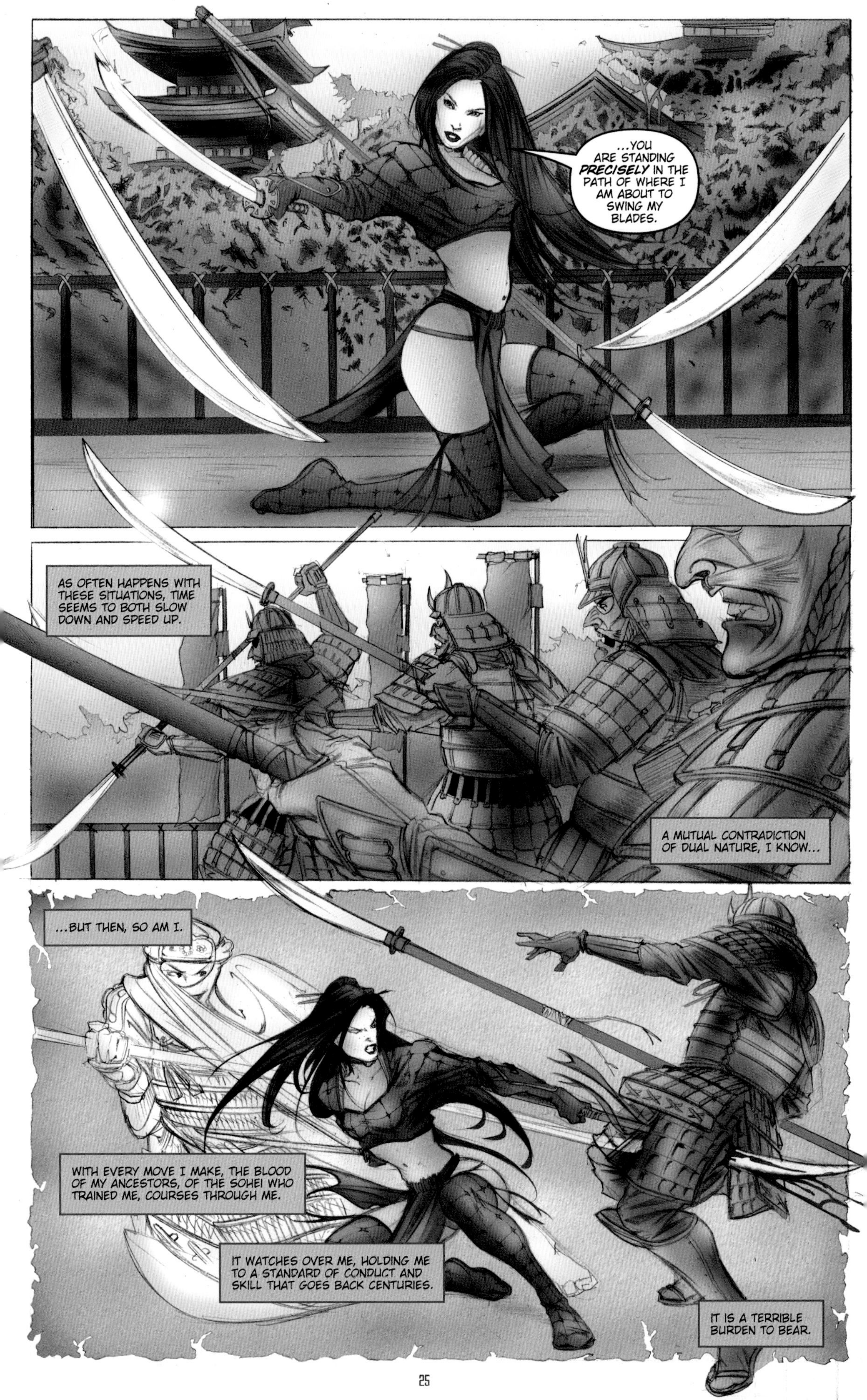
...YOU ARE STANDING PRECISELY IN THE PATH OF WHERE I AM ABOUT TO SWING MY BLADES.
AS OFTEN HAPPENS WITH THESE SITUATIONS, TIME SEEMS TO BOTH SLOW DOWN AND SPEED UP.
A MUTUAL CONTRADICTION OF DUAL NATURE, I KNOW...
...BUT THEN, SO AM I.
WITH EVERY MOVE I MAKE, THE BLOOD OF MY ANCESTORS, OF THE SOHEI WHO TRAINED ME, COURSES THROUGH ME.
IT WATCHES OVER ME, HOLDING ME TO A STANDARD OF CONDUCT AND SKILL THAT GOES BACK CENTURIES.
IT IS A TERRIBLE BURDEN TO BEAR.

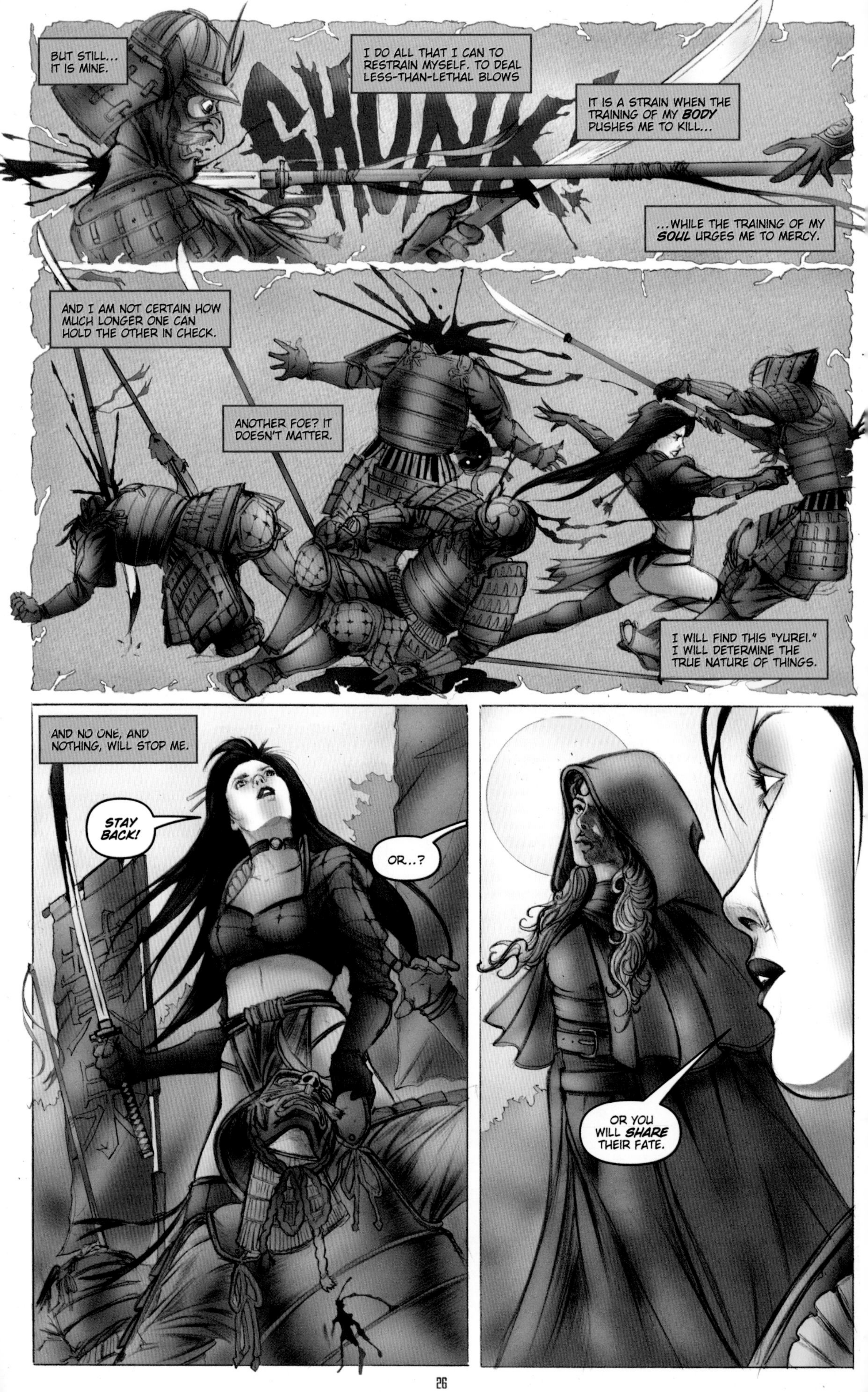
BUT STILL... IT IS MINE.
I DO ALL THAT I CAN TO RESTRAIN MYSELF. TO DEAL LESS-THAN-LETHAL BLOWS
SHUNK!
IT IS A STRAIN WHEN THE TRAINING OF MY BODY PUSHES ME TO KILL...
...WHILE THE TRAINING OF MY SOUL URGES ME TO MERCY.
AND I AM NOT CERTAIN HOW MUCH LONGER ONE CAN HOLD THE OTHER IN CHECK.
ANOTHER FOE? IT DOESN'T MATTER.
I WILL FIND THIS "YUREI." I WILL DETERMINE THE TRUE NATURE OF THINGS.
AND NO ONE, AND NOTHING, WILL STOP ME.
STAY BACK!
OR..?
OR YOU WILL SHARE THEIR FATE.

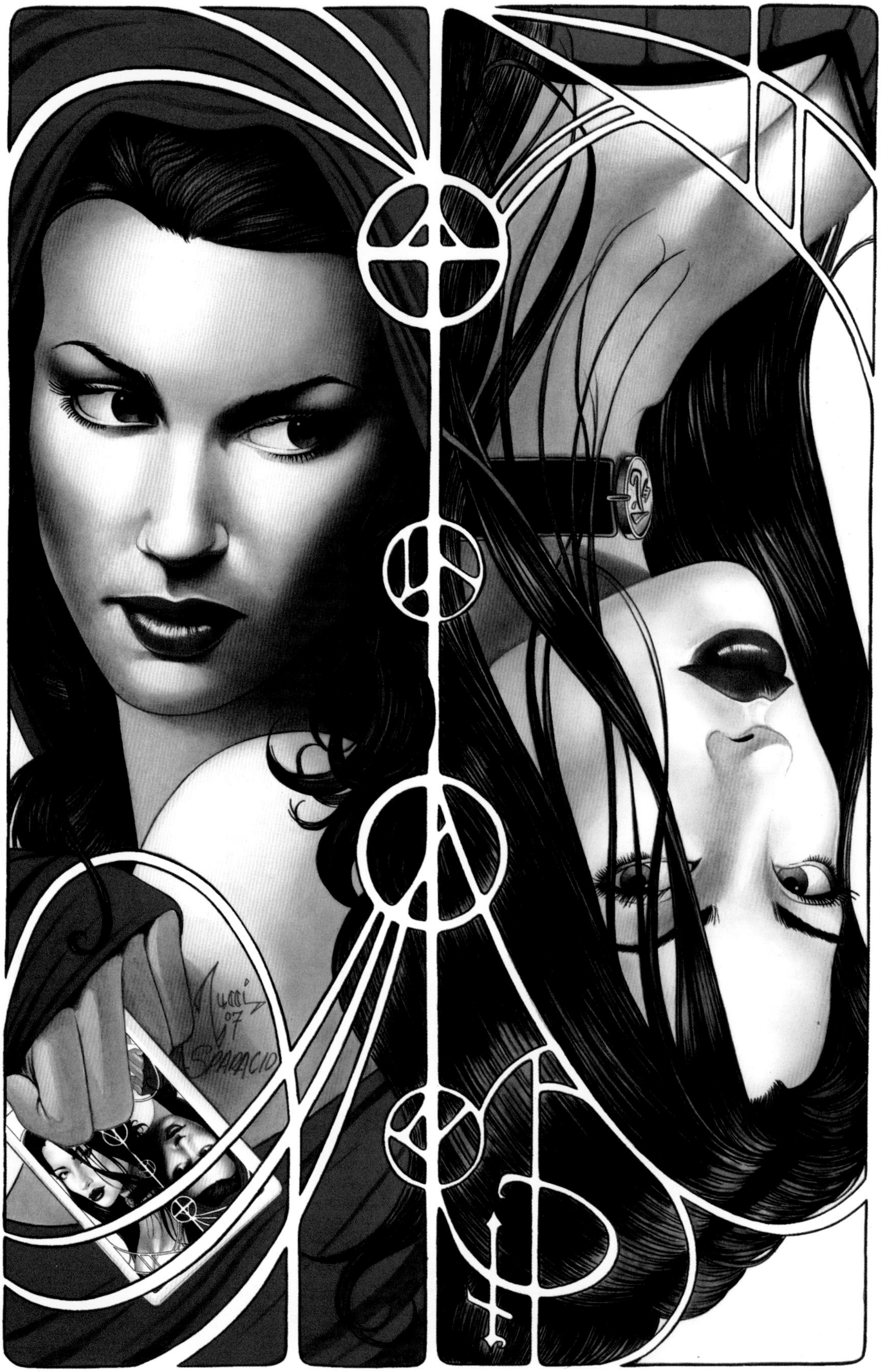

Art by Billy Tucci
Colors by Mark Sparacio

Chapter 2

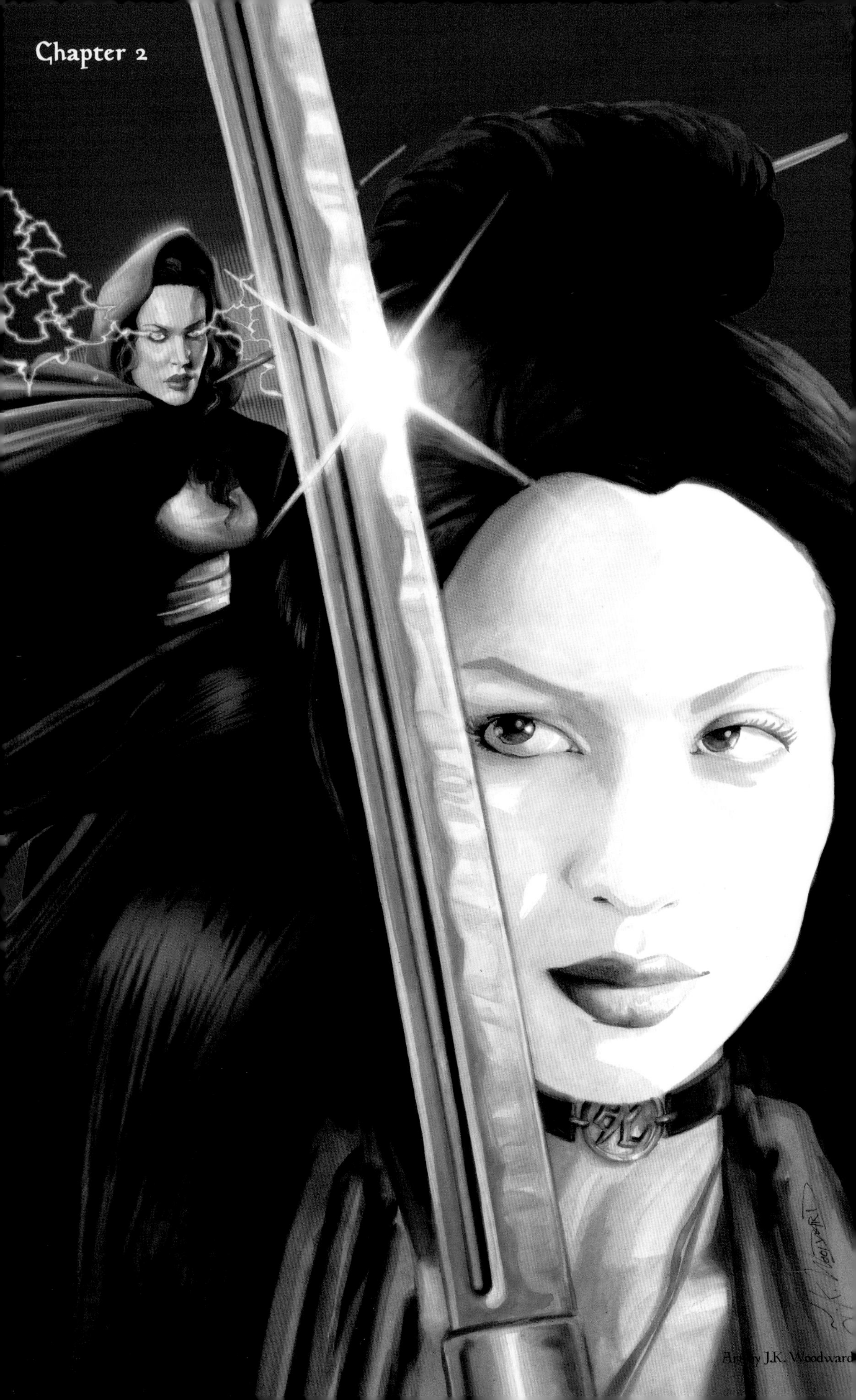

Art by J.K. Woodward

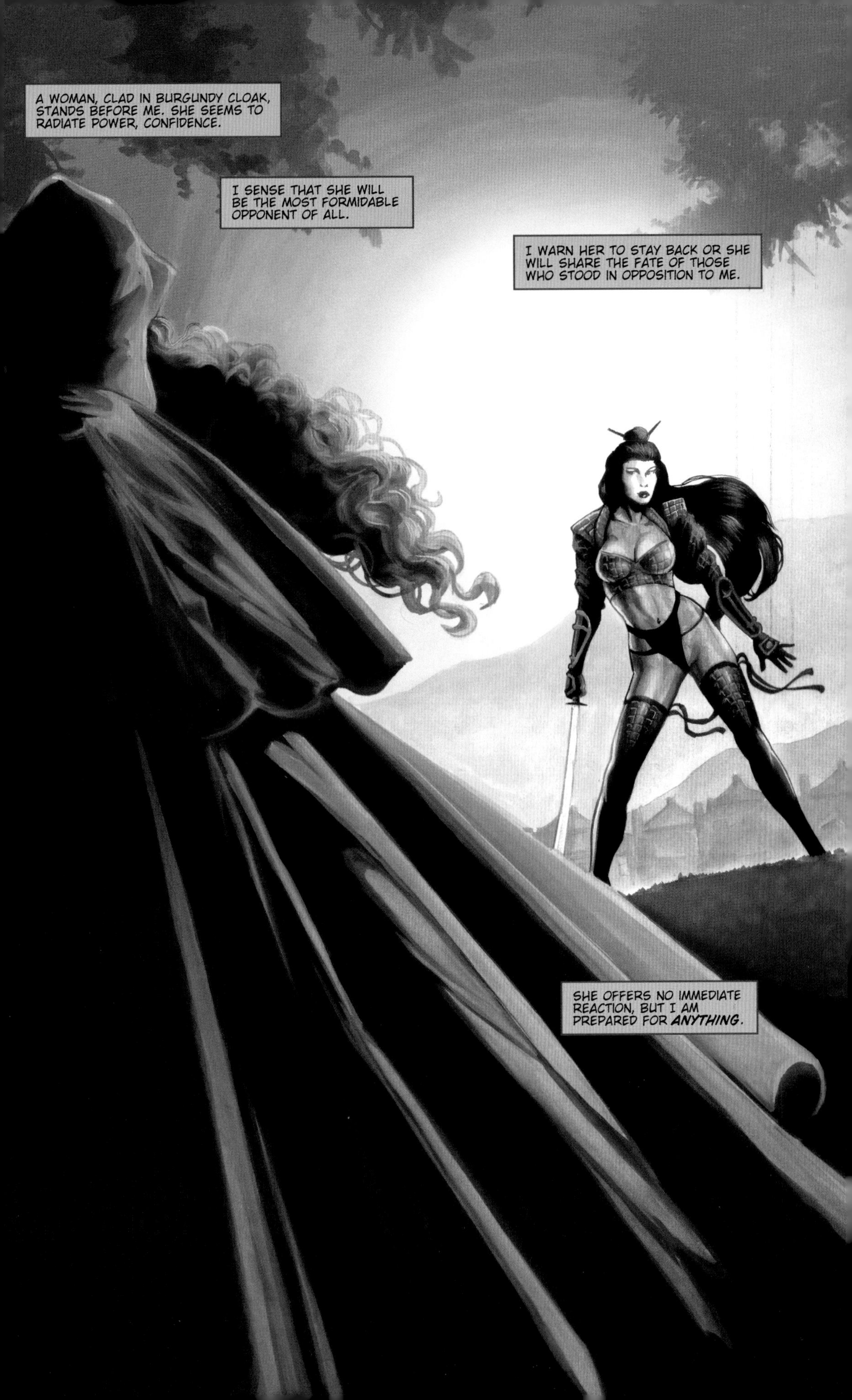
A WOMAN, CLAD IN BURGUNDY CLOAK, STANDS BEFORE ME. SHE SEEMS TO RADIATE POWER, CONFIDENCE.
I SENSE THAT SHE WILL BE THE MOST FORMIDABLE OPPONENT OF ALL.
I WARN HER TO STAY BACK OR SHE WILL SHARE THE FATE OF THOSE WHO STOOD IN OPPOSITION TO ME.
SHE OFFERS NO IMMEDIATE REACTION, BUT I AM PREPARED FOR ***ANYTHING***.

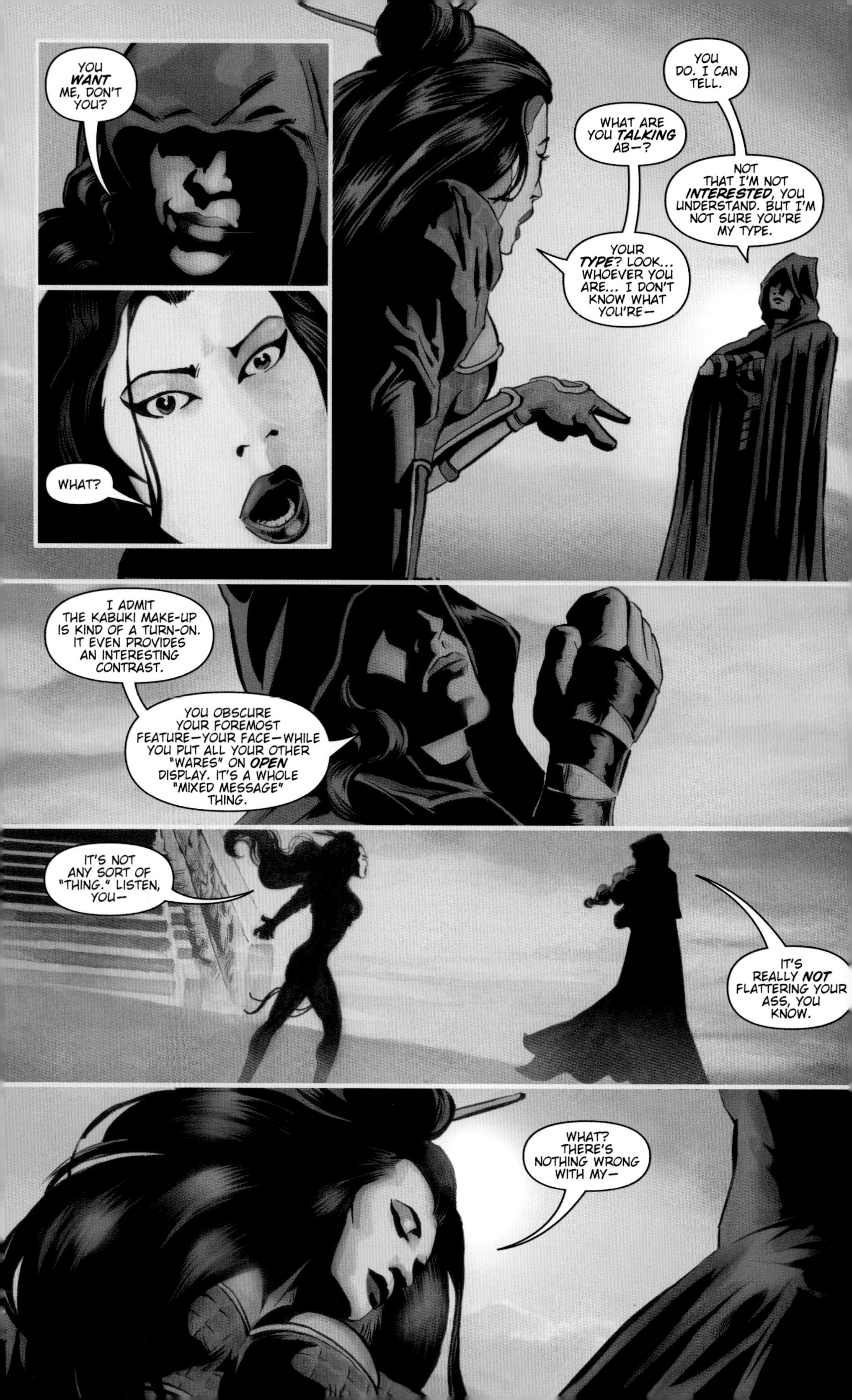

YOU WANT ME, DON'T YOU?
WHAT?
WHAT ARE YOU TALKING AB—?
YOU DO. I CAN TELL.
NOT THAT I'M NOT INTERESTED, YOU UNDERSTAND. BUT I'M NOT SURE YOU'RE MY TYPE.
YOUR TYPE? LOOK... WHOEVER YOU ARE... I DON'T KNOW WHAT YOU'RE—
I ADMIT THE KABUKI MAKE-UP IS KIND OF A TURN-ON. IT EVEN PROVIDES AN INTERESTING CONTRAST.
YOU OBSCURE YOUR FOREMOST FEATURE—YOUR FACE—WHILE YOU PUT ALL YOUR OTHER "WARES" ON OPEN DISPLAY. IT'S A WHOLE "MIXED MESSAGE" THING.
IT'S NOT ANY SORT OF "THING." LISTEN, YOU—
IT'S REALLY NOT FLATTERING YOUR ASS, YOU KNOW.
WHAT? THERE'S NOTHING WRONG WITH MY—

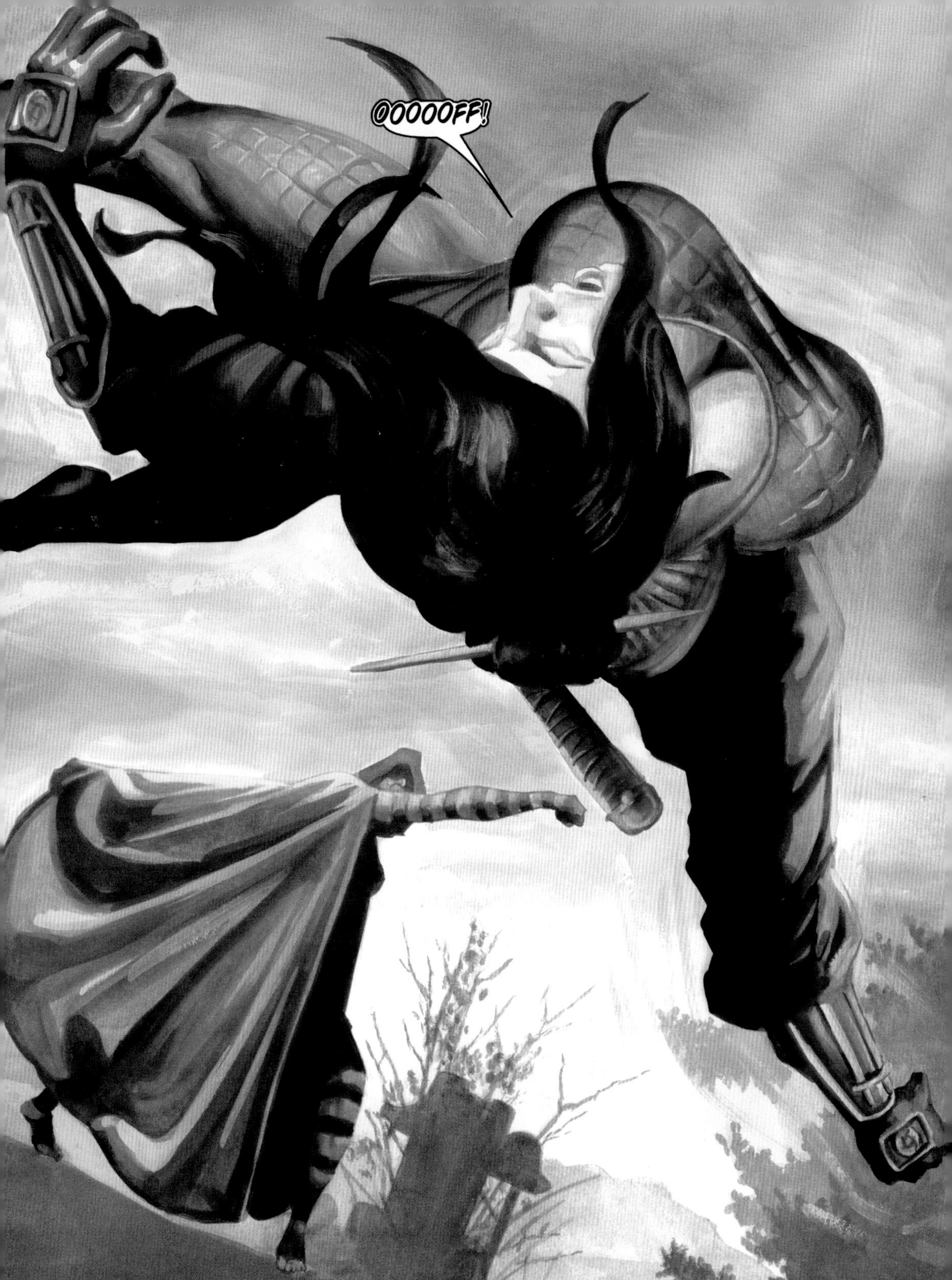
OOOOOFF!

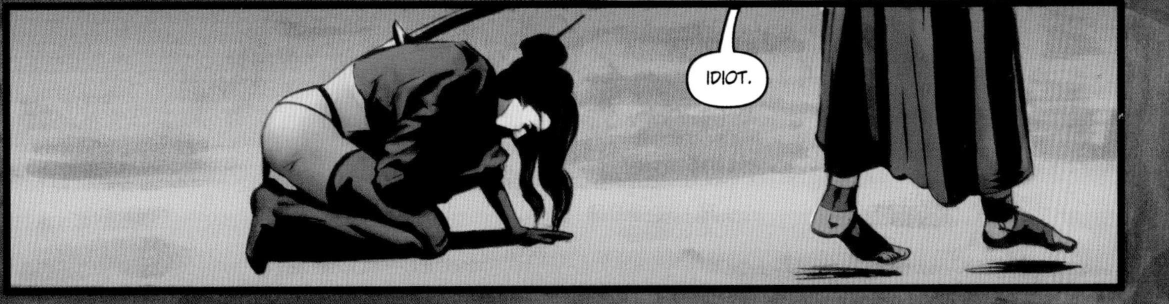
IDIOT.

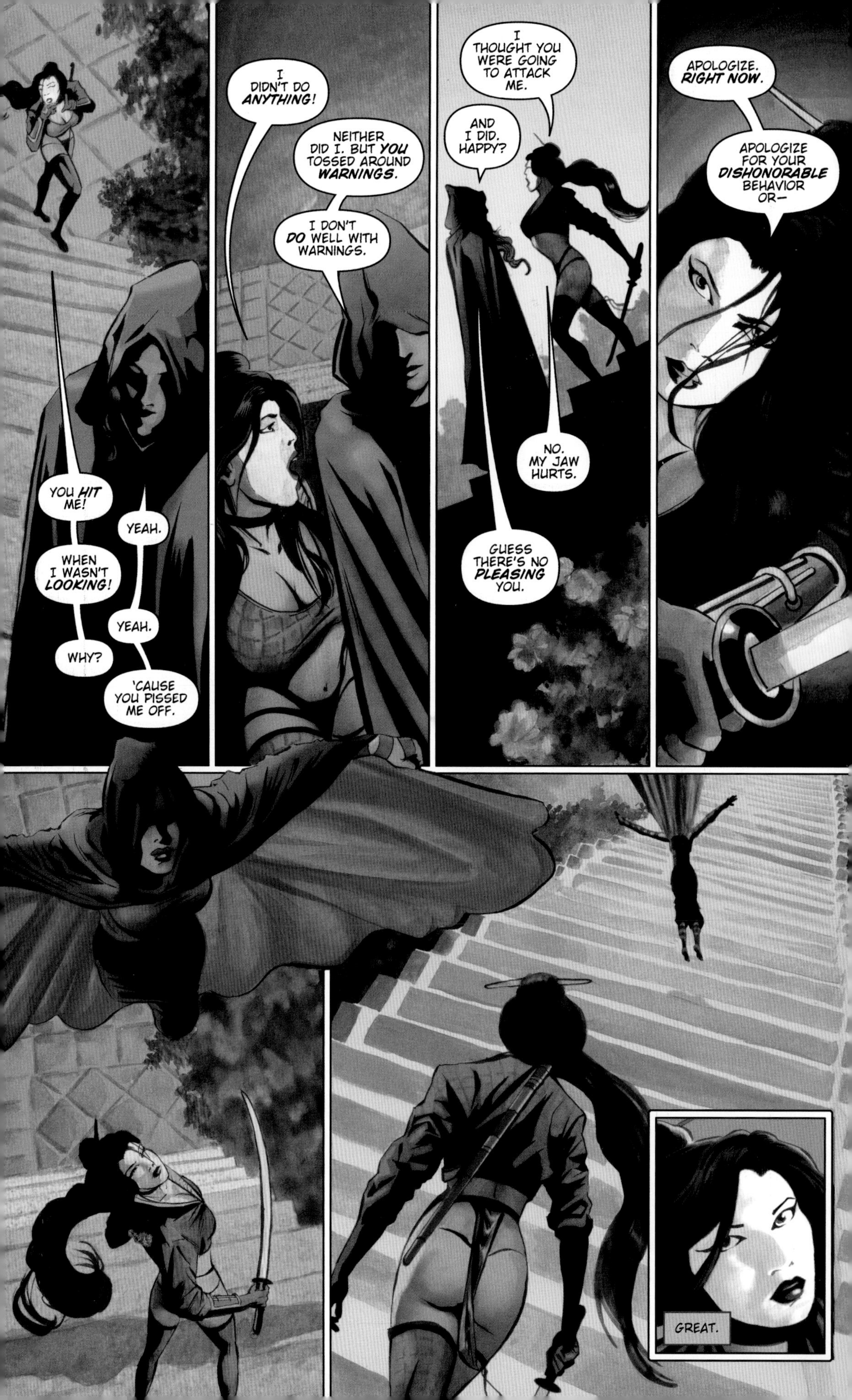
YOU HIT ME!
YEAH.
WHEN I WASN'T LOOKING!
YEAH.
WHY?
'CAUSE YOU PISSED ME OFF.
I DIDN'T DO ANYTHING!
NEITHER DID I. BUT YOU TOSSED AROUND WARNINGS.
I DON'T DO WELL WITH WARNINGS.
I THOUGHT YOU WERE GOING TO ATTACK ME.
AND I DID. HAPPY?
NO. MY JAW HURTS.
GUESS THERE'S NO PLEASING YOU.
APOLOGIZE. RIGHT NOW.
APOLOGIZE FOR YOUR DISHONORABLE BEHAVIOR OR—
GREAT.

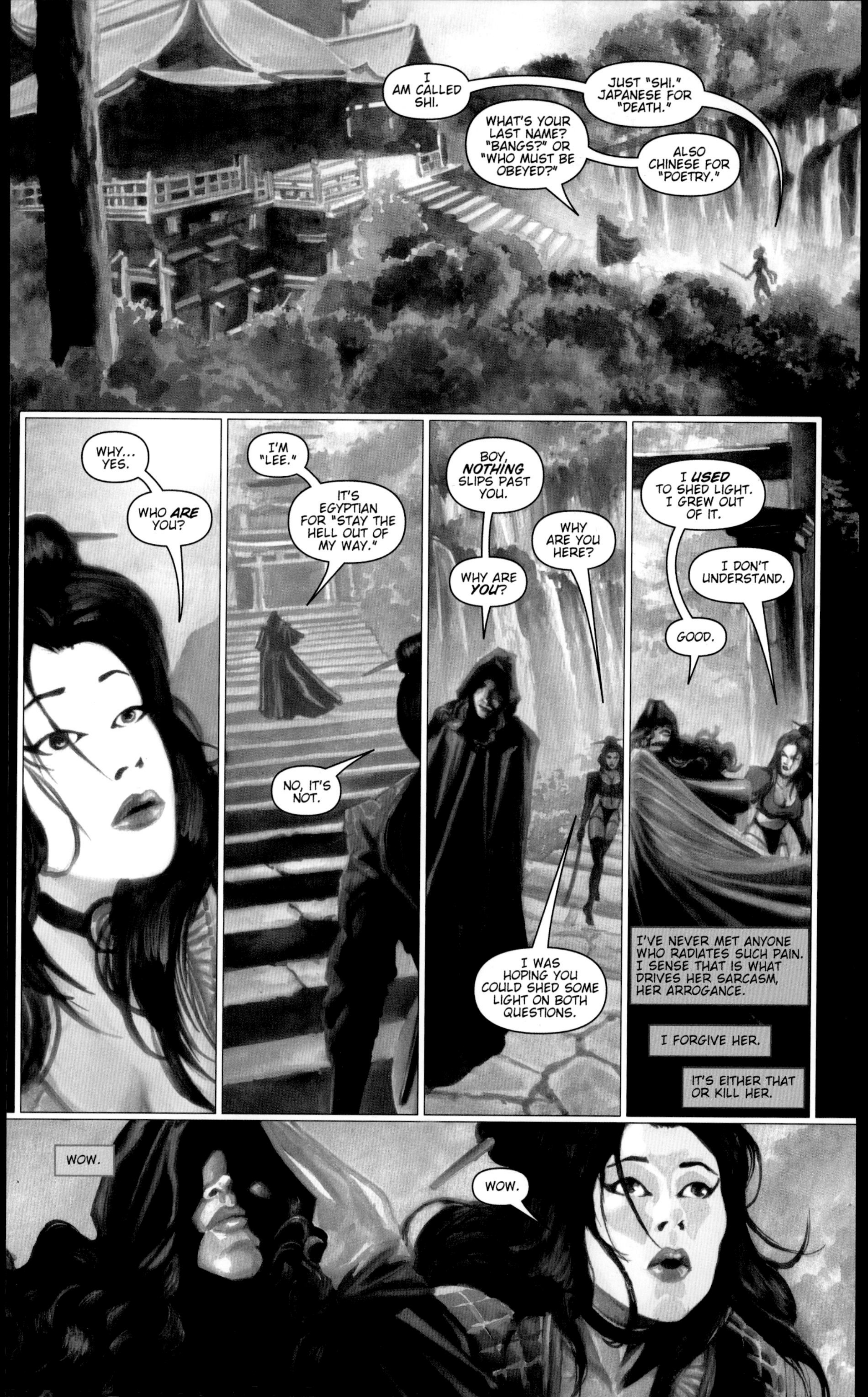
I AM CALLED SHI.
WHAT'S YOUR LAST NAME? "BANGS?" OR "WHO MUST BE OBEYED?"
JUST "SHI." JAPANESE FOR "DEATH."
ALSO CHINESE FOR "POETRY."
WHY... YES.
WHO ARE YOU?
I'M "LEE."
IT'S EGYPTIAN FOR "STAY THE HELL OUT OF MY WAY."
NO, IT'S NOT.
BOY, NOTHING SLIPS PAST YOU.
WHY ARE YOU HERE?
WHY ARE YOU?
I WAS HOPING YOU COULD SHED SOME LIGHT ON BOTH QUESTIONS.
I USED TO SHED LIGHT. I GREW OUT OF IT.
I DON'T UNDERSTAND.
GOOD.
I'VE NEVER MET ANYONE WHO RADIATES SUCH PAIN. I SENSE THAT IS WHAT DRIVES HER SARCASM, HER ARROGANCE.
I FORGIVE HER.
IT'S EITHER THAT OR KILL HER.
WOW.
WOW.

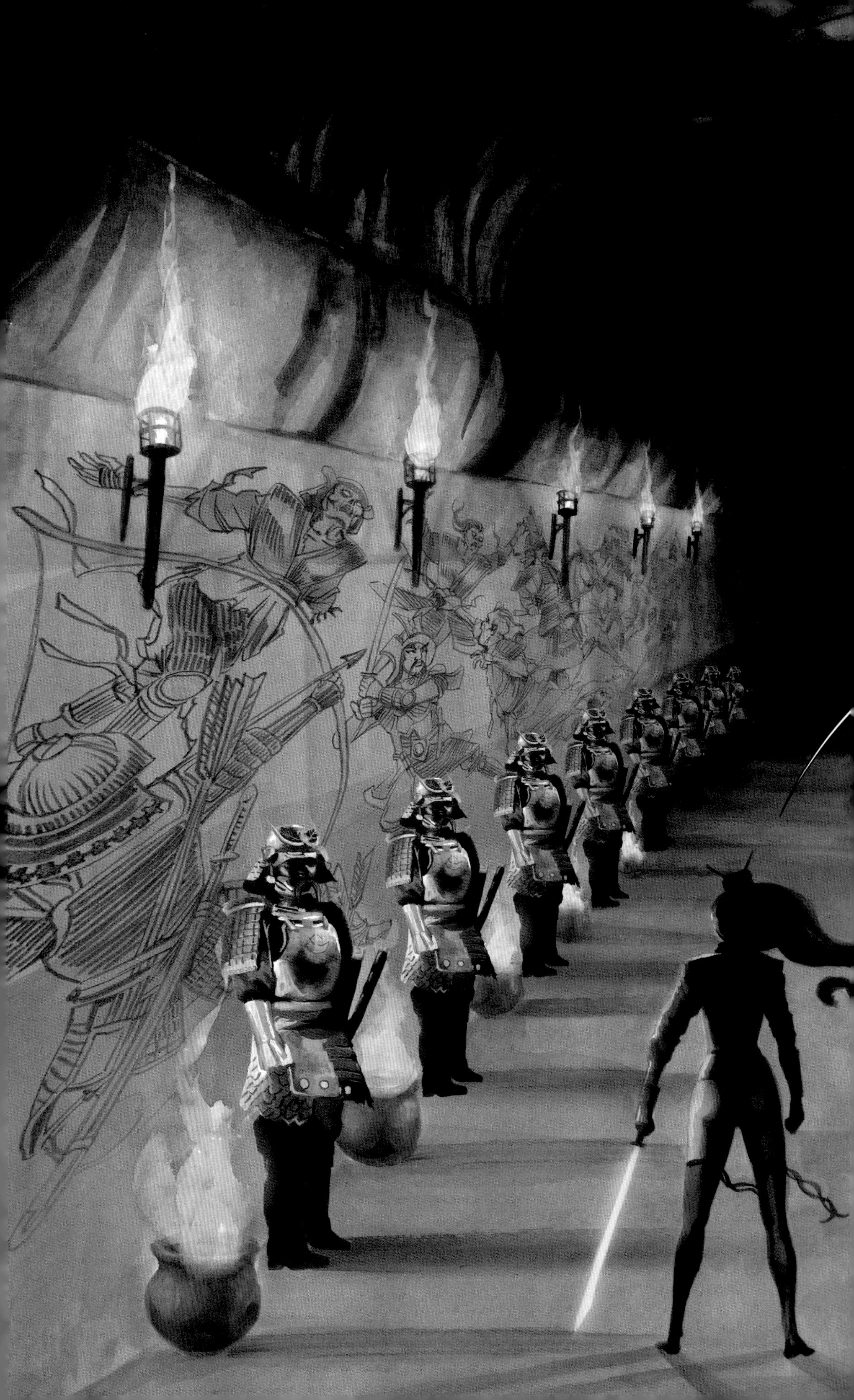

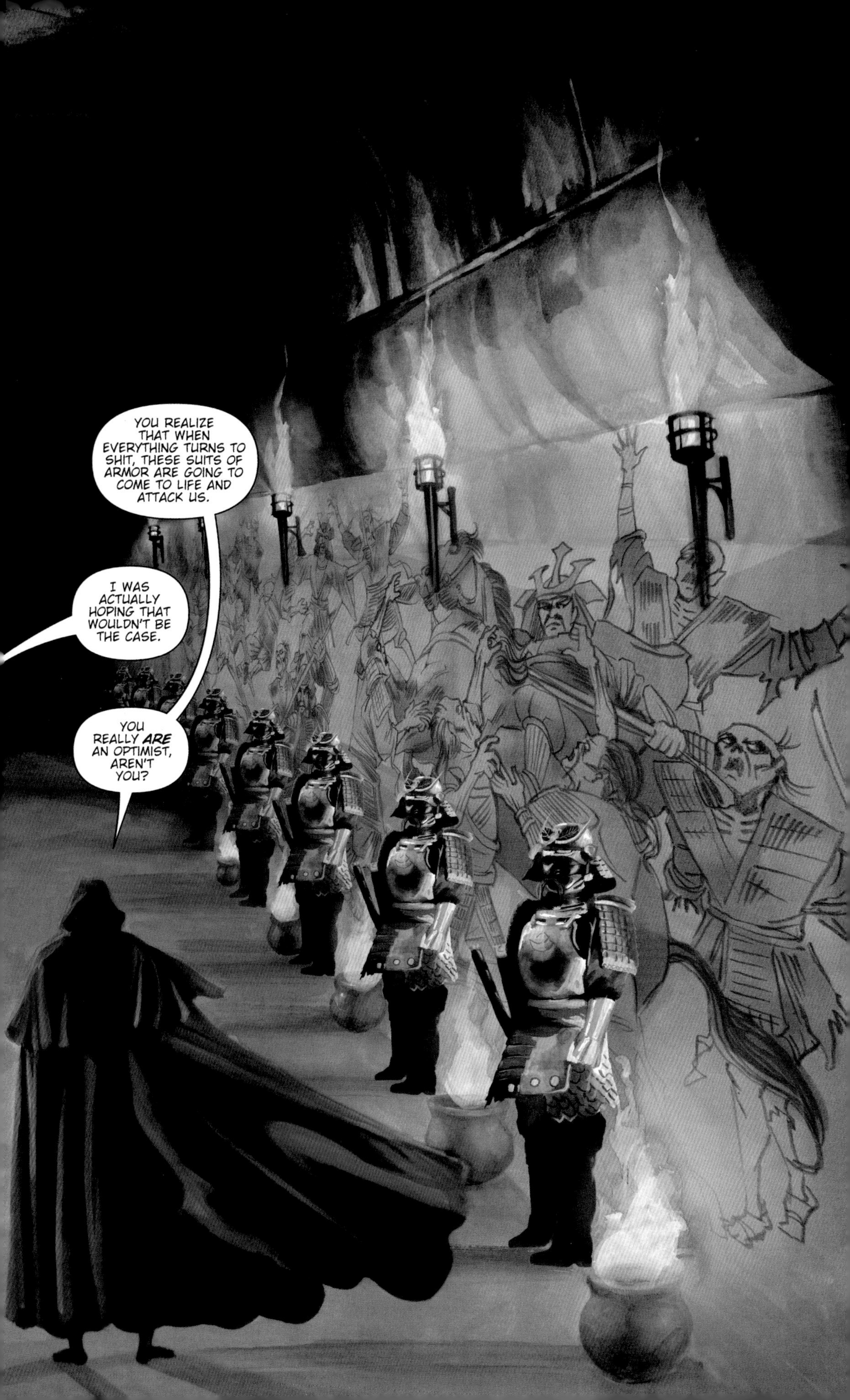
YOU REALIZE THAT WHEN EVERYTHING TURNS TO SHIT, THESE SUITS OF ARMOR ARE GOING TO COME TO LIFE AND ATTACK US.
I WAS ACTUALLY HOPING THAT WOULDN'T BE THE CASE.
YOU REALLY ARE AN OPTIMIST, AREN'T YOU?

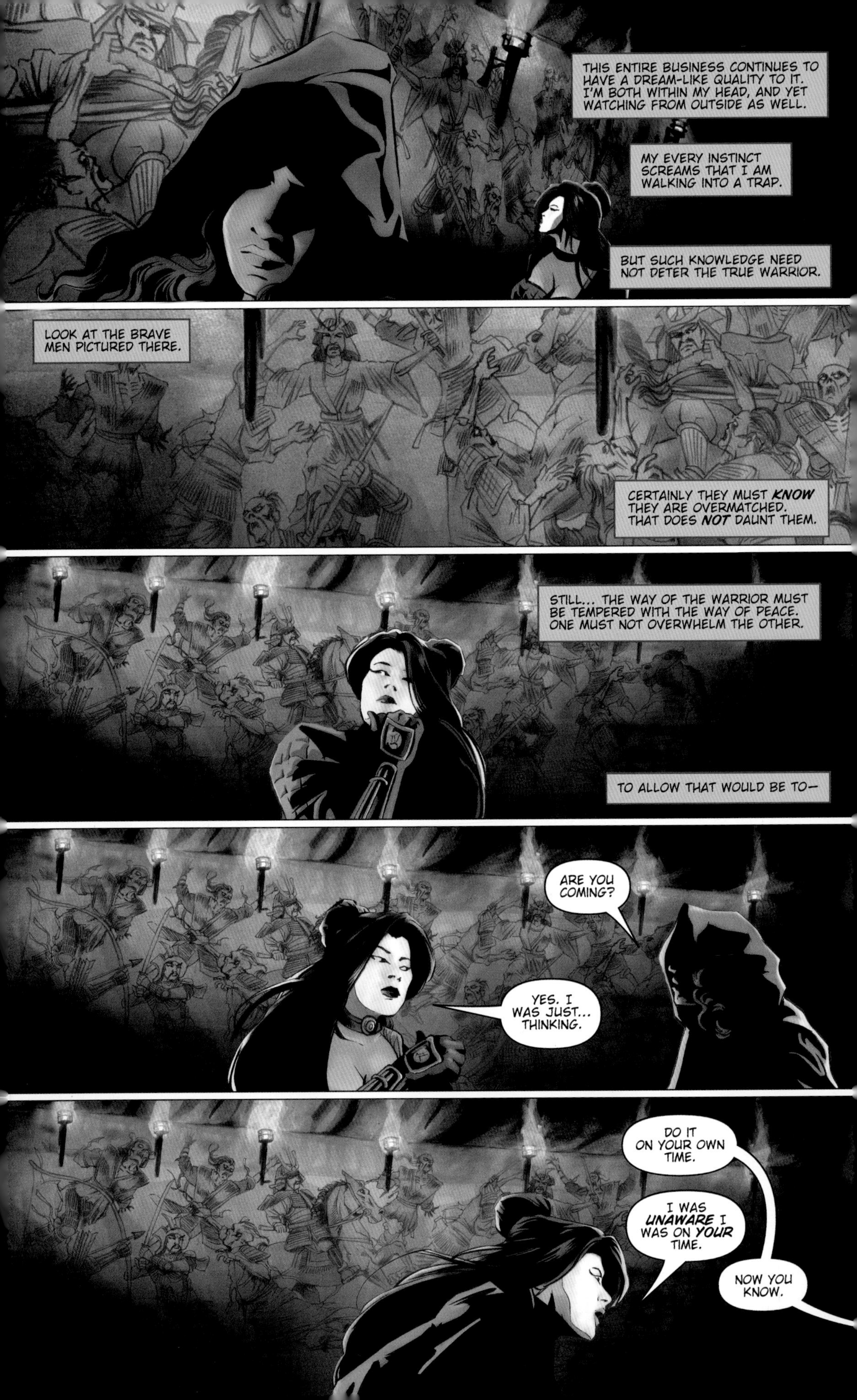
THIS ENTIRE BUSINESS CONTINUES TO HAVE A DREAM-LIKE QUALITY TO IT. I'M BOTH WITHIN MY HEAD, AND YET WATCHING FROM OUTSIDE AS WELL.
MY EVERY INSTINCT SCREAMS THAT I AM WALKING INTO A TRAP.
BUT SUCH KNOWLEDGE NEED NOT DETER THE TRUE WARRIOR.
LOOK AT THE BRAVE MEN PICTURED THERE.
CERTAINLY THEY MUST *KNOW* THEY ARE OVERMATCHED. THAT DOES *NOT* DAUNT THEM.
STILL... THE WAY OF THE WARRIOR MUST BE TEMPERED WITH THE WAY OF PEACE. ONE MUST NOT OVERWHELM THE OTHER.
TO ALLOW THAT WOULD BE TO—
ARE YOU COMING?
YES. I WAS JUST... THINKING.
DO IT ON YOUR OWN TIME.
I WAS *UNAWARE* I WAS ON *YOUR* TIME.
NOW YOU KNOW.

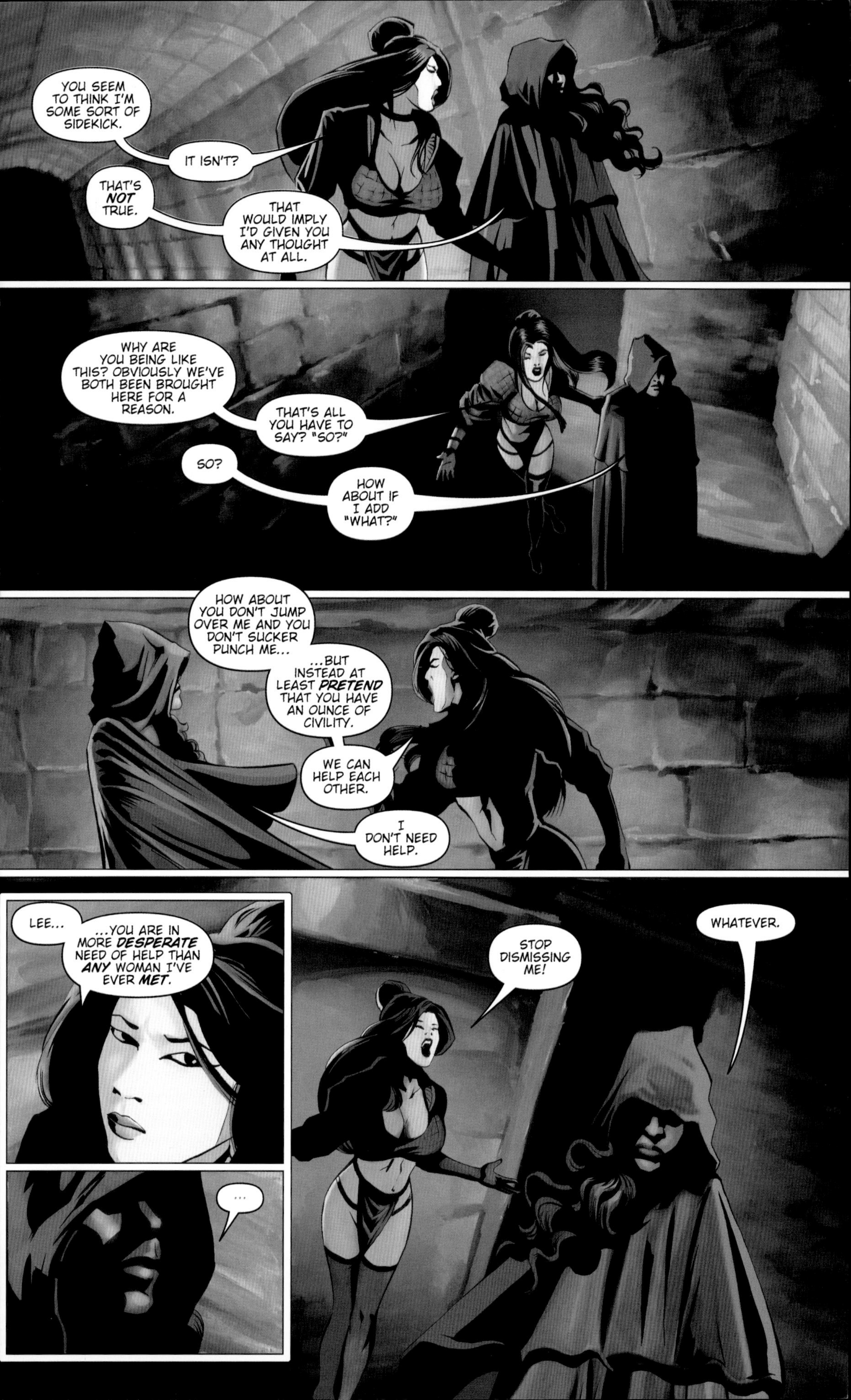
YOU SEEM TO THINK I'M SOME SORT OF SIDEKICK.
IT ISN'T?
THAT'S ***NOT*** TRUE.
THAT WOULD IMPLY I'D GIVEN YOU ANY THOUGHT AT ALL.
WHY ARE YOU BEING LIKE THIS? OBVIOUSLY WE'VE BOTH BEEN BROUGHT HERE FOR A REASON.
THAT'S ALL YOU HAVE TO SAY? "SO?"
SO?
HOW ABOUT IF I ADD "WHAT?"
HOW ABOUT YOU DON'T JUMP OVER ME AND YOU DON'T SUCKER PUNCH ME...
...BUT INSTEAD AT LEAST ***PRETEND*** THAT YOU HAVE AN OUNCE OF CIVILITY.
WE CAN HELP EACH OTHER.
I DON'T NEED HELP.
LEE...
...YOU ARE IN MORE ***DESPERATE*** NEED OF HELP THAN ***ANY*** WOMAN I'VE EVER ***MET***.
...
STOP DISMISSING ME!
WHATEVER.

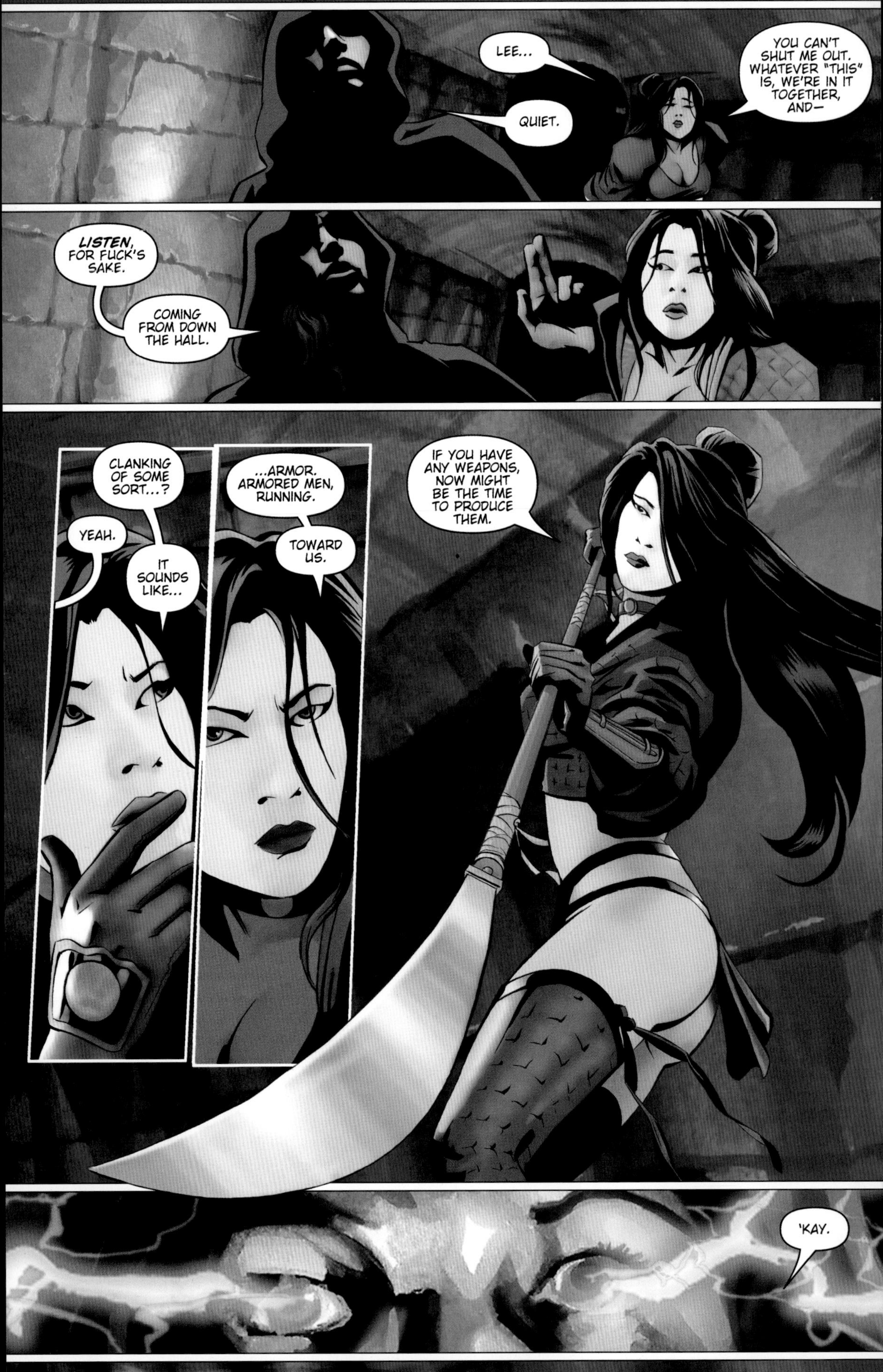
LEE...
YOU CAN'T SHUT ME OUT. WHATEVER "THIS" IS, WE'RE IN IT TOGETHER, AND—
QUIET.
LISTEN, FOR FUCK'S SAKE.
COMING FROM DOWN THE HALL.
CLANKING OF SOME SORT...?
YEAH.
IT SOUNDS LIKE...
...ARMOR. ARMORED MEN, RUNNING.
TOWARD US.
IF YOU HAVE ANY WEAPONS, NOW MIGHT BE THE TIME TO PRODUCE THEM.
'KAY.

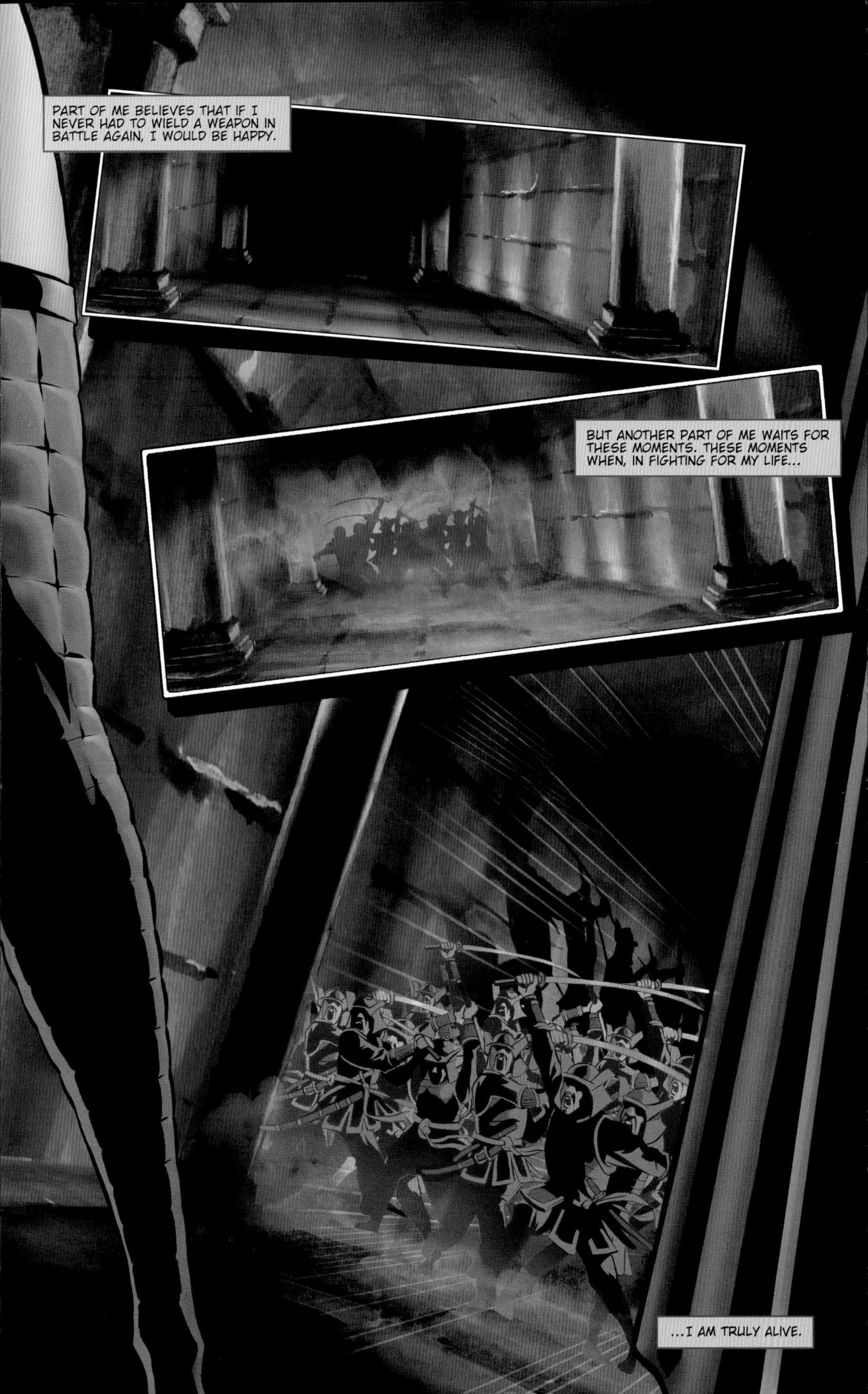
PART OF ME BELIEVES THAT IF I NEVER HAD TO WIELD A WEAPON IN BATTLE AGAIN, I WOULD BE HAPPY.
BUT ANOTHER PART OF ME WAITS FOR THESE MOMENTS. THESE MOMENTS WHEN, IN FIGHTING FOR MY LIFE...
...I AM TRULY ALIVE.

GET READY. WHEN I GIVE THE SIGNAL...

YEAH. RIGHT.

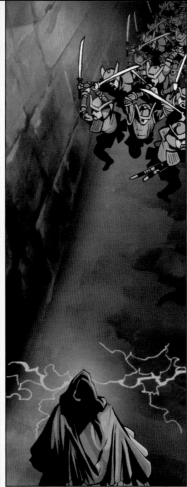

ARE *THEY* WAITING FOR YOUR SIGNAL, TOO?

I... I DON'T *UNDERSTAND.*

AND HERE I THOUGHT YOU HAD ALL THE ANSWERS.

GREETINGS.

WELCOME TO MY HOME.

SHE'S... BEAUTIFUL. SHE'S GLORIOUS.

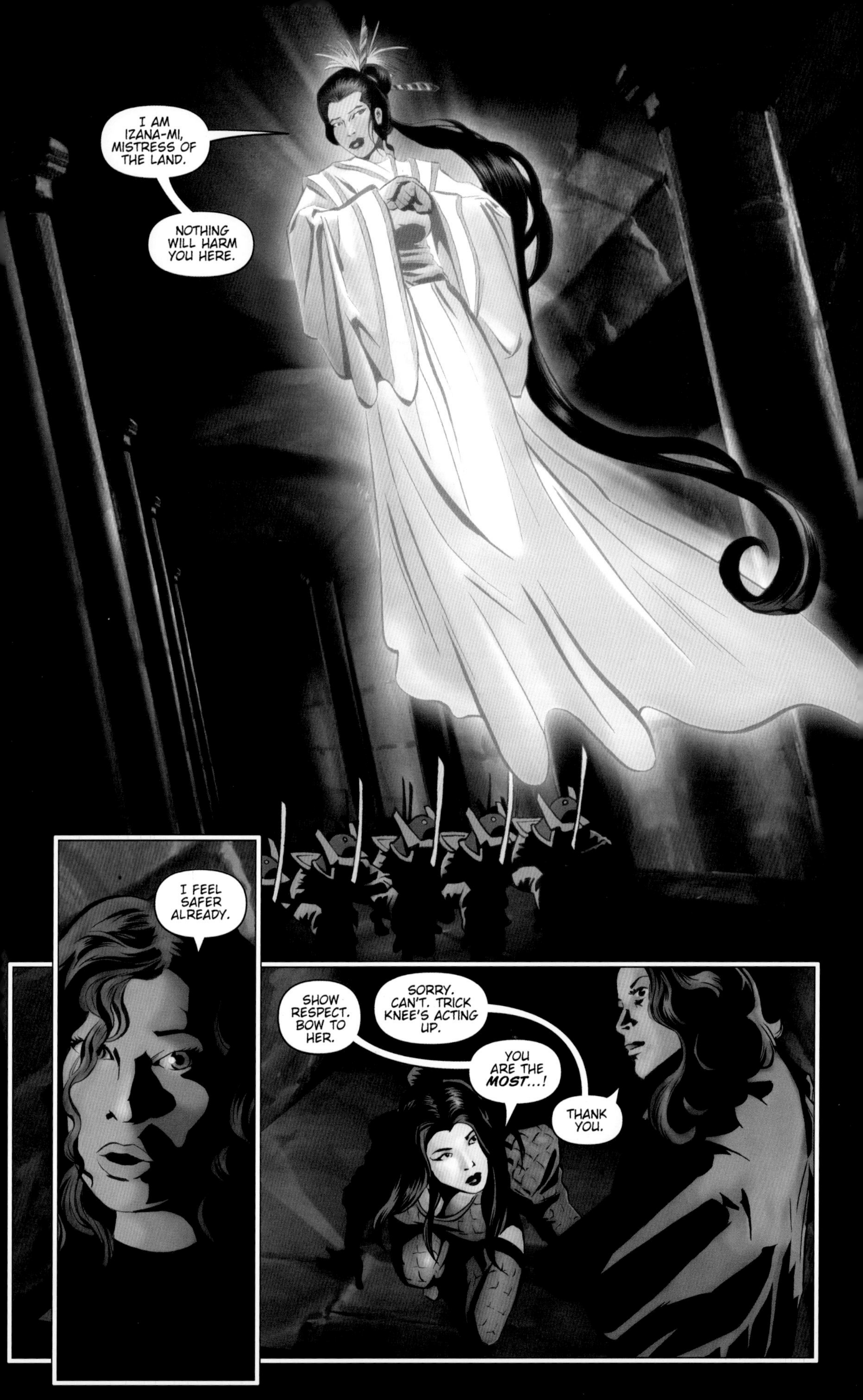
I AM IZANA-MI, MISTRESS OF THE LAND.
NOTHING WILL HARM YOU HERE.
I FEEL SAFER ALREADY.
SHOW RESPECT. BOW TO HER.
SORRY. CAN'T. TRICK KNEE'S ACTING UP.
YOU ARE THE MOST...!
THANK YOU.

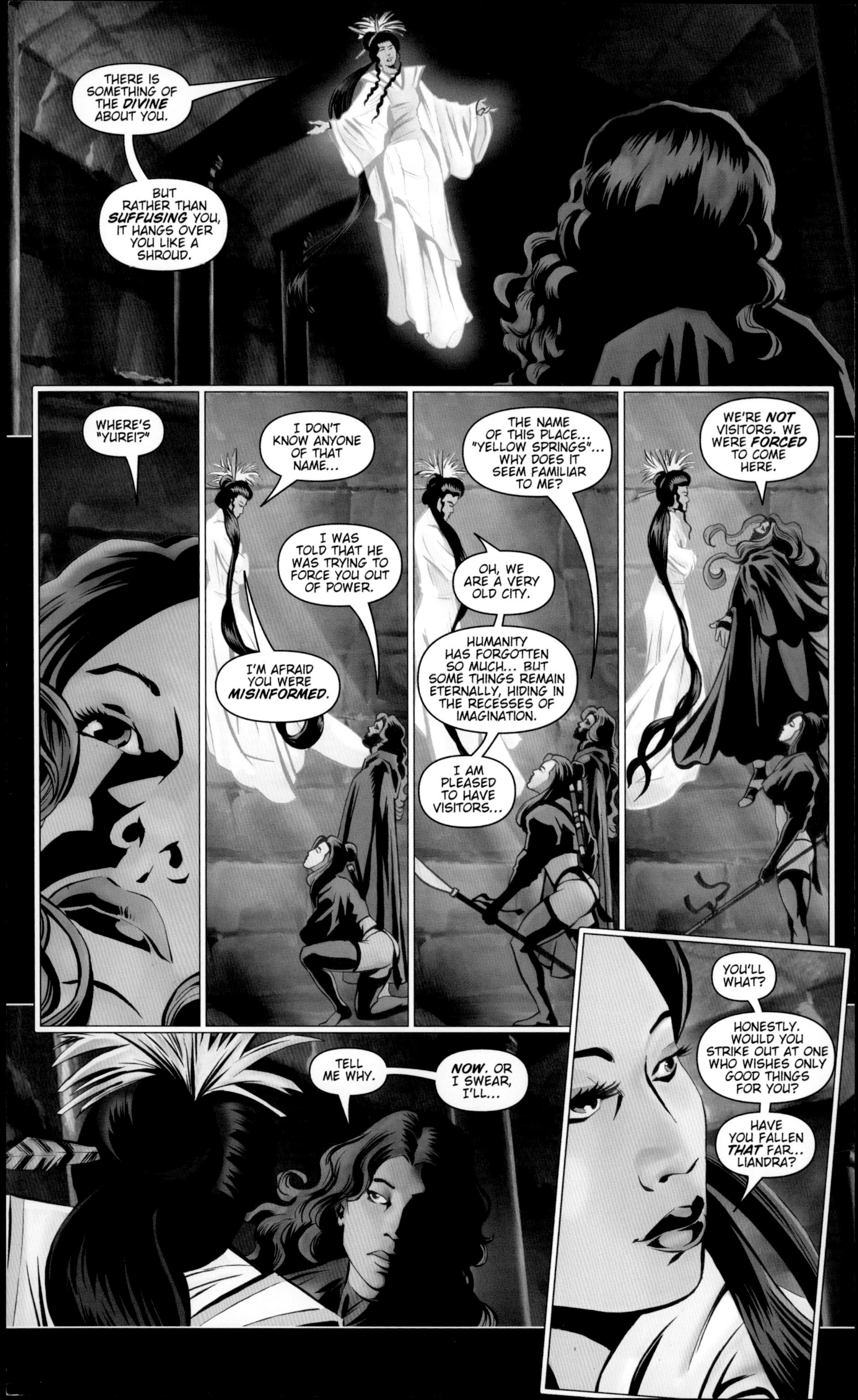

THERE IS SOMETHING OF THE DIVINE ABOUT YOU.
BUT RATHER THAN SUFFUSING YOU, IT HANGS OVER YOU LIKE A SHROUD.
WHERE'S "YUREI?"
I DON'T KNOW ANYONE OF THAT NAME...
I WAS TOLD THAT HE WAS TRYING TO FORCE YOU OUT OF POWER.
I'M AFRAID YOU WERE MISINFORMED.
THE NAME OF THIS PLACE... "YELLOW SPRINGS"... WHY DOES IT SEEM FAMILIAR TO ME?
OH, WE ARE A VERY OLD CITY.
HUMANITY HAS FORGOTTEN SO MUCH... BUT SOME THINGS REMAIN ETERNALLY, HIDING IN THE RECESSES OF IMAGINATION.
I AM PLEASED TO HAVE VISITORS...
WE'RE NOT VISITORS. WE WERE FORCED TO COME HERE.
TELL ME WHY.
NOW. OR I SWEAR, I'LL...
YOU'LL WHAT?
HONESTLY. WOULD YOU STRIKE OUT AT ONE WHO WISHES ONLY GOOD THINGS FOR YOU?
HAVE YOU FALLEN THAT FAR... LIANDRA?

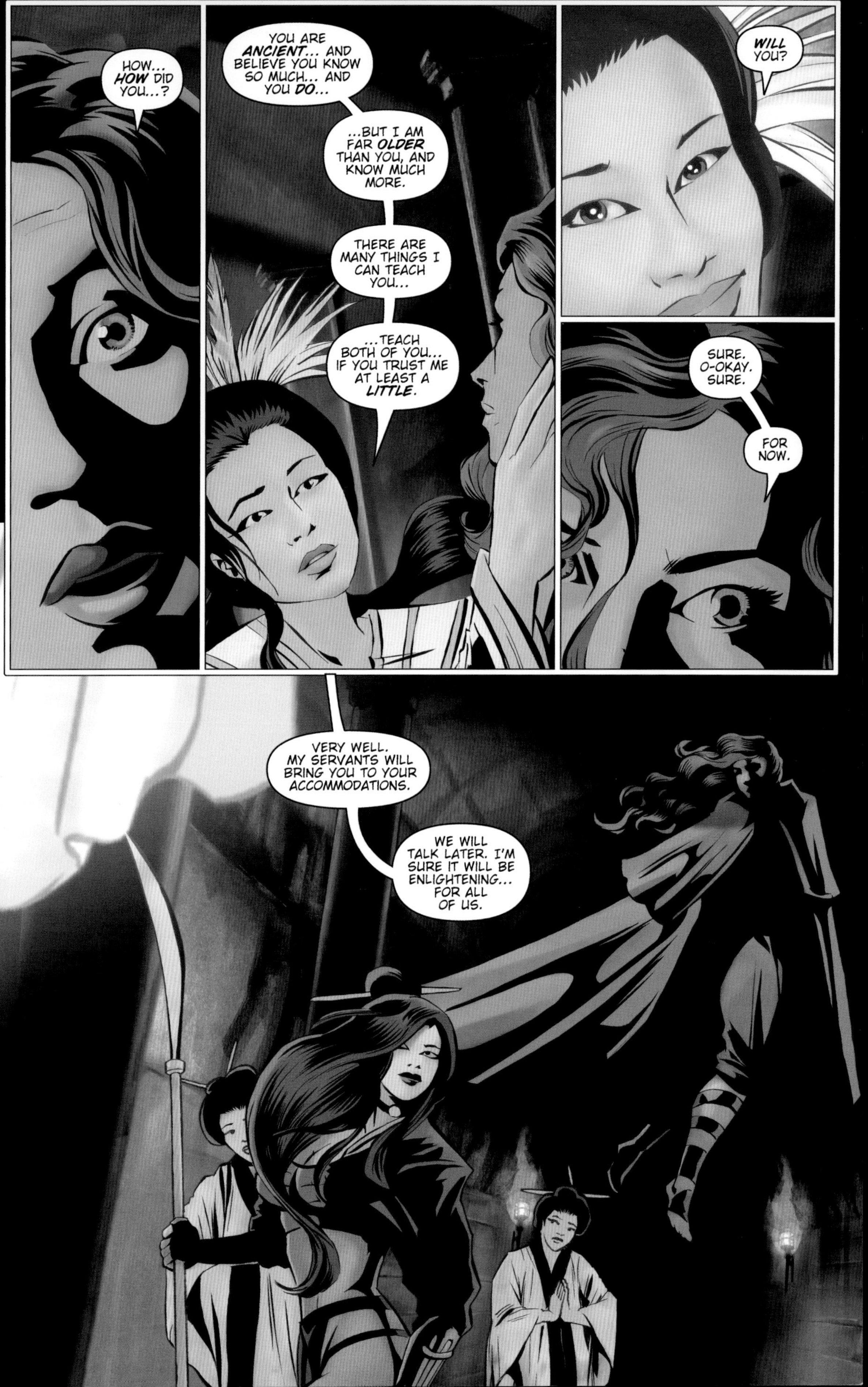

HOW... *HOW* DID YOU...?
YOU ARE *ANCIENT*... AND BELIEVE YOU KNOW SO MUCH... AND YOU *DO*...
...BUT I AM FAR *OLDER* THAN YOU, AND KNOW MUCH MORE.
THERE ARE MANY THINGS I CAN TEACH YOU...
...TEACH BOTH OF YOU... IF YOU TRUST ME AT LEAST A *LITTLE*.
WILL YOU?
SURE. O-OKAY. SURE.
FOR NOW.
VERY WELL. MY SERVANTS WILL BRING YOU TO YOUR ACCOMMODATIONS.
WE WILL TALK LATER. I'M SURE IT WILL BE ENLIGHTENING... FOR ALL OF US.

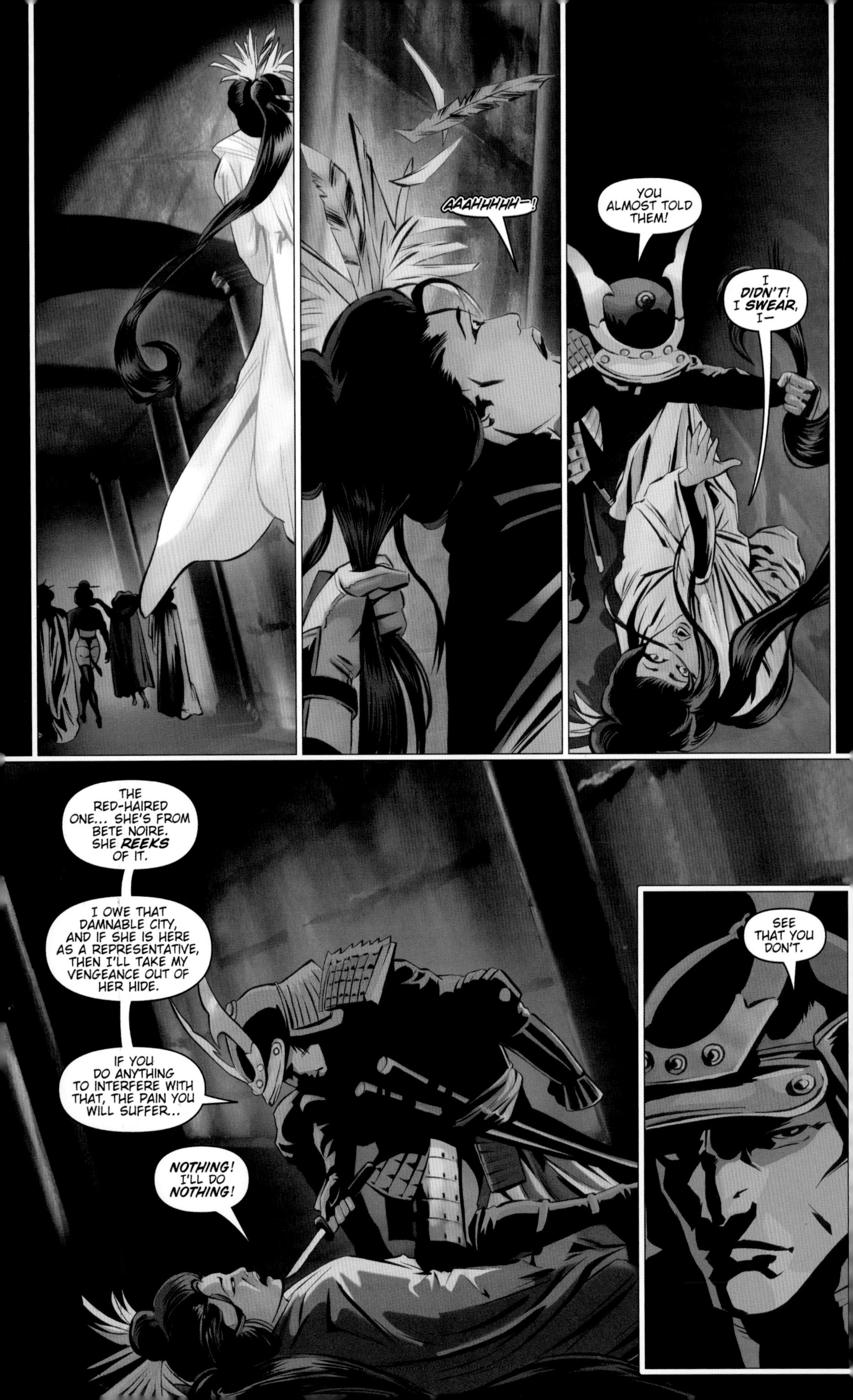
AAAHHHHH—!
YOU ALMOST TOLD THEM!
I DIDN'T! I SWEAR, I—
THE RED-HAIRED ONE... SHE'S FROM BETE NOIRE. SHE REEKS OF IT.
I OWE THAT DAMNABLE CITY, AND IF SHE IS HERE AS A REPRESENTATIVE, THEN I'LL TAKE MY VENGEANCE OUT OF HER HIDE.
IF YOU DO ANYTHING TO INTERFERE WITH THAT, THE PAIN YOU WILL SUFFER...
NOTHING! I'LL DO NOTHING!
SEE THAT YOU DON'T.

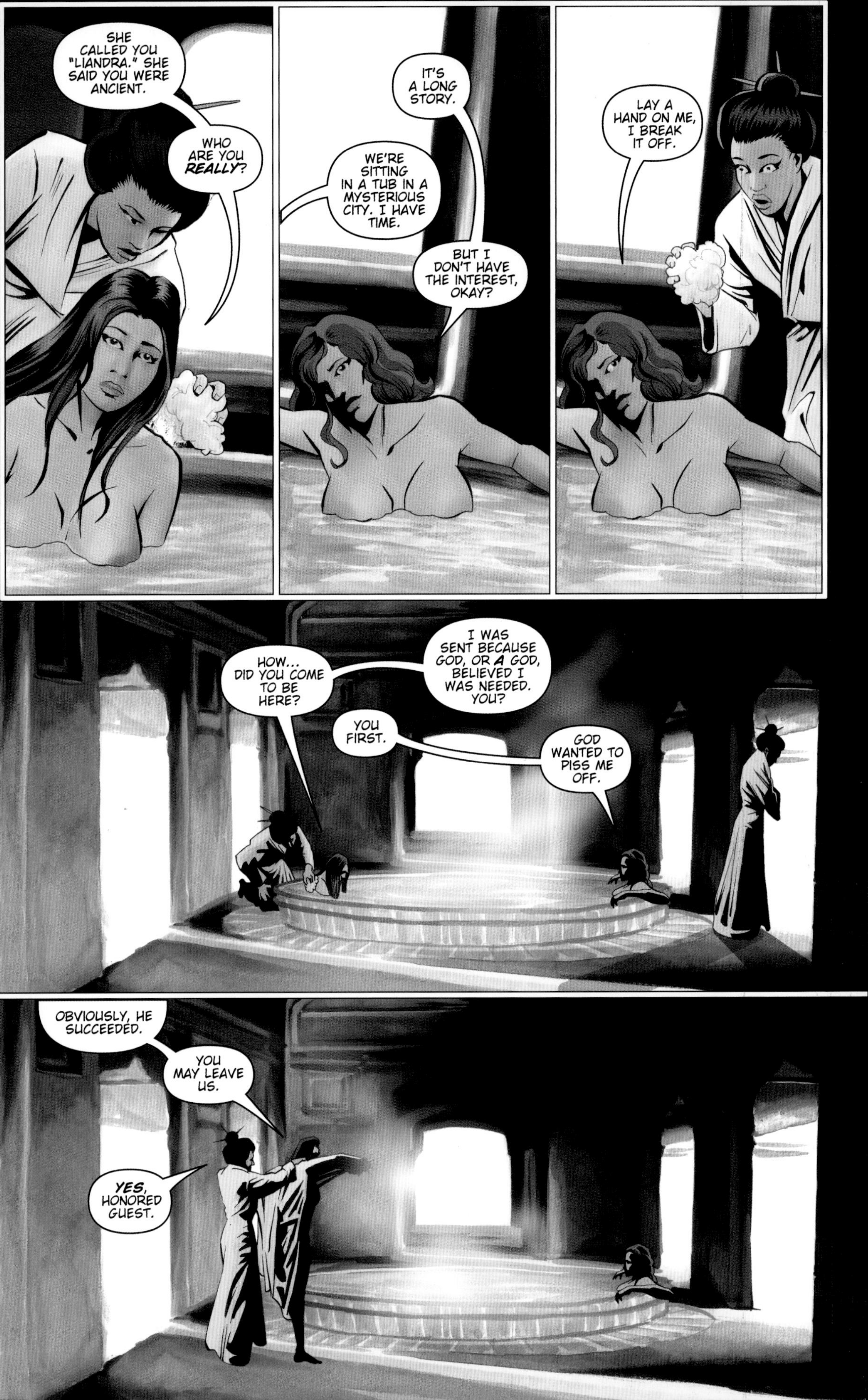
SHE CALLED YOU "LIANDRA." SHE SAID YOU WERE ANCIENT.
WHO ARE YOU *REALLY*?
IT'S A LONG STORY.
WE'RE SITTING IN A TUB IN A MYSTERIOUS CITY. I HAVE TIME.
BUT I DON'T HAVE THE INTEREST, OKAY?
LAY A HAND ON ME, I BREAK IT OFF.
HOW... DID YOU COME TO BE HERE?
I WAS SENT BECAUSE GOD, OR *A* GOD, BELIEVED I WAS NEEDED. YOU?
YOU FIRST.
GOD WANTED TO PISS ME OFF.
OBVIOUSLY, HE SUCCEEDED.
YOU MAY LEAVE US.
YES, HONORED GUEST.

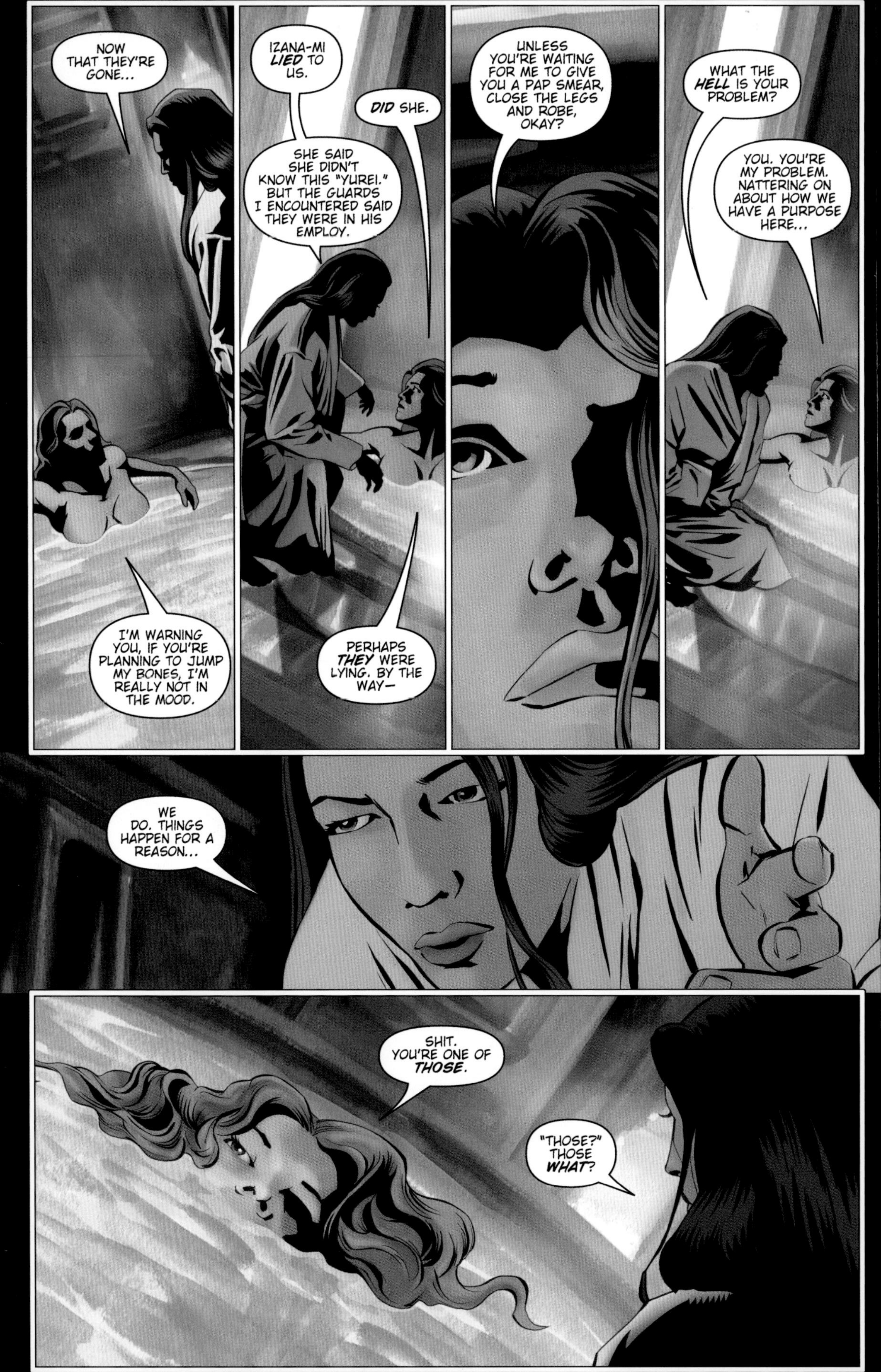
NOW THAT THEY'RE GONE...
I'M WARNING YOU, IF YOU'RE PLANNING TO JUMP MY BONES, I'M REALLY NOT IN THE MOOD.
IZANA-MI *LIED* TO US.
SHE SAID SHE DIDN'T KNOW THIS "YUREI." BUT THE GUARDS I ENCOUNTERED SAID THEY WERE IN HIS EMPLOY.
DID SHE.
PERHAPS *THEY* WERE LYING. BY THE WAY—
UNLESS YOU'RE WAITING FOR ME TO GIVE YOU A PAP SMEAR, CLOSE THE LEGS AND ROBE, OKAY?
WHAT THE *HELL* IS YOUR PROBLEM?
YOU. YOU'RE MY PROBLEM. NATTERING ON ABOUT HOW WE HAVE A PURPOSE HERE...
WE DO. THINGS HAPPEN FOR A REASON...
SHIT. YOU'RE ONE OF *THOSE*.
"THOSE?" THOSE *WHAT*?

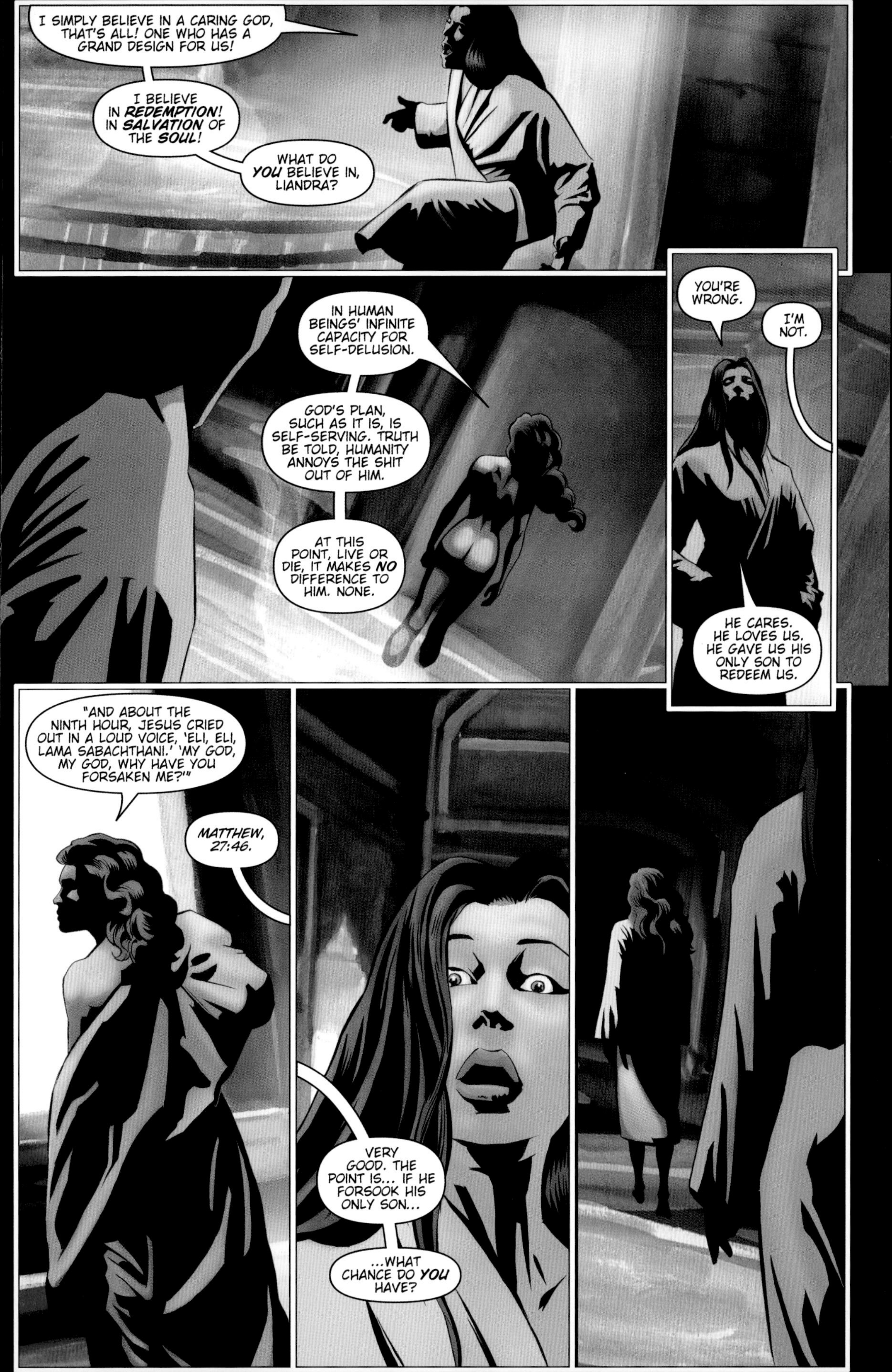
I SIMPLY BELIEVE IN A CARING GOD, THAT'S ALL! ONE WHO HAS A GRAND DESIGN FOR US!
I BELIEVE IN **REDEMPTION**! IN **SALVATION** OF THE **SOUL**!
WHAT DO ***YOU*** BELIEVE IN, LIANDRA?
IN HUMAN BEINGS' INFINITE CAPACITY FOR SELF-DELUSION.
GOD'S PLAN, SUCH AS IT IS, IS SELF-SERVING. TRUTH BE TOLD, HUMANITY ANNOYS THE SHIT OUT OF HIM.
AT THIS POINT, LIVE OR DIE, IT MAKES ***NO*** DIFFERENCE TO HIM. NONE.
YOU'RE WRONG.
I'M NOT.
HE CARES. HE LOVES US. HE GAVE US HIS ONLY SON TO REDEEM US.
"AND ABOUT THE NINTH HOUR, JESUS CRIED OUT IN A LOUD VOICE, 'ELI, ELI, LAMA SABACHTHANI.' 'MY GOD, MY GOD, WHY HAVE YOU FORSAKEN ME?'"
MATTHEW, 27:46.
VERY GOOD. THE POINT IS... IF HE FORSOOK HIS ONLY SON...
...WHAT CHANCE DO ***YOU*** HAVE?

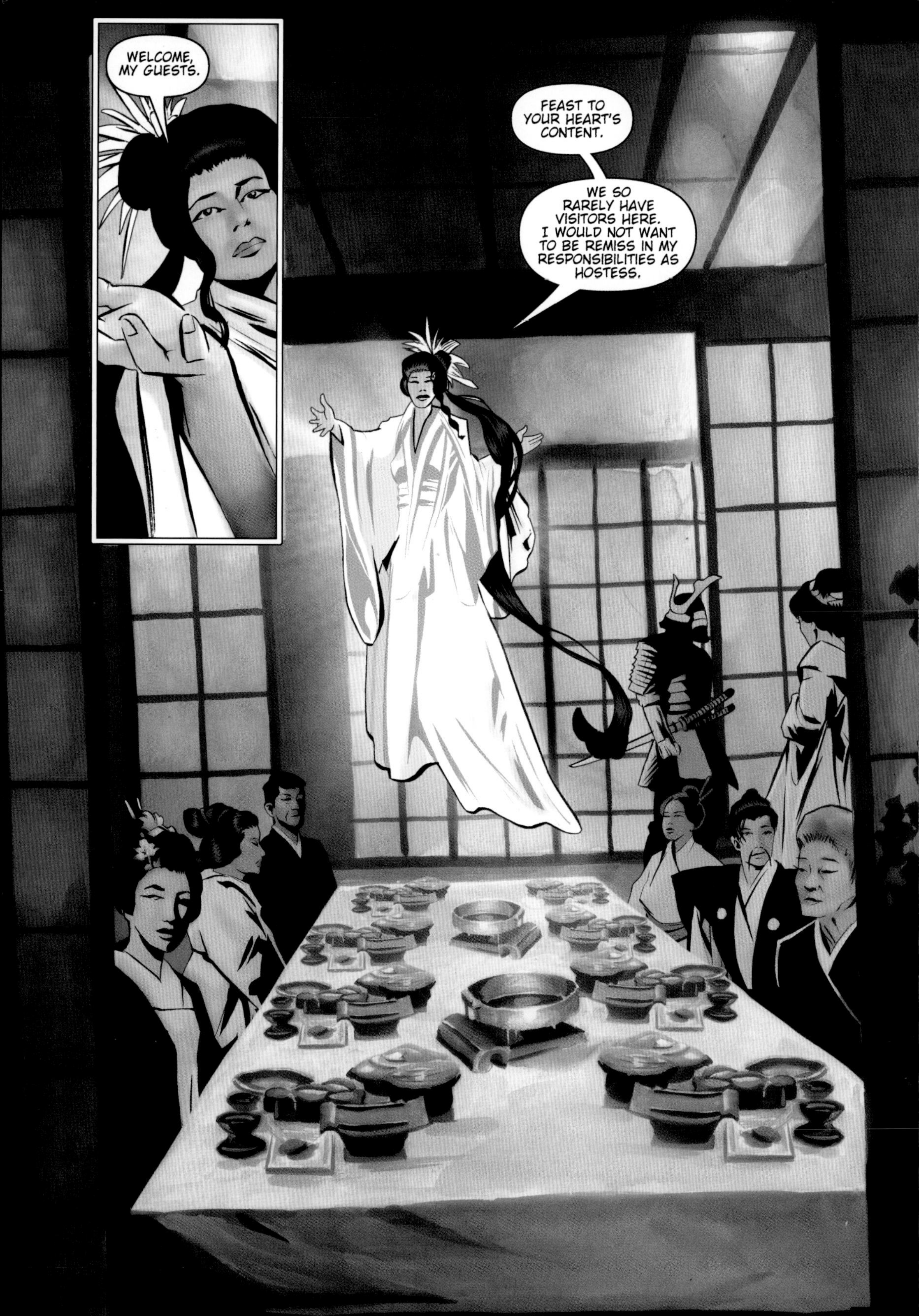
WELCOME, MY GUESTS.
FEAST TO YOUR HEART'S CONTENT.
WE SO RARELY HAVE VISITORS HERE. I WOULD NOT WANT TO BE REMISS IN MY RESPONSIBILITIES AS HOSTESS.

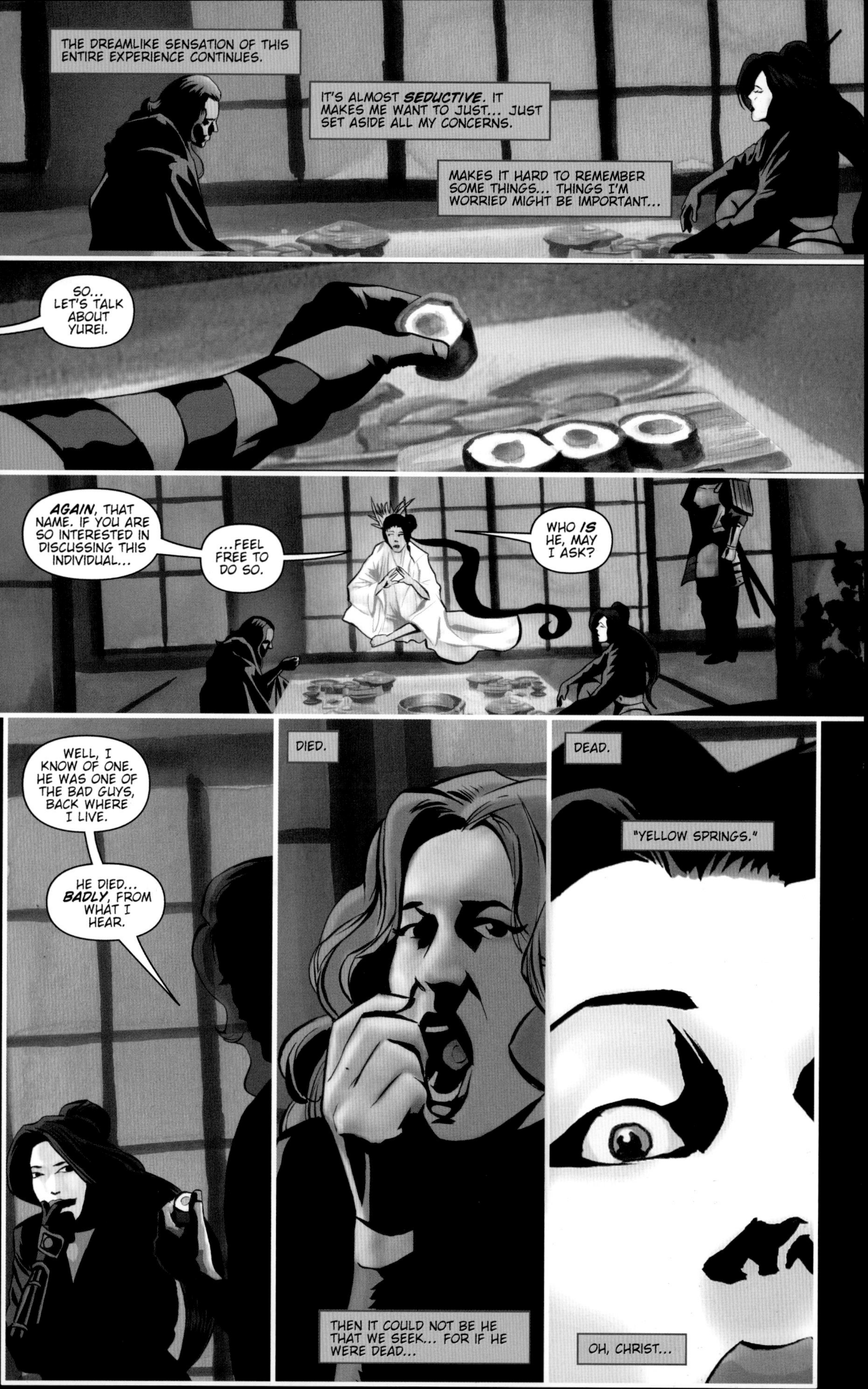
THE DREAMLIKE SENSATION OF THIS ENTIRE EXPERIENCE CONTINUES.
IT'S ALMOST SEDUCTIVE. IT MAKES ME WANT TO JUST... JUST SET ASIDE ALL MY CONCERNS.
MAKES IT HARD TO REMEMBER SOME THINGS... THINGS I'M WORRIED MIGHT BE IMPORTANT...
SO... LET'S TALK ABOUT YUREI.
AGAIN, THAT NAME. IF YOU ARE SO INTERESTED IN DISCUSSING THIS INDIVIDUAL...
...FEEL FREE TO DO SO.
WHO IS HE, MAY I ASK?
WELL, I KNOW OF ONE. HE WAS ONE OF THE BAD GUYS, BACK WHERE I LIVE.
HE DIED... BADLY, FROM WHAT I HEAR.
DIED.
THEN IT COULD NOT BE HE THAT WE SEEK... FOR IF HE WERE DEAD...
DEAD.
"YELLOW SPRINGS."
OH, CHRIST...

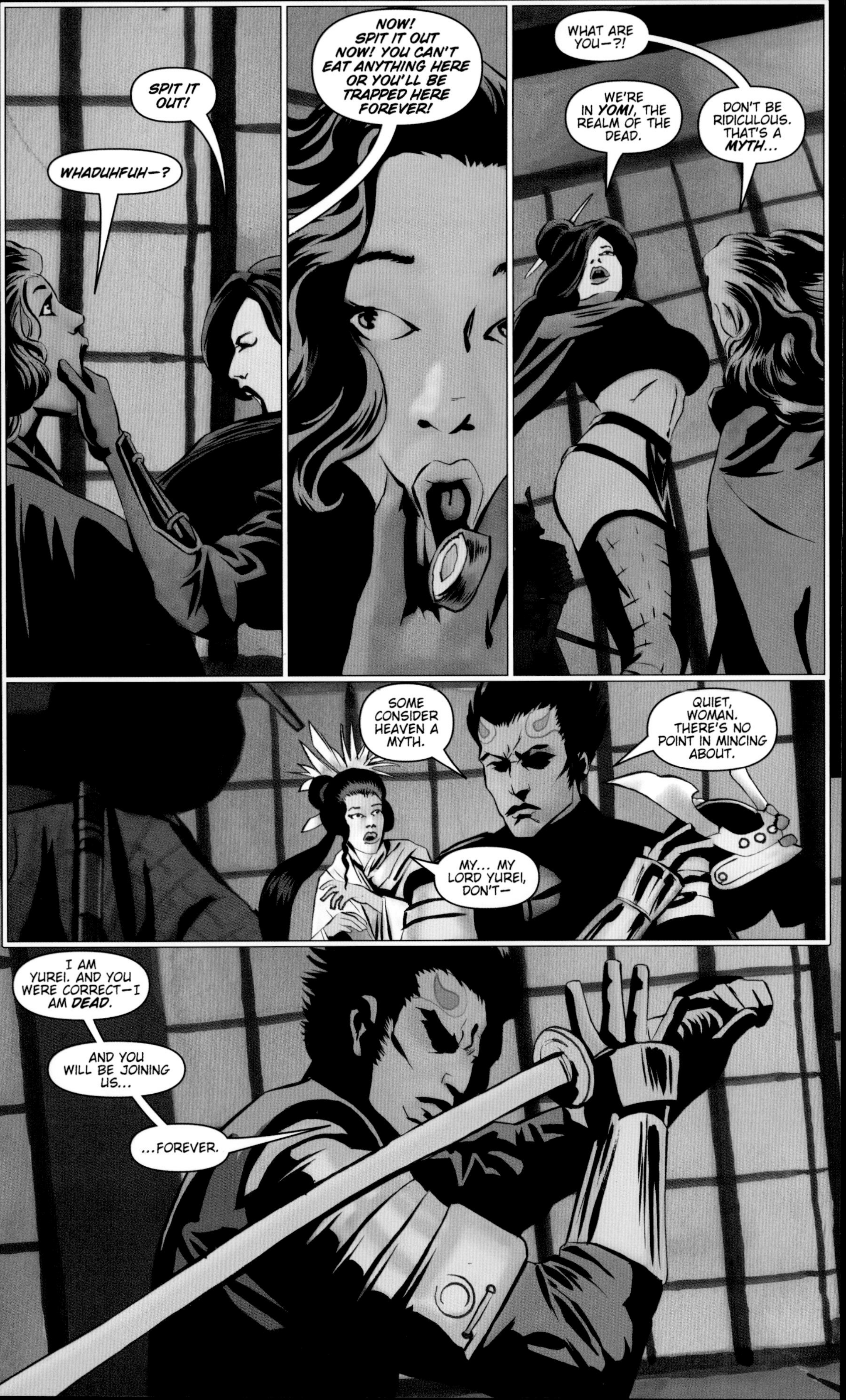
SPIT IT OUT!
WHADUHFUH—?
NOW! SPIT IT OUT NOW! YOU CAN'T EAT ANYTHING HERE OR YOU'LL BE TRAPPED HERE FOREVER!
WHAT ARE YOU—?!
WE'RE IN YOMI, THE REALM OF THE DEAD.
DON'T BE RIDICULOUS. THAT'S A MYTH...
SOME CONSIDER HEAVEN A MYTH.
QUIET, WOMAN. THERE'S NO POINT IN MINCING ABOUT.
MY... MY LORD YUREI, DON'T—
I AM YUREI. AND YOU WERE CORRECT—I AM DEAD.
AND YOU WILL BE JOINING US...
...FOREVER.

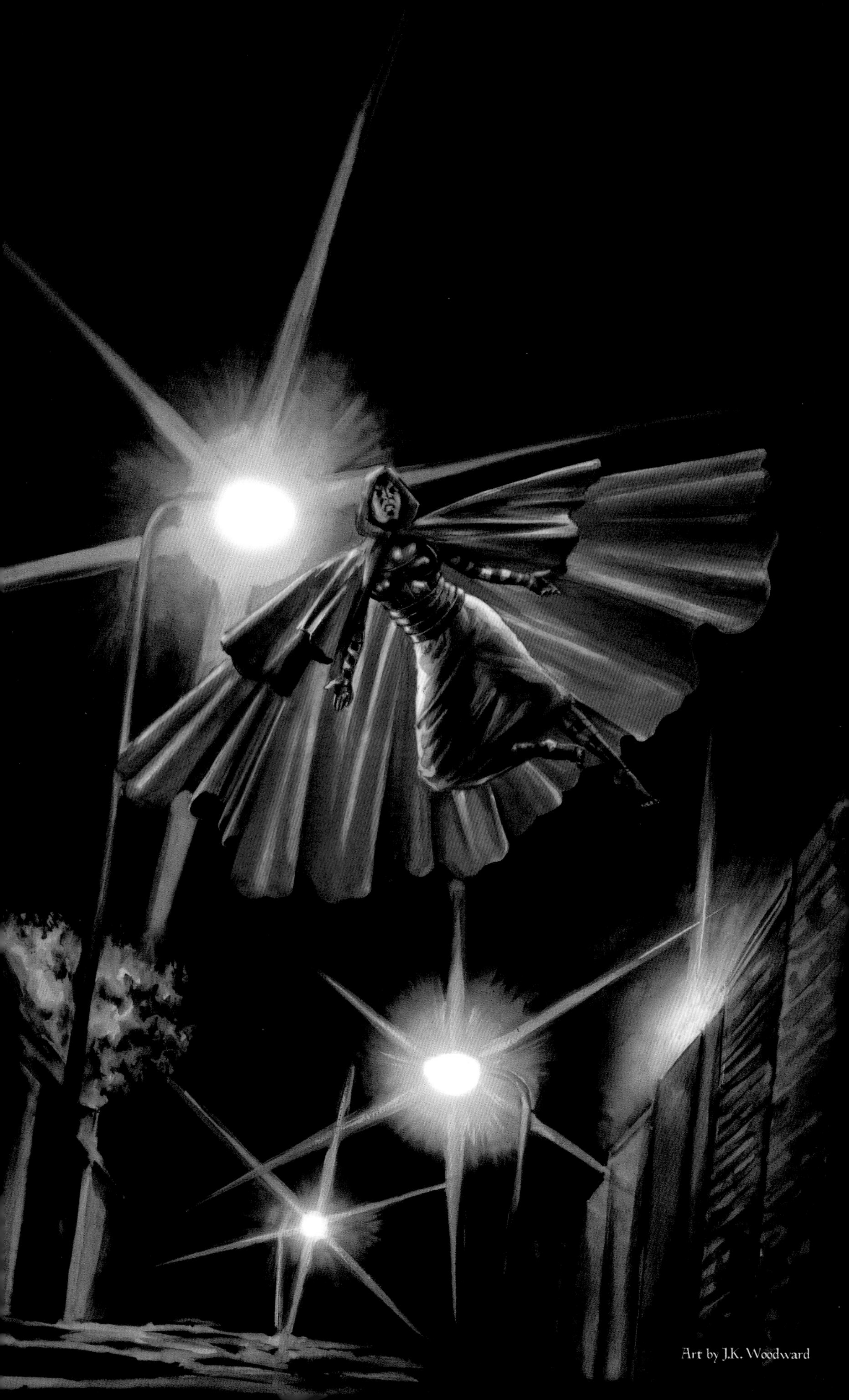
Art by J.K. Woodward

Chapter 3

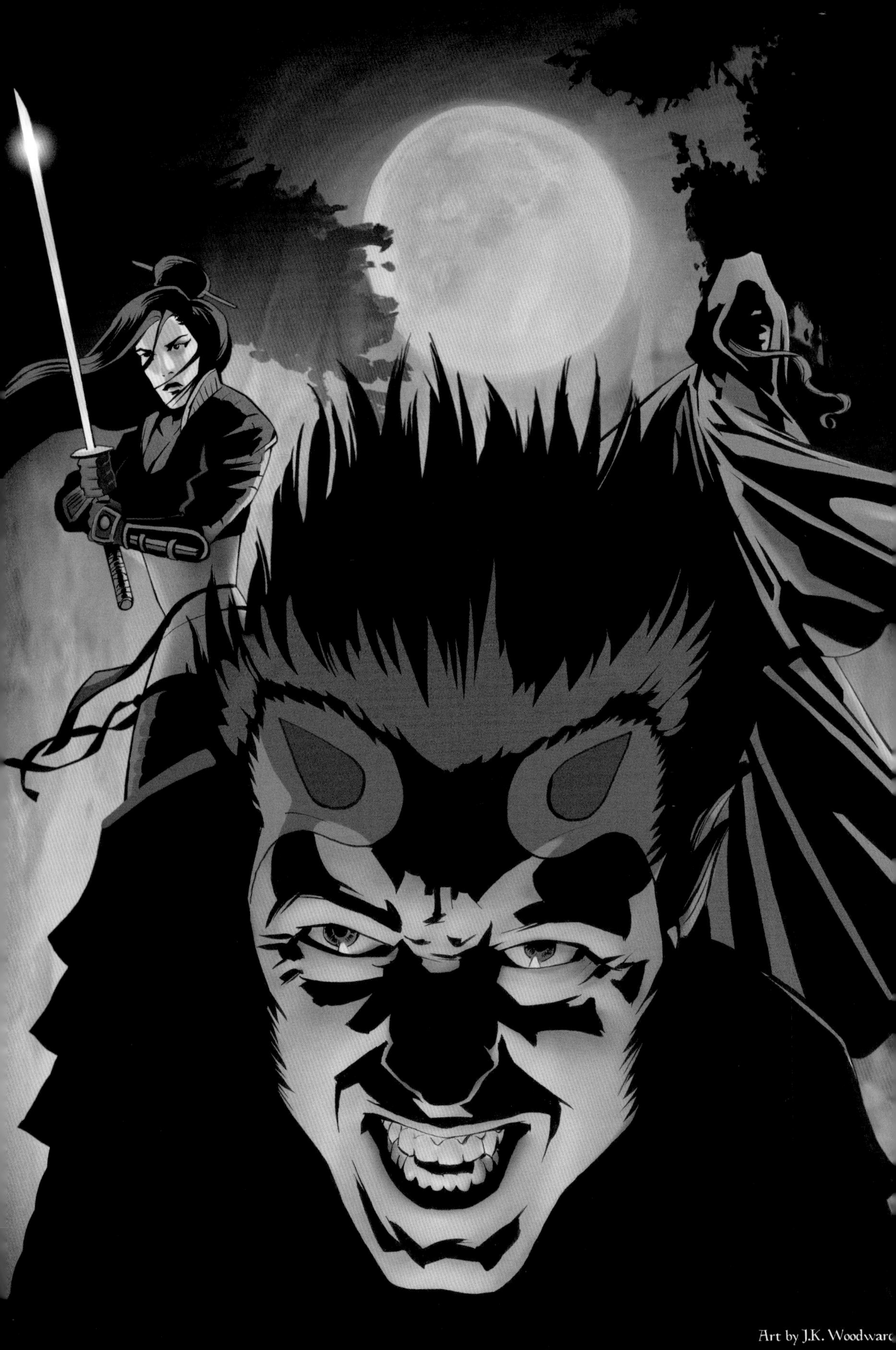

Art by J.K. Woodward

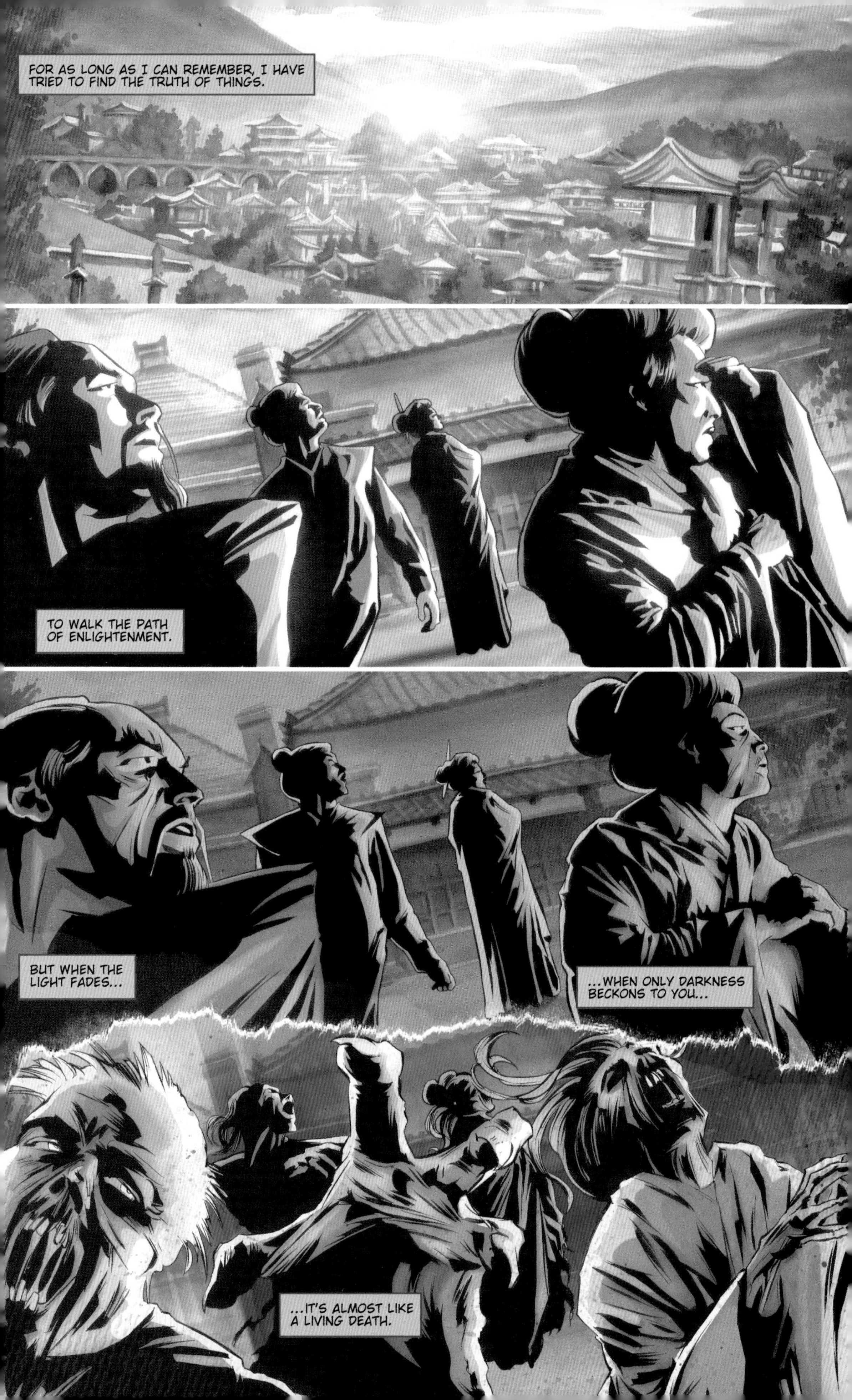
FOR AS LONG AS I CAN REMEMBER, I HAVE TRIED TO FIND THE TRUTH OF THINGS.
TO WALK THE PATH OF ENLIGHTENMENT.
BUT WHEN THE LIGHT FADES...
...WHEN ONLY DARKNESS BECKONS TO YOU...
...IT'S ALMOST LIKE A LIVING DEATH.

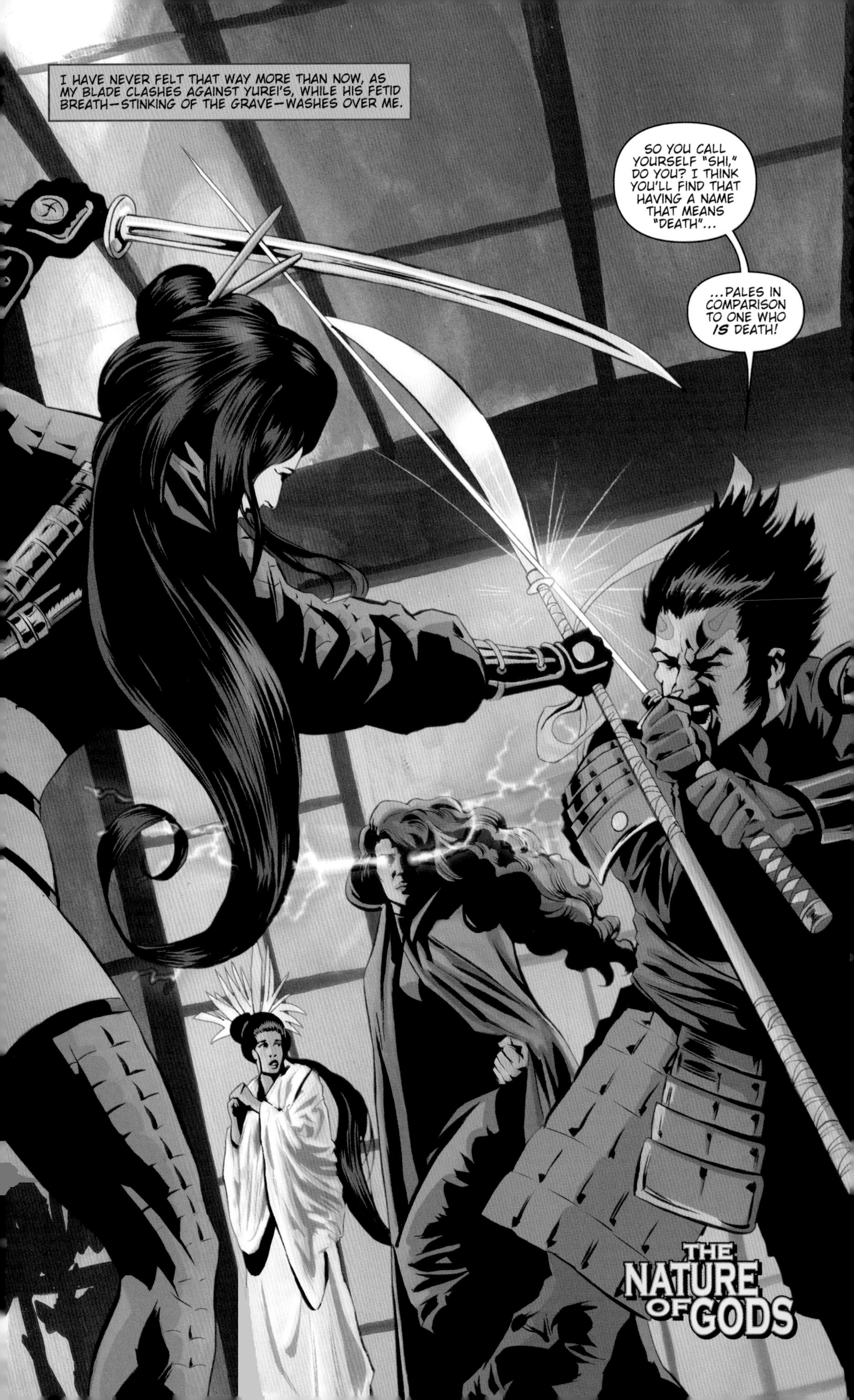
I HAVE NEVER FELT THAT WAY MORE THAN NOW, AS MY BLADE CLASHES AGAINST YUREI'S, WHILE HIS FETID BREATH—STINKING OF THE GRAVE—WASHES OVER ME.
SO YOU CALL YOURSELF "SHI," DO YOU? I THINK YOU'LL FIND THAT HAVING A NAME THAT MEANS "DEATH"...
...PALES IN COMPARISON TO ONE WHO *IS* DEATH!
THE NATURE OF GODS

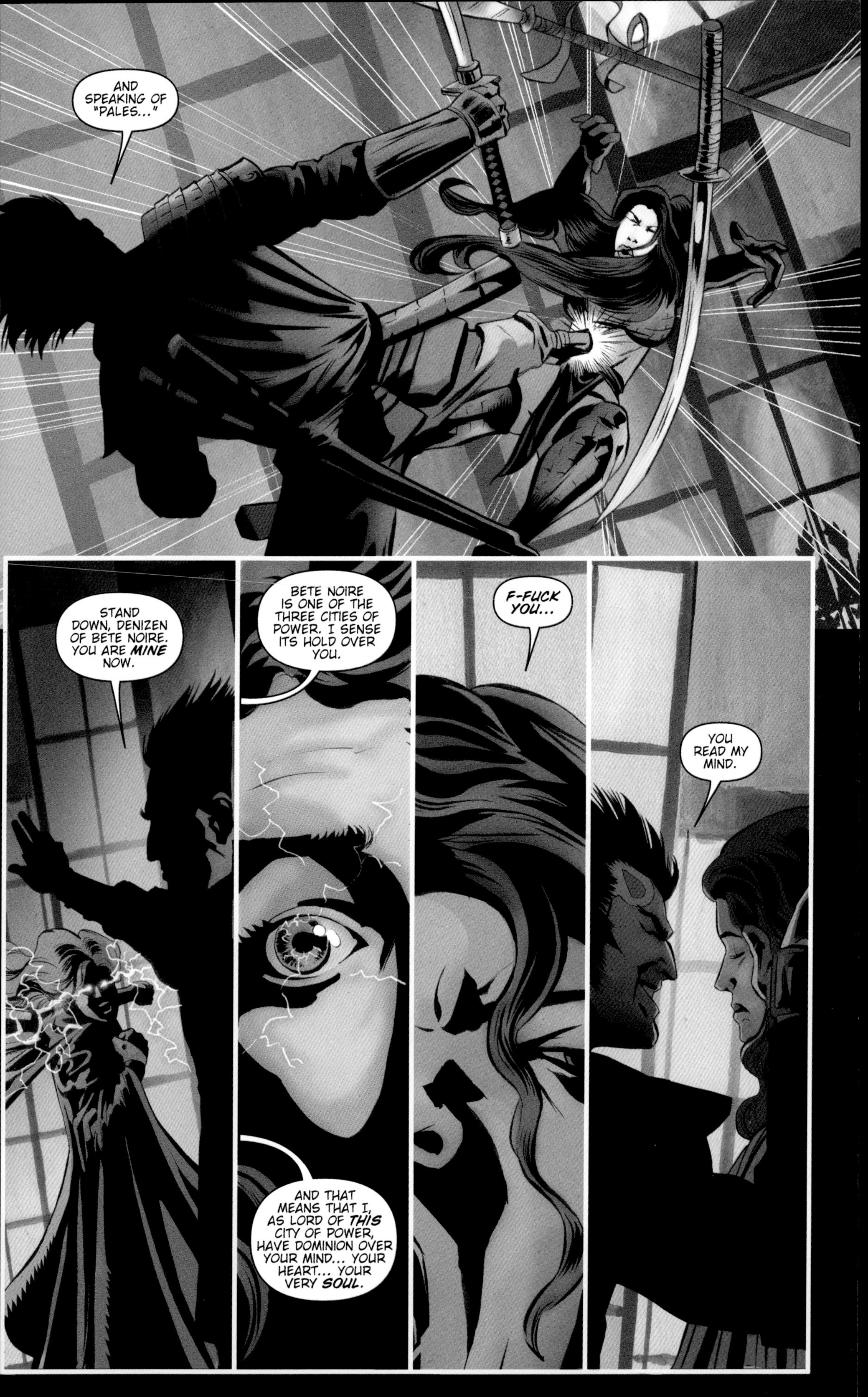
AND SPEAKING OF "PALES..."
STAND DOWN, DENIZEN OF BETE NOIRE. YOU ARE *MINE* NOW.
BETE NOIRE IS ONE OF THE THREE CITIES OF POWER. I SENSE ITS HOLD OVER YOU.
AND THAT MEANS THAT I, AS LORD OF *THIS* CITY OF POWER, HAVE DOMINION OVER YOUR MIND... YOUR HEART... YOUR VERY *SOUL*.
F-FUCK YOU...
YOU READ MY MIND.

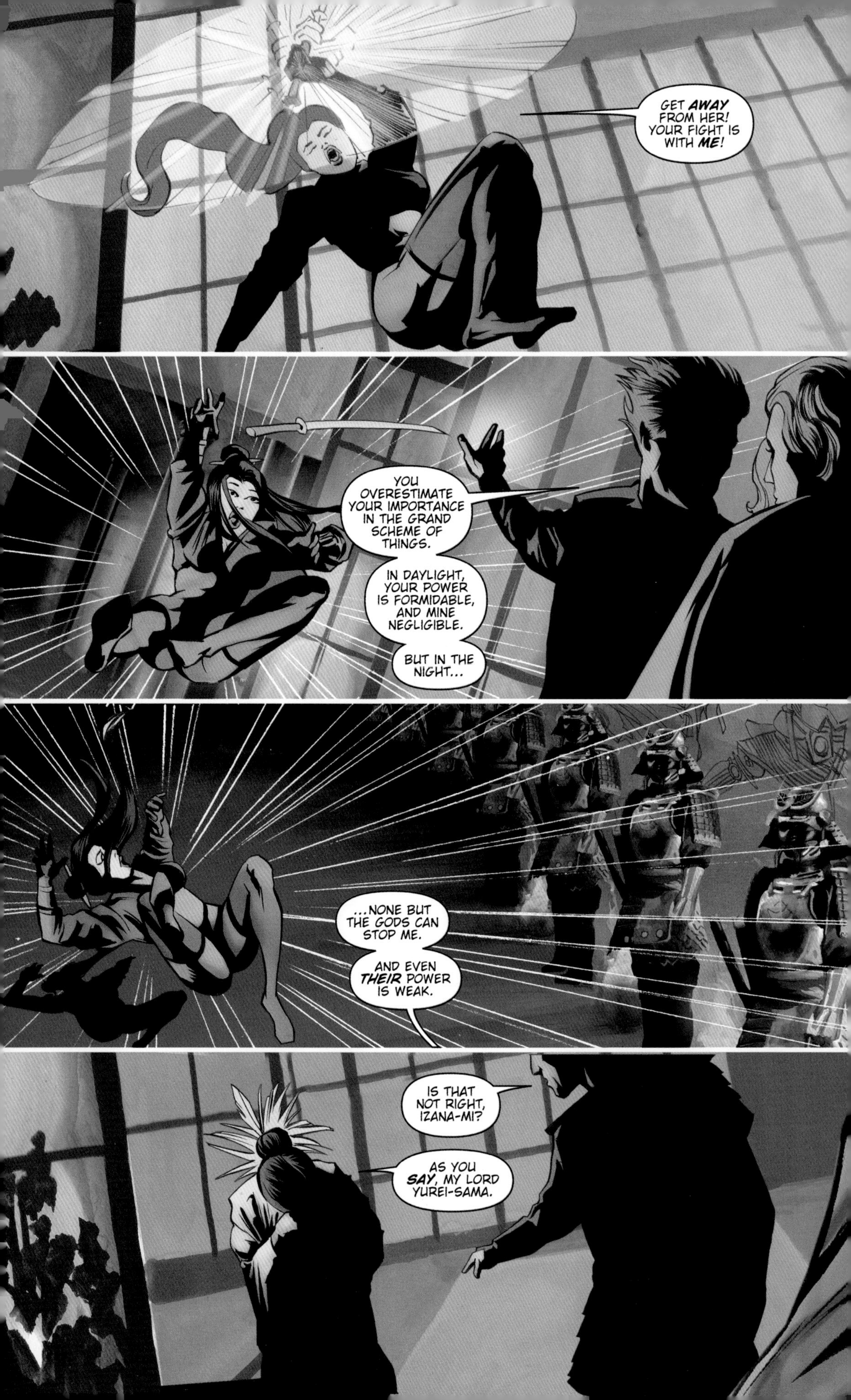
GET AWAY FROM HER! YOUR FIGHT IS WITH ME!
YOU OVERESTIMATE YOUR IMPORTANCE IN THE GRAND SCHEME OF THINGS.
IN DAYLIGHT, YOUR POWER IS FORMIDABLE, AND MINE NEGLIGIBLE.
BUT IN THE NIGHT...
...NONE BUT THE GODS CAN STOP ME.
AND EVEN THEIR POWER IS WEAK.
IS THAT NOT RIGHT, IZANA-MI?
AS YOU SAY, MY LORD YUREI-SAMA.

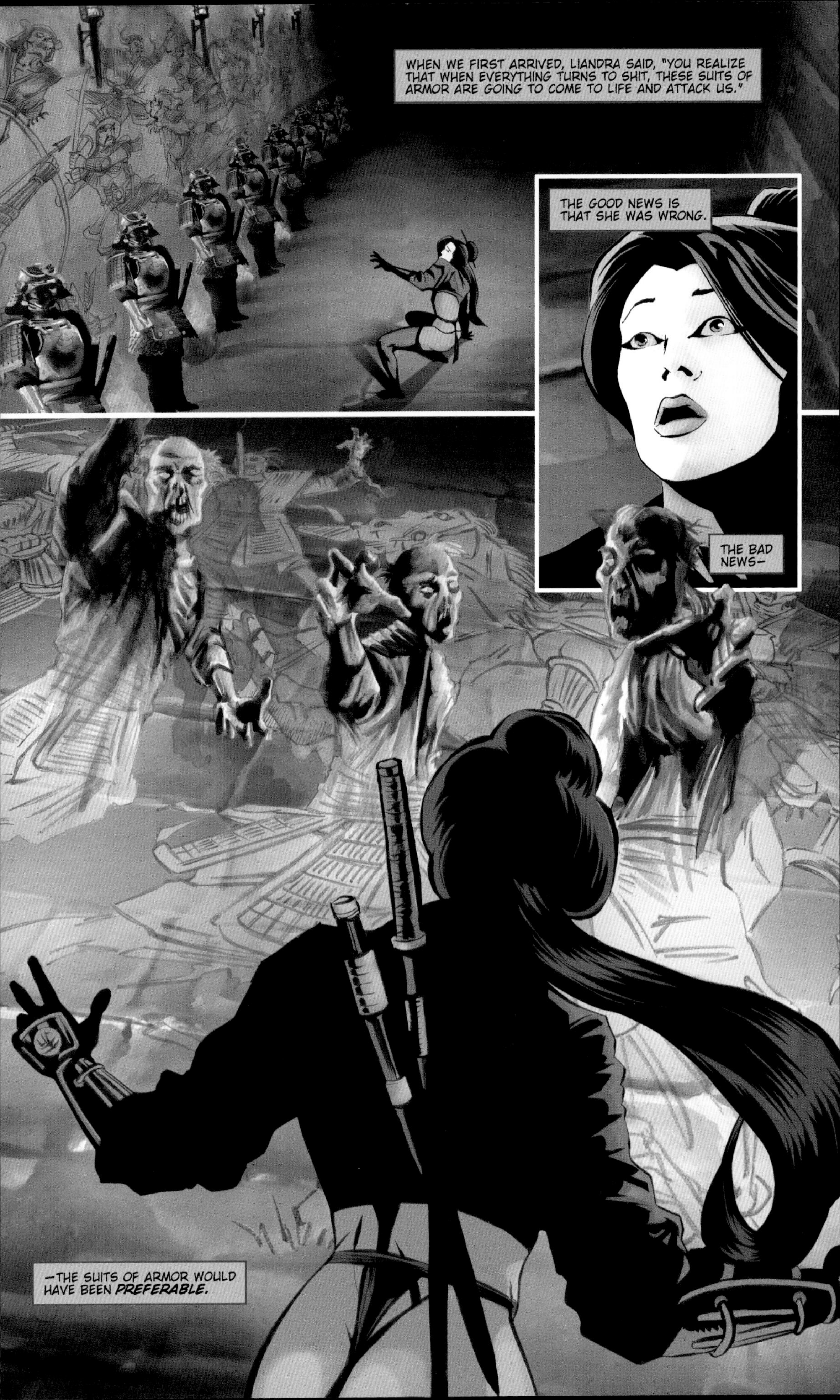
WHEN WE FIRST ARRIVED, LIANDRA SAID, "YOU REALIZE THAT WHEN EVERYTHING TURNS TO SHIT, THESE SUITS OF ARMOR ARE GOING TO COME TO LIFE AND ATTACK US."
THE GOOD NEWS IS THAT SHE WAS WRONG.
THE BAD NEWS–
–THE SUITS OF ARMOR WOULD HAVE BEEN *PREFERABLE.*

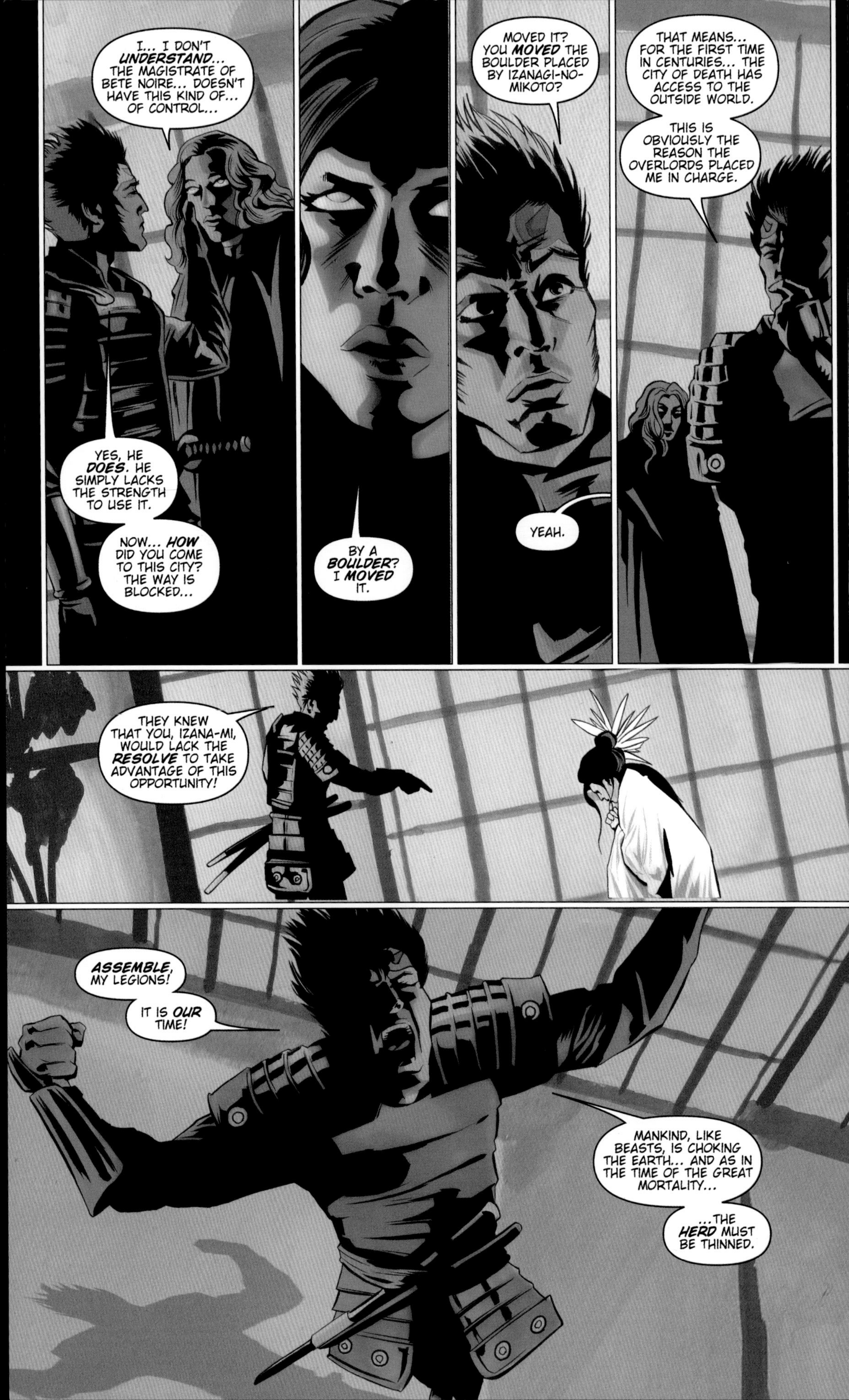

I... I DON'T UNDERSTAND... THE MAGISTRATE OF BETE NOIRE... DOESN'T HAVE THIS KIND OF... OF CONTROL...
YES, HE DOES. HE SIMPLY LACKS THE STRENGTH TO USE IT.
NOW... HOW DID YOU COME TO THIS CITY? THE WAY IS BLOCKED...
BY A BOULDER? I MOVED IT.
MOVED IT? YOU MOVED THE BOULDER PLACED BY IZANAGI-NO-MIKOTO?
YEAH.
THAT MEANS... FOR THE FIRST TIME IN CENTURIES... THE CITY OF DEATH HAS ACCESS TO THE OUTSIDE WORLD.
THIS IS OBVIOUSLY THE REASON THE OVERLORDS PLACED ME IN CHARGE.
THEY KNEW THAT YOU, IZANA-MI, WOULD LACK THE RESOLVE TO TAKE ADVANTAGE OF THIS OPPORTUNITY!
ASSEMBLE, MY LEGIONS!
IT IS OUR TIME!
MANKIND, LIKE BEASTS, IS CHOKING THE EARTH... AND AS IN THE TIME OF THE GREAT MORTALITY...
...THE HERD MUST BE THINNED.

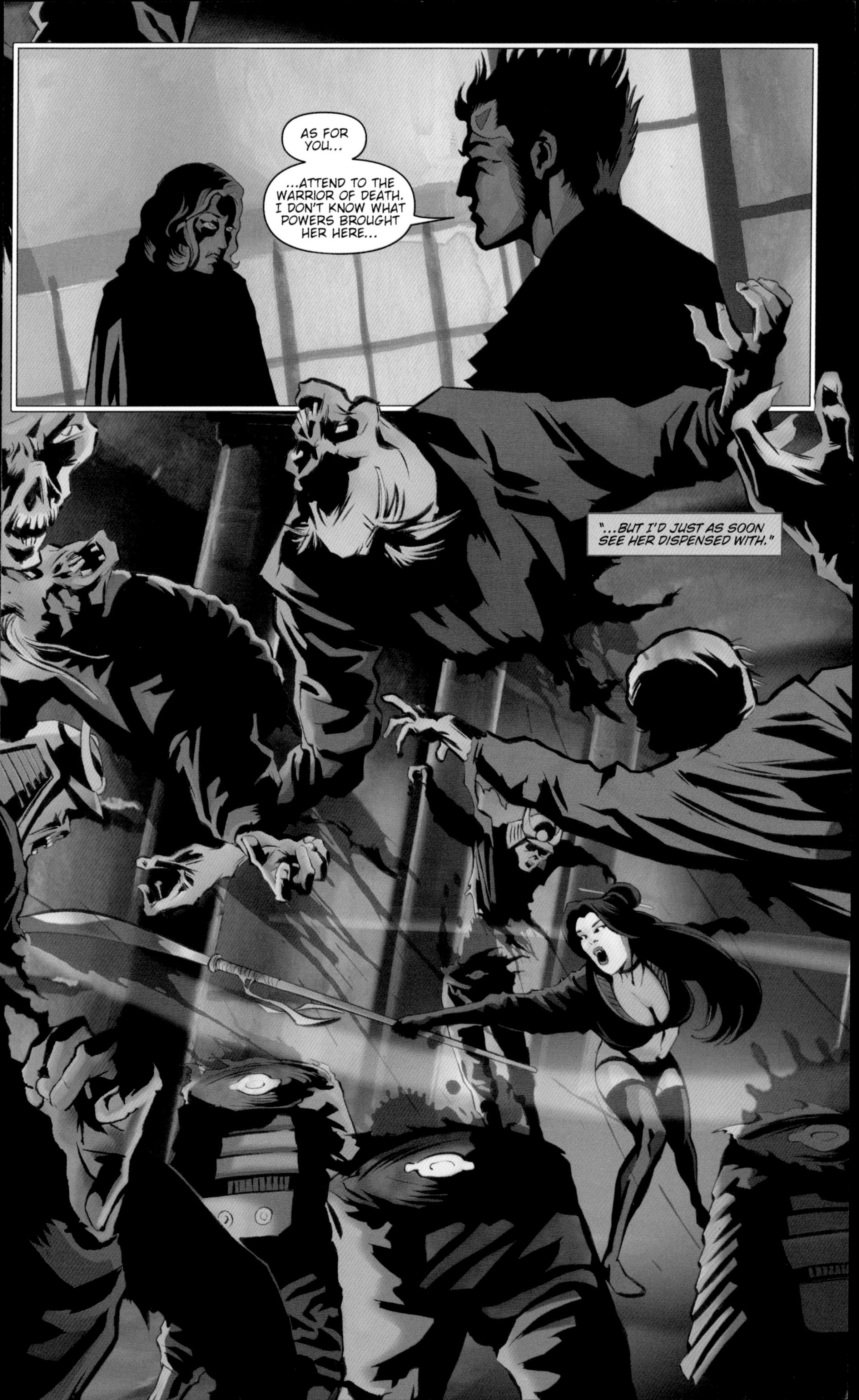
AS FOR YOU...
...ATTEND TO THE WARRIOR OF DEATH. I DON'T KNOW WHAT POWERS BROUGHT HER HERE...
"...BUT I'D JUST AS SOON SEE HER DISPENSED WITH."

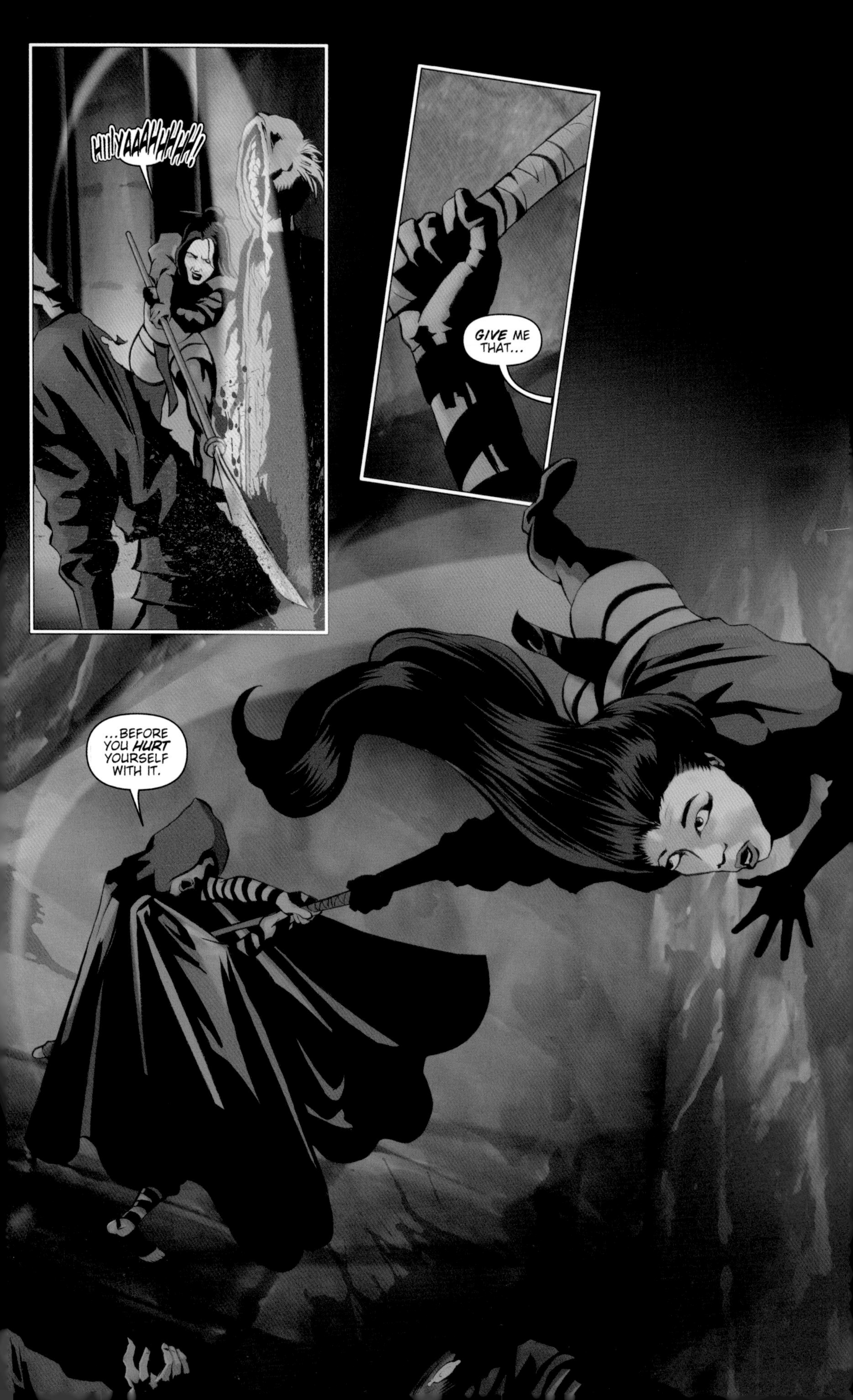
HIIIYAAAHHHHH!!
GIVE ME THAT...
...BEFORE YOU HURT YOURSELF WITH IT.

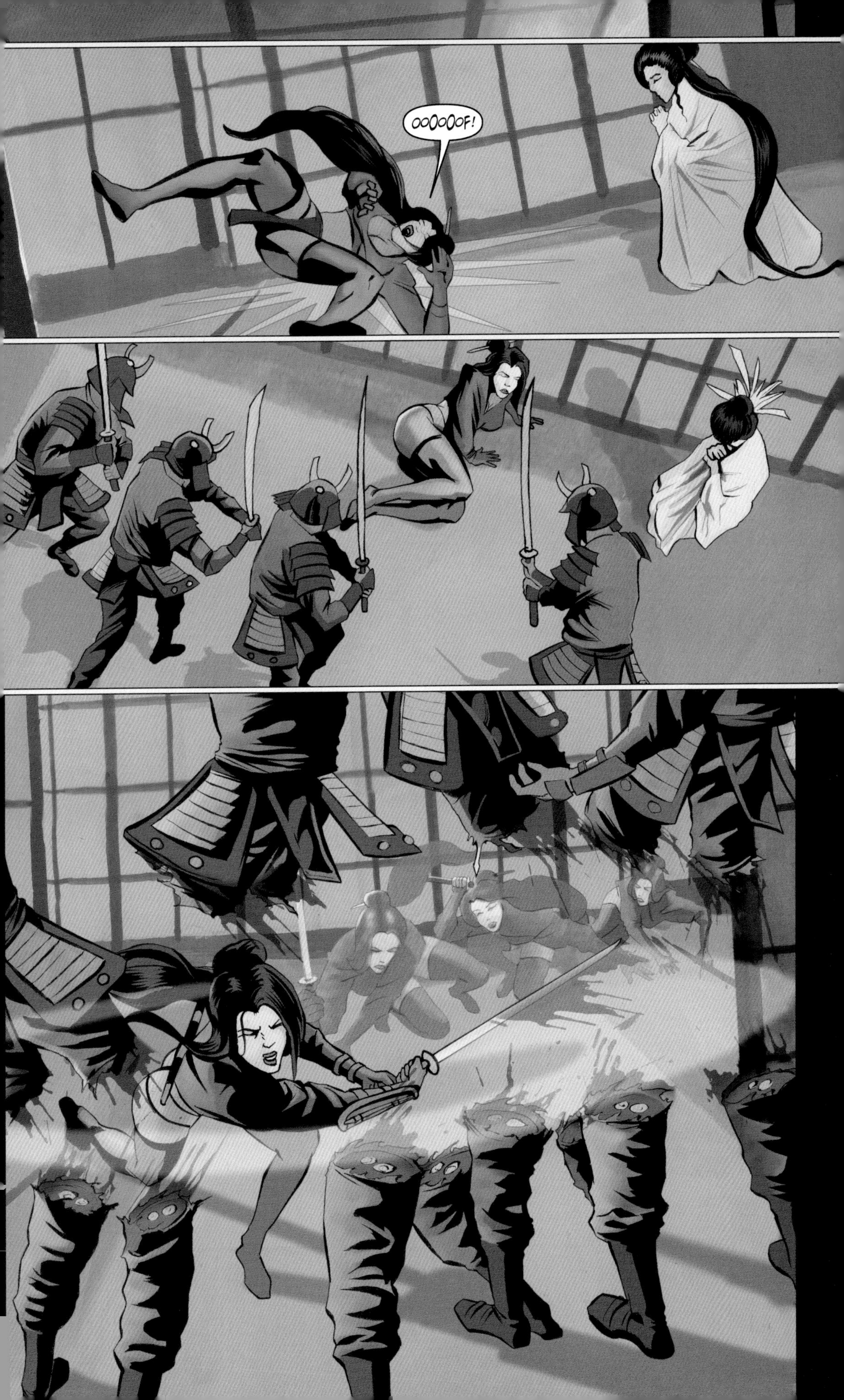
OOOOOOF!

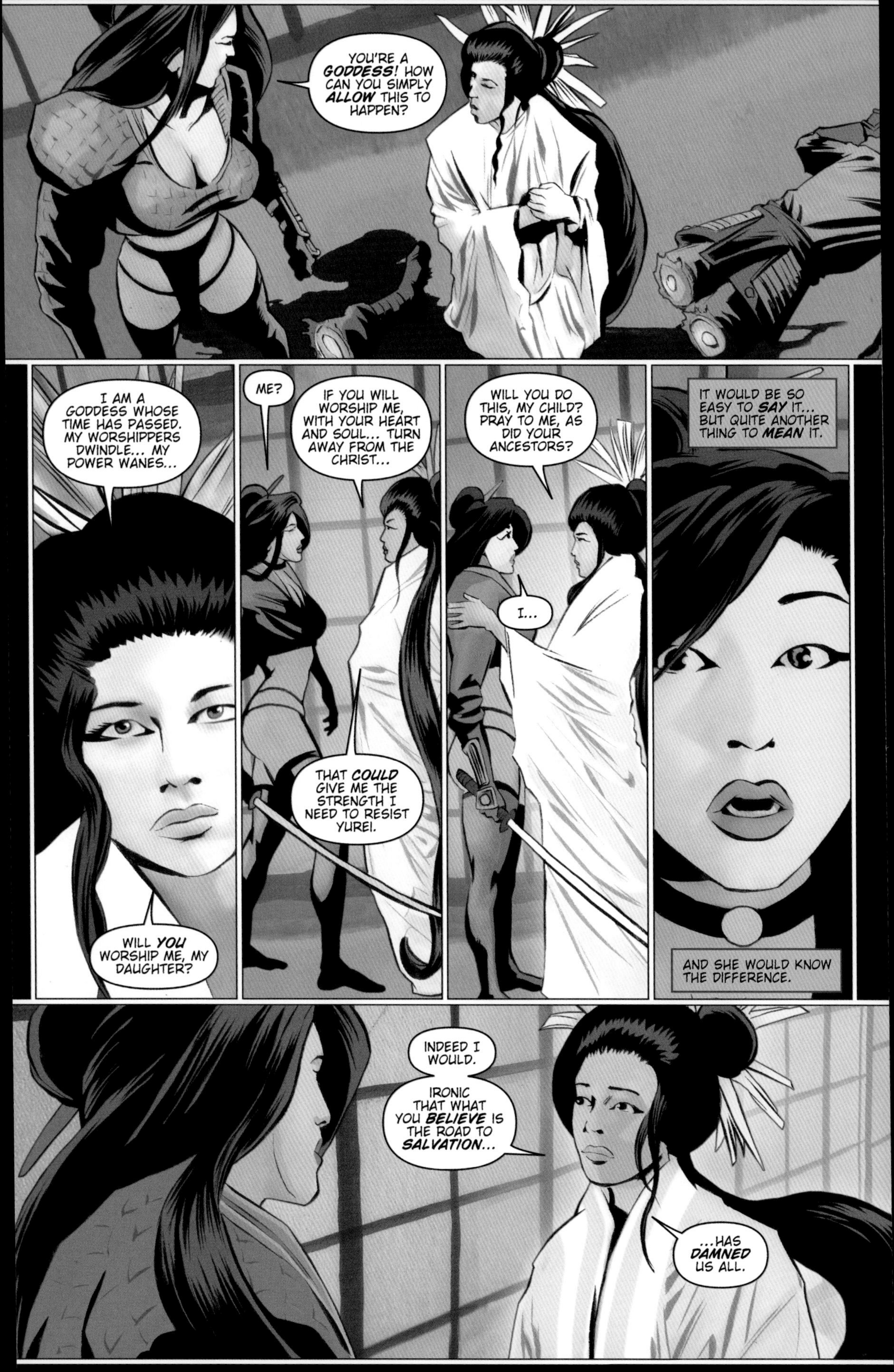
YOU'RE A GODDESS! HOW CAN YOU SIMPLY ALLOW THIS TO HAPPEN?
I AM A GODDESS WHOSE TIME HAS PASSED. MY WORSHIPPERS DWINDLE... MY POWER WANES...
WILL YOU WORSHIP ME, MY DAUGHTER?
ME?
IF YOU WILL WORSHIP ME, WITH YOUR HEART AND SOUL... TURN AWAY FROM THE CHRIST...
THAT COULD GIVE ME THE STRENGTH I NEED TO RESIST YUREI.
WILL YOU DO THIS, MY CHILD? PRAY TO ME, AS DID YOUR ANCESTORS?
I...
IT WOULD BE SO EASY TO SAY IT... BUT QUITE ANOTHER THING TO MEAN IT.
AND SHE WOULD KNOW THE DIFFERENCE.
INDEED I WOULD.
IRONIC THAT WHAT YOU BELIEVE IS THE ROAD TO SALVATION...
...HAS DAMNED US ALL.

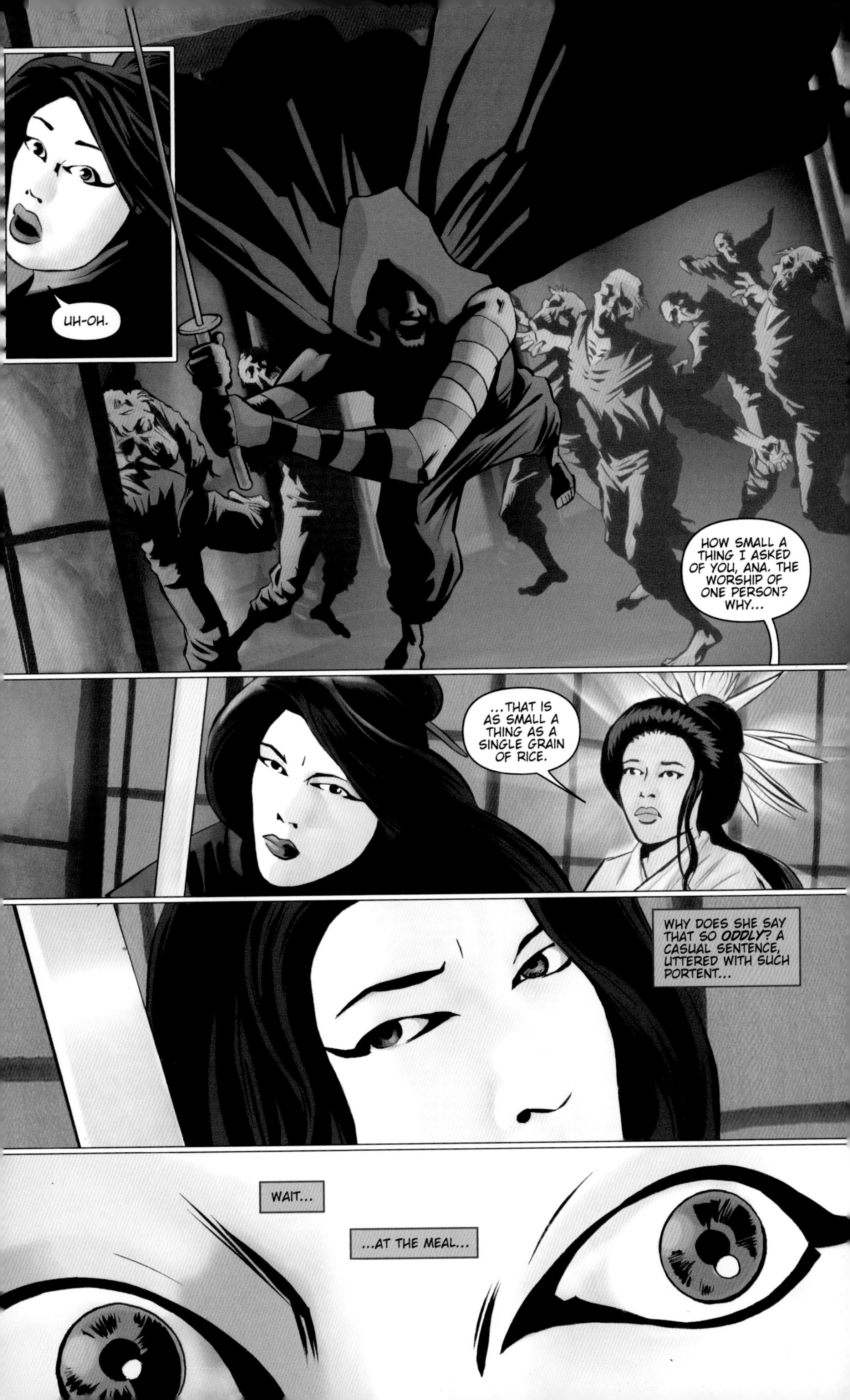
UH-OH.
HOW SMALL A THING I ASKED OF YOU, ANA. THE WORSHIP OF ONE PERSON? WHY...
...THAT IS AS SMALL A THING AS A SINGLE GRAIN OF RICE.
WHY DOES SHE SAY THAT SO *ODDLY*? A CASUAL SENTENCE, UTTERED WITH SUCH PORTENT...
WAIT...
...AT THE MEAL...

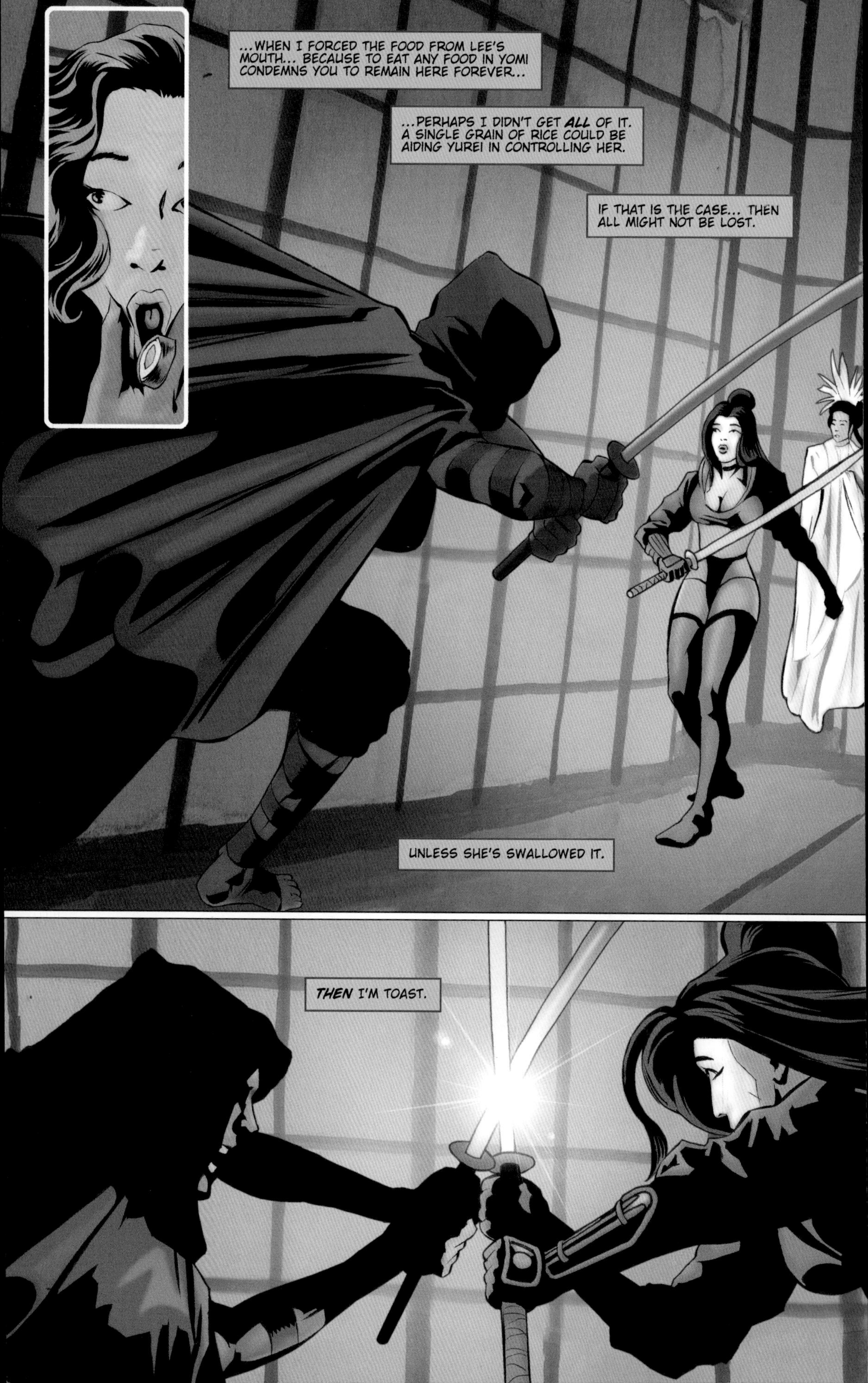
...WHEN I FORCED THE FOOD FROM LEE'S MOUTH... BECAUSE TO EAT ANY FOOD IN YOMI CONDEMNS YOU TO REMAIN HERE FOREVER...
...PERHAPS I DIDN'T GET ALL OF IT. A SINGLE GRAIN OF RICE COULD BE AIDING YUREI IN CONTROLLING HER.
IF THAT IS THE CASE... THEN ALL MIGHT NOT BE LOST.
UNLESS SHE'S SWALLOWED IT.
THEN I'M TOAST.

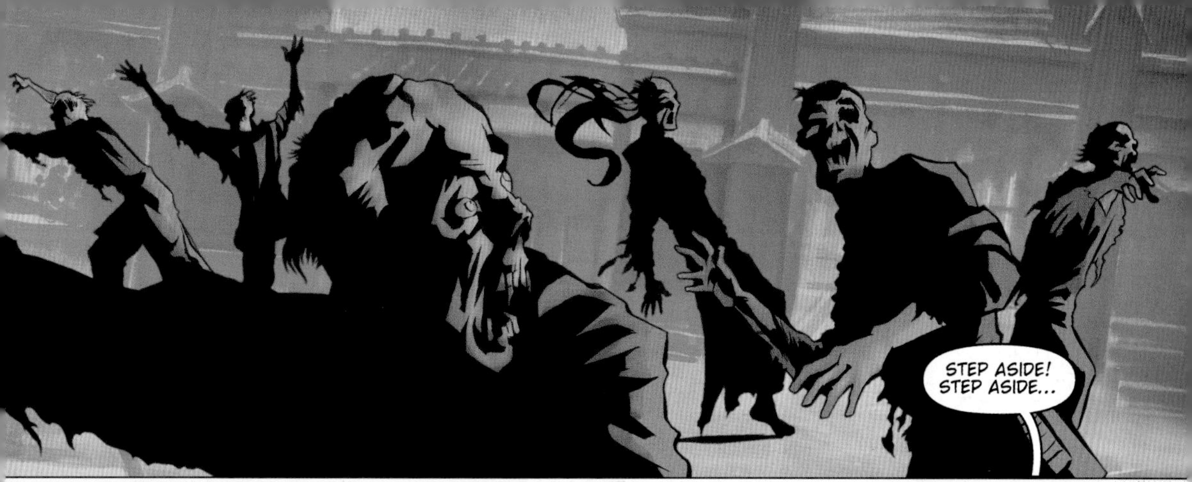
STEP ASIDE! STEP ASIDE...

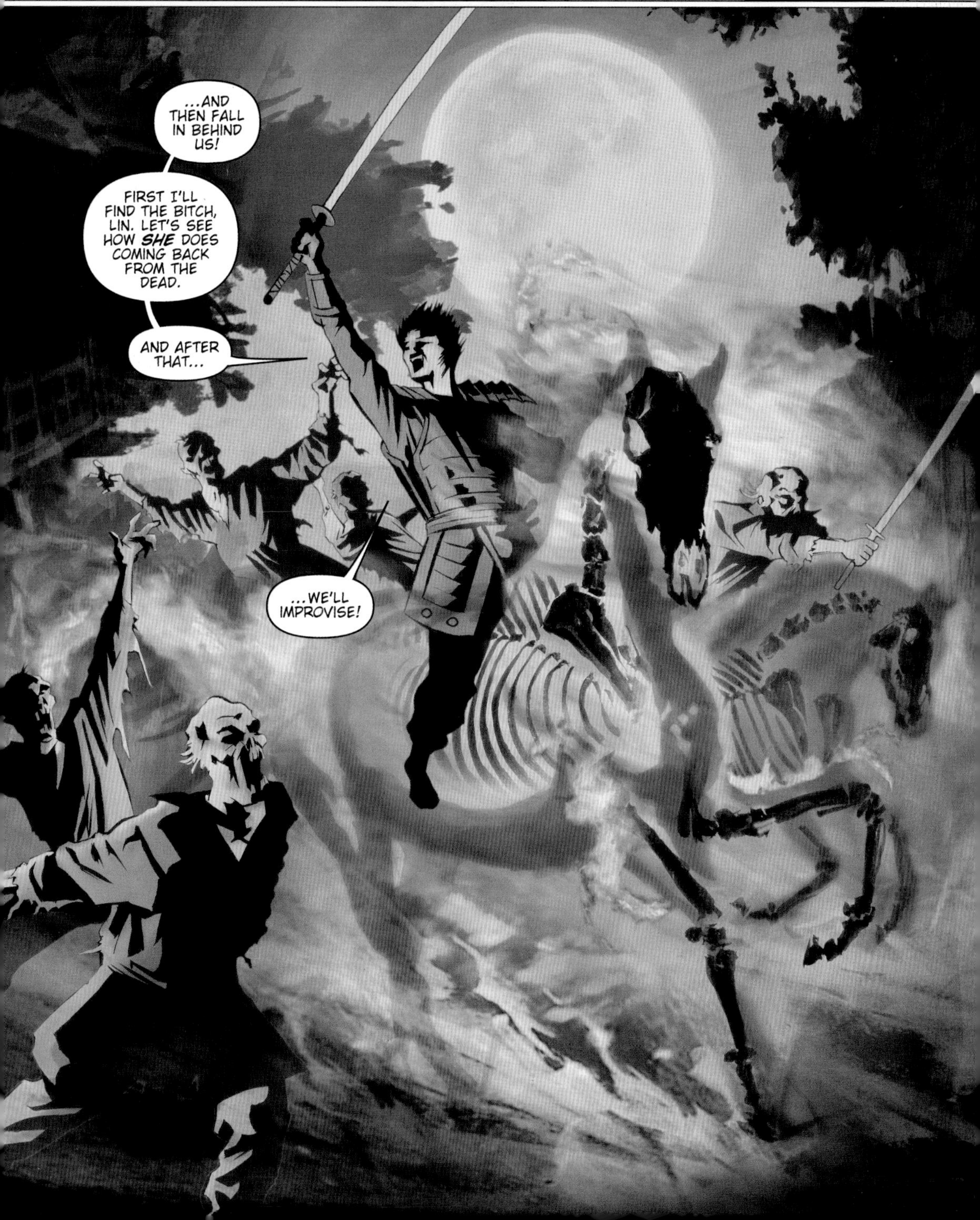
...AND THEN FALL IN BEHIND US!
FIRST I'LL FIND THE BITCH, LIN. LET'S SEE HOW *SHE* DOES COMING BACK FROM THE DEAD.
AND AFTER THAT...
...WE'LL IMPROVISE!

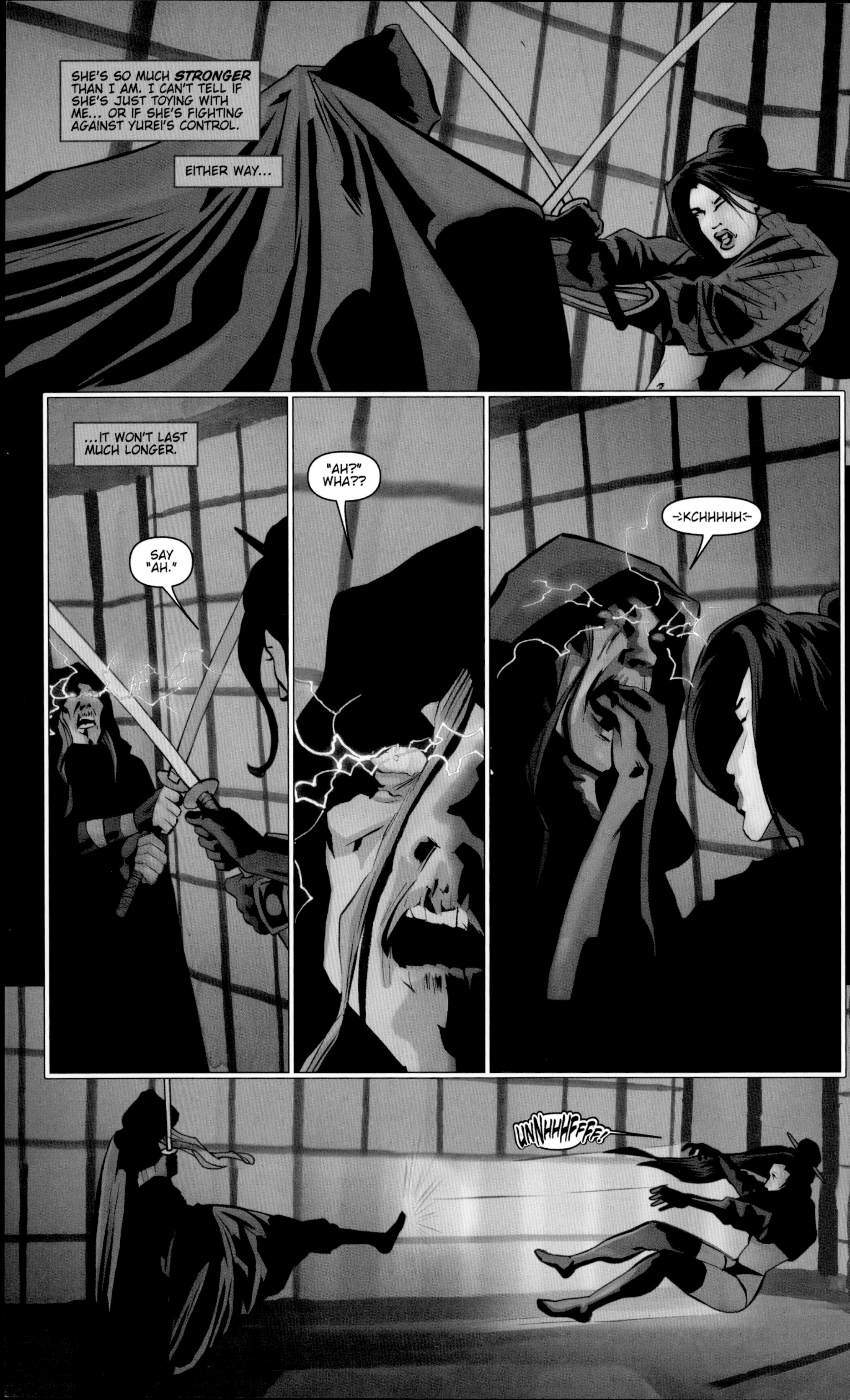
SHE'S SO MUCH STRONGER THAN I AM. I CAN'T TELL IF SHE'S JUST TOYING WITH ME... OR IF SHE'S FIGHTING AGAINST YUREI'S CONTROL.
EITHER WAY...
...IT WON'T LAST MUCH LONGER.
SAY "AH."
"AH?" WHA??
KCHHHHH
UNNHHHFFF!!

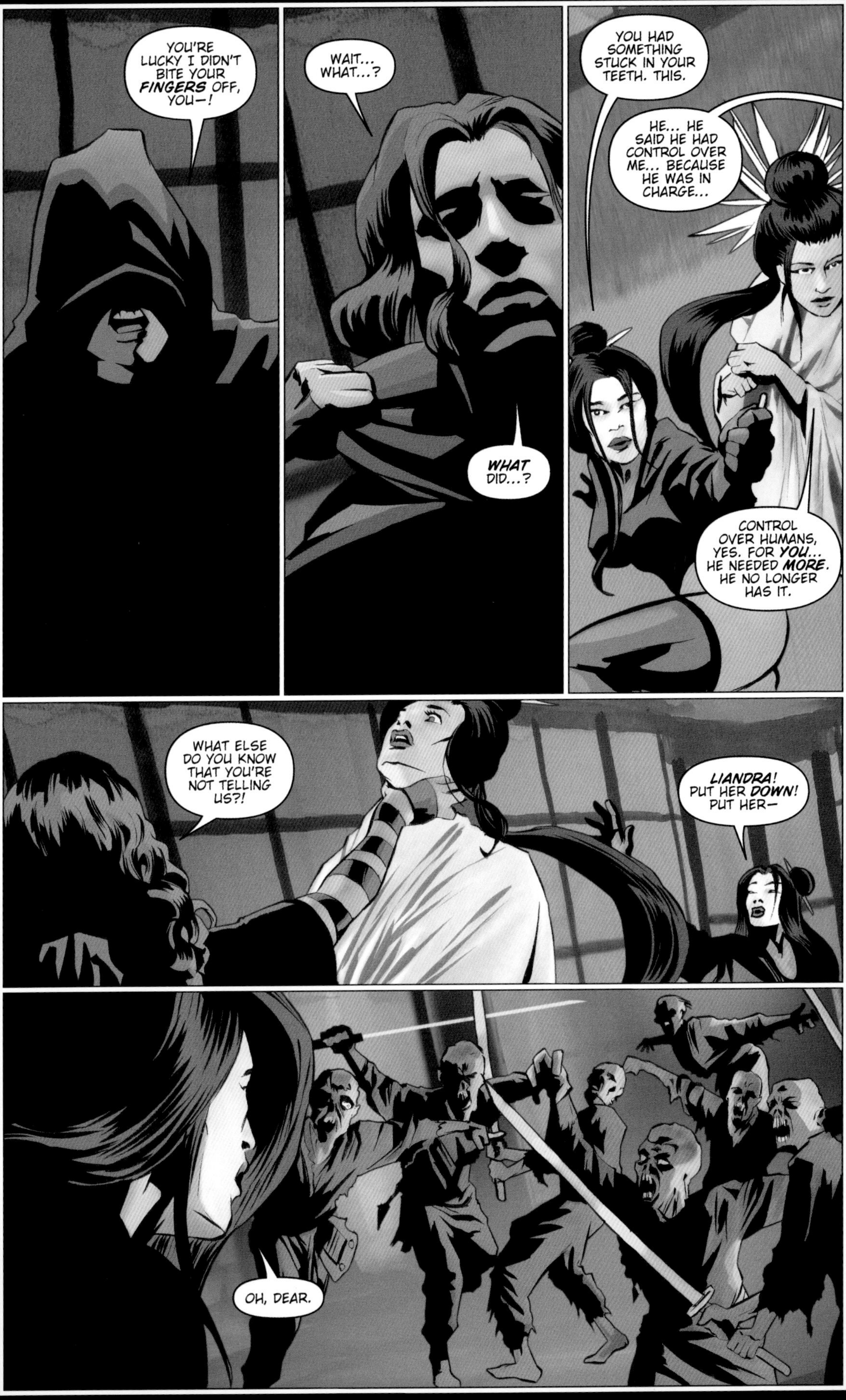

YOU'RE LUCKY I DIDN'T BITE YOUR **FINGERS** OFF, YOU—!
WAIT... WHAT...?
WHAT DID...?
YOU HAD SOMETHING STUCK IN YOUR TEETH. THIS.
HE... HE SAID HE HAD CONTROL OVER ME... BECAUSE HE WAS IN CHARGE...
CONTROL OVER HUMANS, YES. FOR ***YOU***... HE NEEDED ***MORE***. HE NO LONGER HAS IT.
WHAT ELSE DO YOU KNOW THAT YOU'RE NOT TELLING US?!
LIANDRA! PUT HER ***DOWN***! PUT HER—
OH, DEAR.

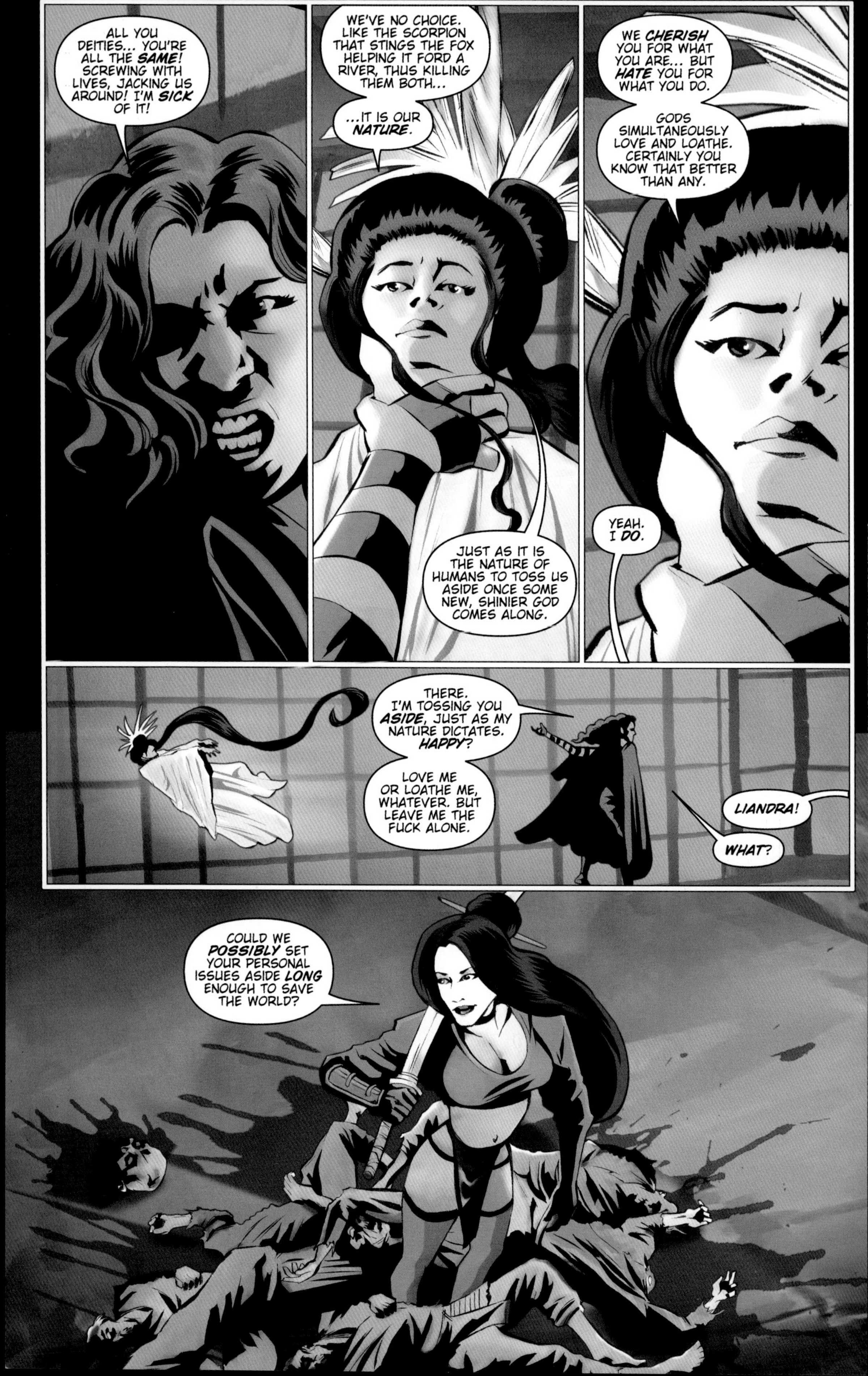
ALL YOU DEITIES... YOU'RE ALL THE SAME! SCREWING WITH LIVES, JACKING US AROUND! I'M SICK OF IT!
WE'VE NO CHOICE. LIKE THE SCORPION THAT STINGS THE FOX HELPING IT FORD A RIVER, THUS KILLING THEM BOTH...
...IT IS OUR NATURE.
JUST AS IT IS THE NATURE OF HUMANS TO TOSS US ASIDE ONCE SOME NEW, SHINIER GOD COMES ALONG.
WE CHERISH YOU FOR WHAT YOU ARE... BUT HATE YOU FOR WHAT YOU DO.
GODS SIMULTANEOUSLY LOVE AND LOATHE. CERTAINLY YOU KNOW THAT BETTER THAN ANY.
YEAH. I DO.
THERE. I'M TOSSING YOU ASIDE, JUST AS MY NATURE DICTATES. HAPPY?
LOVE ME OR LOATHE ME, WHATEVER. BUT LEAVE ME THE FUCK ALONE.
LIANDRA!
WHAT?
COULD WE POSSIBLY SET YOUR PERSONAL ISSUES ASIDE LONG ENOUGH TO SAVE THE WORLD?

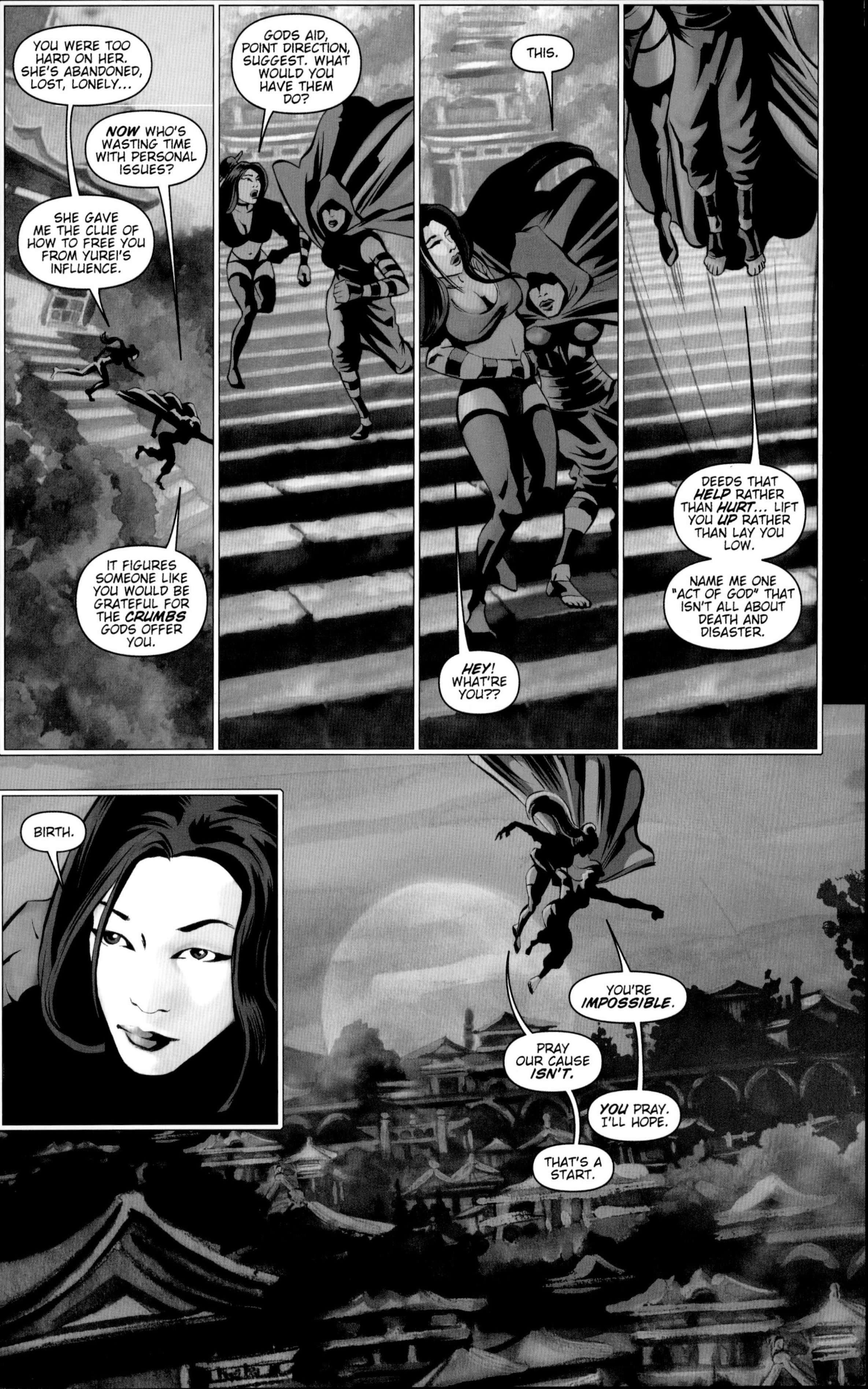
YOU WERE TOO HARD ON HER. SHE'S ABANDONED, LOST, LONELY...
NOW WHO'S WASTING TIME WITH PERSONAL ISSUES?
SHE GAVE ME THE CLUE OF HOW TO FREE YOU FROM YUREI'S INFLUENCE.
IT FIGURES SOMEONE LIKE YOU WOULD BE GRATEFUL FOR THE CRUMBS GODS OFFER YOU.
GODS AID, POINT DIRECTION, SUGGEST. WHAT WOULD YOU HAVE THEM DO?
THIS.
HEY! WHAT'RE YOU??
DEEDS THAT HELP RATHER THAN HURT... LIFT YOU UP RATHER THAN LAY YOU LOW.
NAME ME ONE "ACT OF GOD" THAT ISN'T ALL ABOUT DEATH AND DISASTER.
BIRTH.
YOU'RE IMPOSSIBLE.
PRAY OUR CAUSE ISN'T.
YOU PRAY. I'LL HOPE.
THAT'S A START.

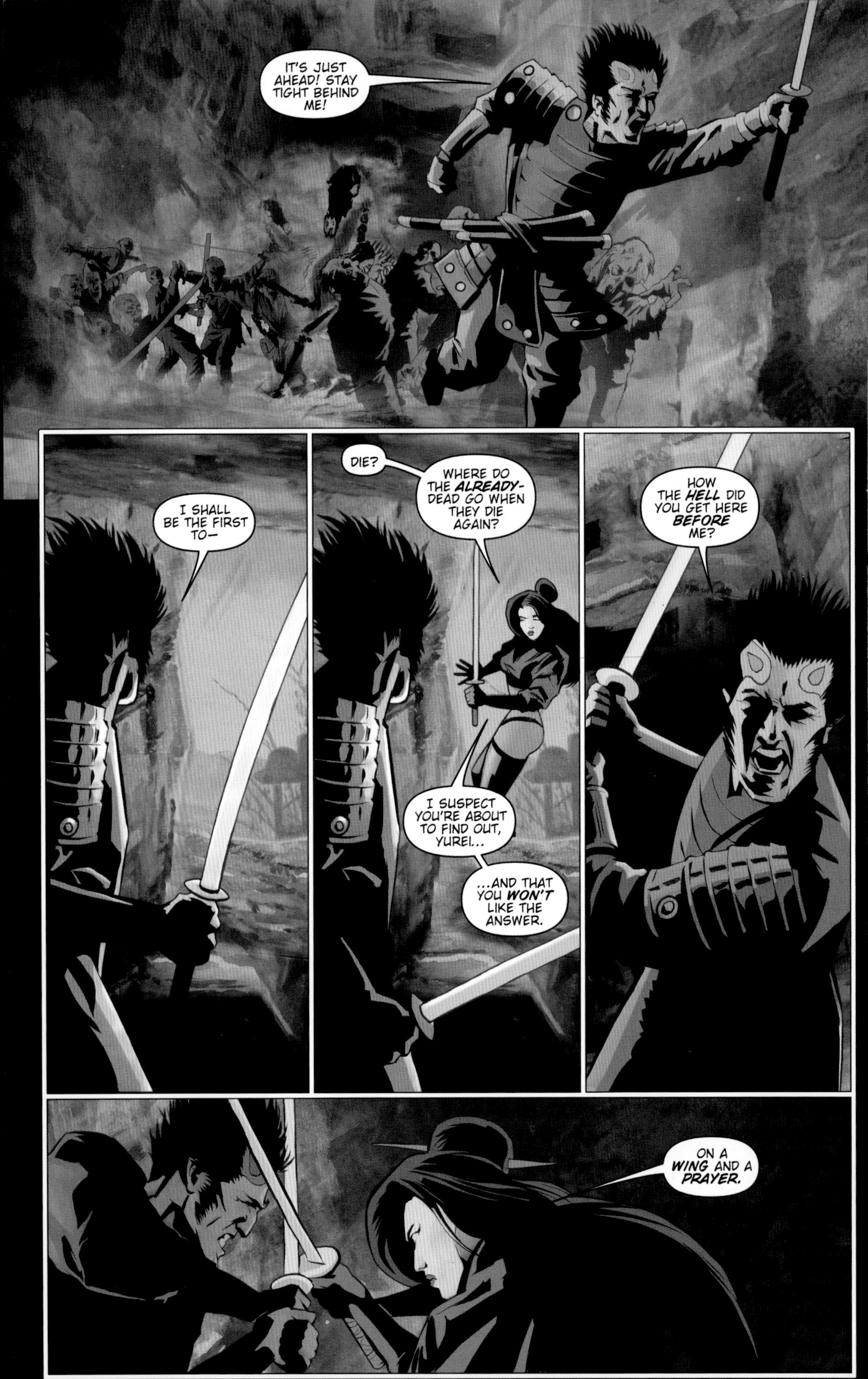
IT'S JUST AHEAD! STAY TIGHT BEHIND ME!
I SHALL BE THE FIRST TO—
DIE?
WHERE DO THE ALREADY-DEAD GO WHEN THEY DIE AGAIN?
I SUSPECT YOU'RE ABOUT TO FIND OUT, YUREI...
...AND THAT YOU WON'T LIKE THE ANSWER.
HOW THE HELL DID YOU GET HERE BEFORE ME?
ON A WING AND A PRAYER.

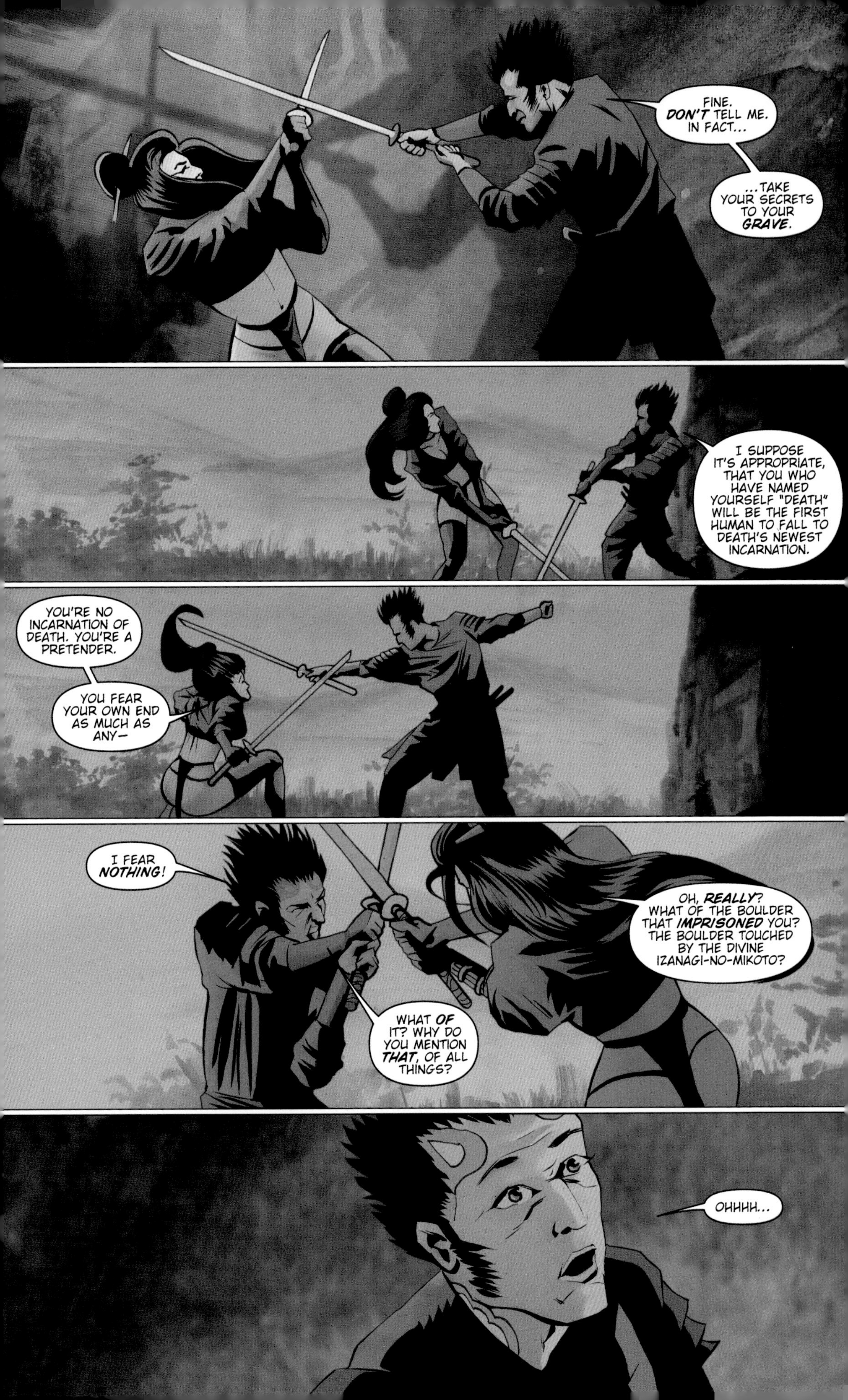
FINE. DON'T TELL ME. IN FACT...
...TAKE YOUR SECRETS TO YOUR GRAVE.
I SUPPOSE IT'S APPROPRIATE, THAT YOU WHO HAVE NAMED YOURSELF "DEATH" WILL BE THE FIRST HUMAN TO FALL TO DEATH'S NEWEST INCARNATION.
YOU'RE NO INCARNATION OF DEATH. YOU'RE A PRETENDER.
YOU FEAR YOUR OWN END AS MUCH AS ANY—
I FEAR NOTHING!
OH, REALLY? WHAT OF THE BOULDER THAT IMPRISONED YOU? THE BOULDER TOUCHED BY THE DIVINE IZANAGI-NO-MIKOTO?
WHAT OF IT? WHY DO YOU MENTION THAT, OF ALL THINGS?
OHHHH...

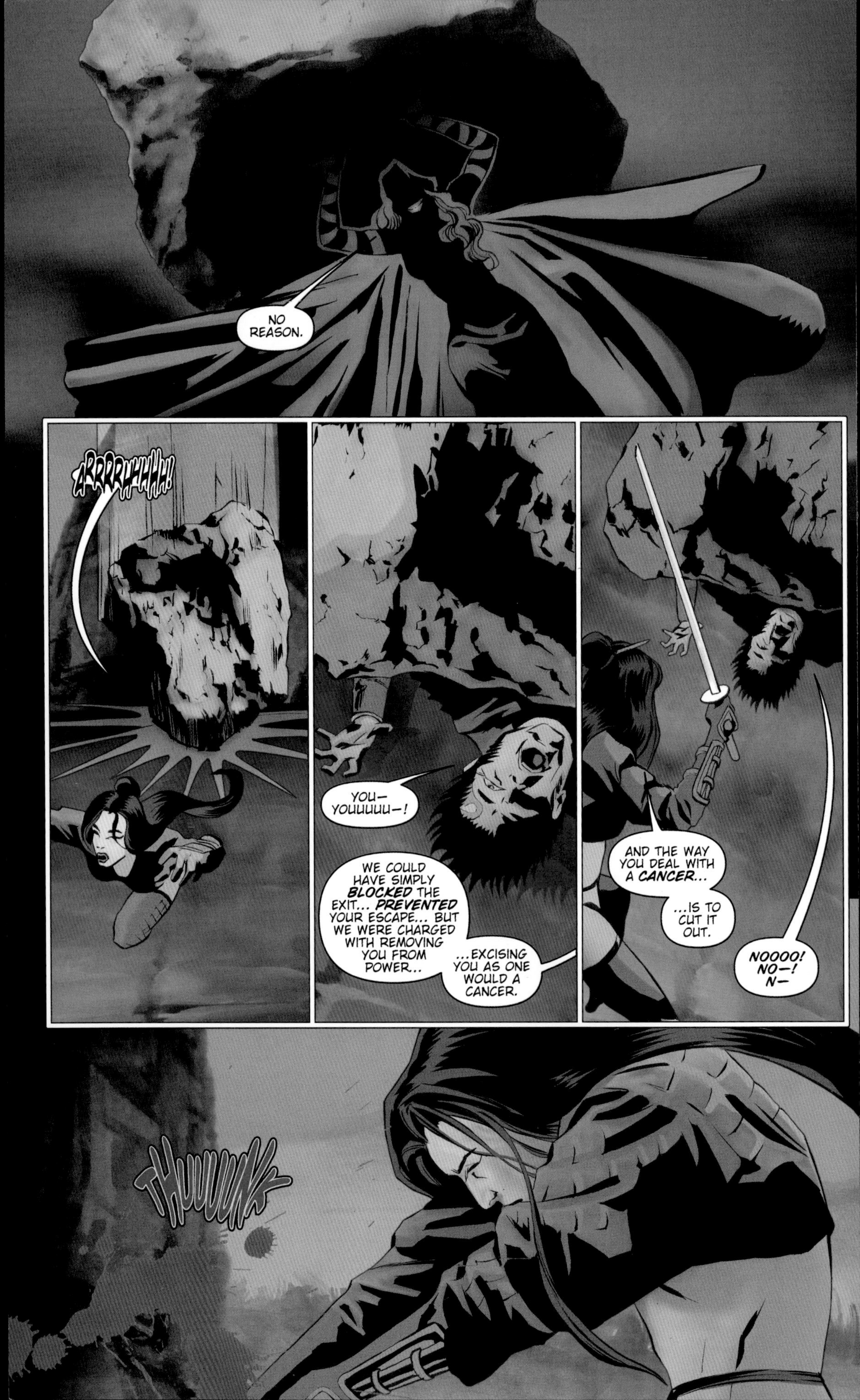
NO REASON.
ARRRRHHHH!
YOU— YOUUUUU—!
WE COULD HAVE SIMPLY **BLOCKED** THE EXIT... **PREVENTED** YOUR ESCAPE... BUT WE WERE CHARGED WITH REMOVING YOU FROM POWER...
...EXCISING YOU AS ONE WOULD A CANCER.
AND THE WAY YOU DEAL WITH A **CANCER**...
...IS TO CUT IT OUT.
NOOOO! NO—! N—
THUUUUNK

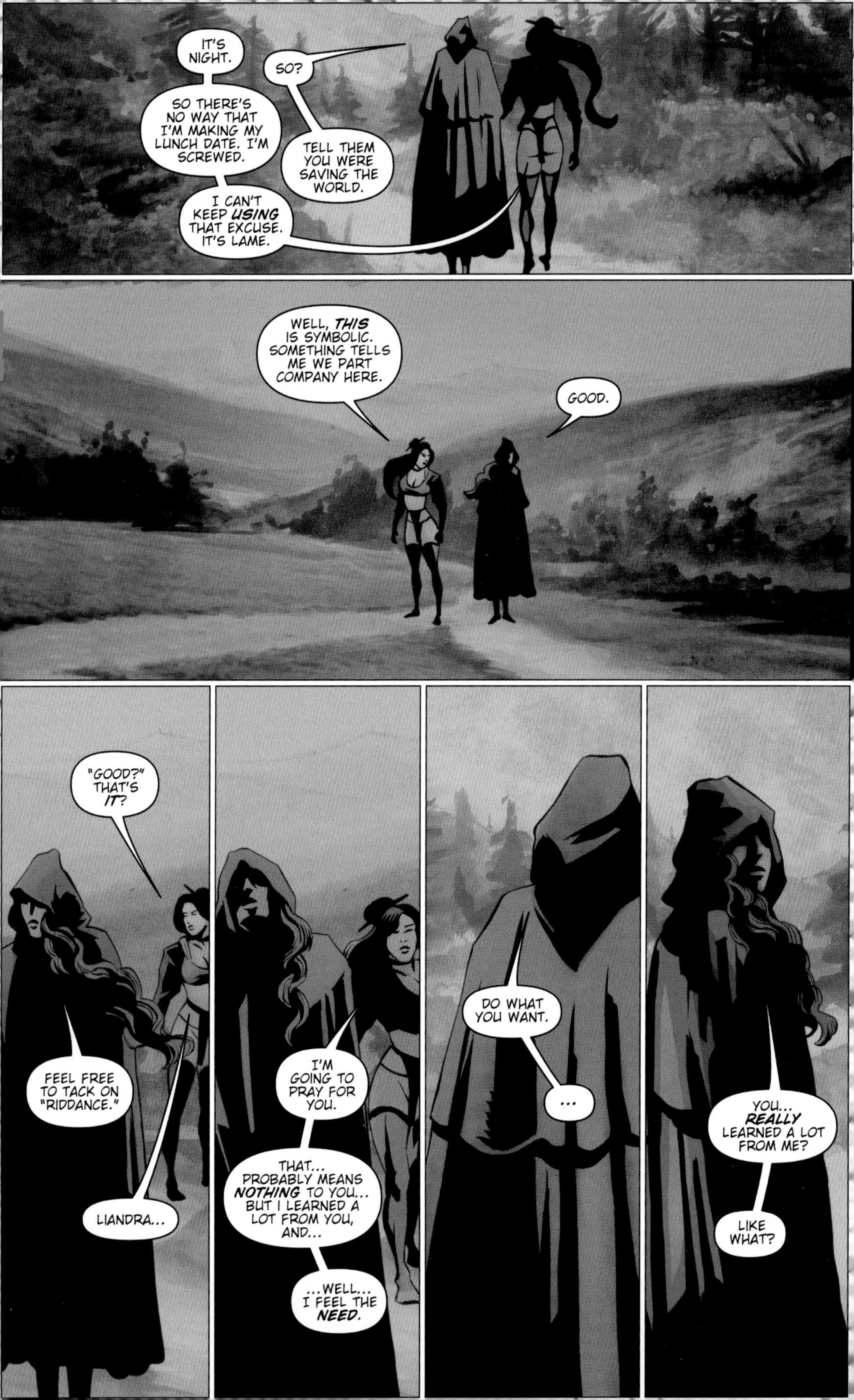
IT'S NIGHT.
SO?
SO THERE'S NO WAY THAT I'M MAKING MY LUNCH DATE. I'M SCREWED.
TELL THEM YOU WERE SAVING THE WORLD.
I CAN'T KEEP *USING* THAT EXCUSE. IT'S LAME.
WELL, *THIS* IS SYMBOLIC. SOMETHING TELLS ME WE PART COMPANY HERE.
GOOD.
"GOOD?" THAT'S *IT*?
FEEL FREE TO TACK ON "RIDDANCE."
LIANDRA...
I'M GOING TO PRAY FOR YOU.
THAT... PROBABLY MEANS *NOTHING* TO YOU... BUT I LEARNED A LOT FROM YOU, AND...
...WELL... I FEEL THE *NEED*.
DO WHAT YOU WANT.
...
YOU... *REALLY* LEARNED A LOT FROM ME?
LIKE WHAT?

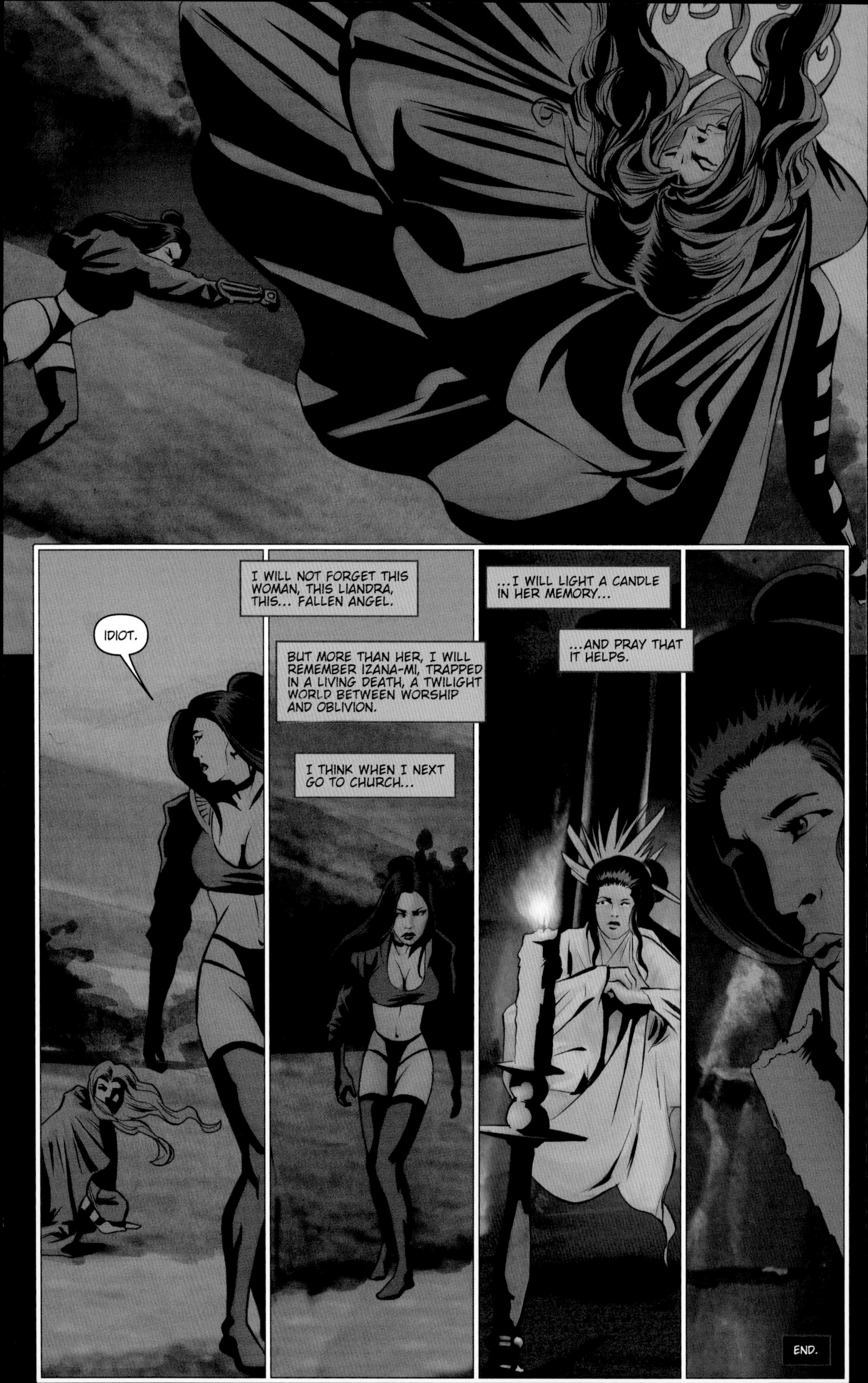
I WILL NOT FORGET THIS WOMAN, THIS LIANDRA, THIS... FALLEN ANGEL.
IDIOT.
BUT MORE THAN HER, I WILL REMEMBER IZANA-MI, TRAPPED IN A LIVING DEATH, A TWILIGHT WORLD BETWEEN WORSHIP AND OBLIVION.
I THINK WHEN I NEXT GO TO CHURCH...
...I WILL LIGHT A CANDLE IN HER MEMORY...
...AND PRAY THAT IT HELPS.
END.

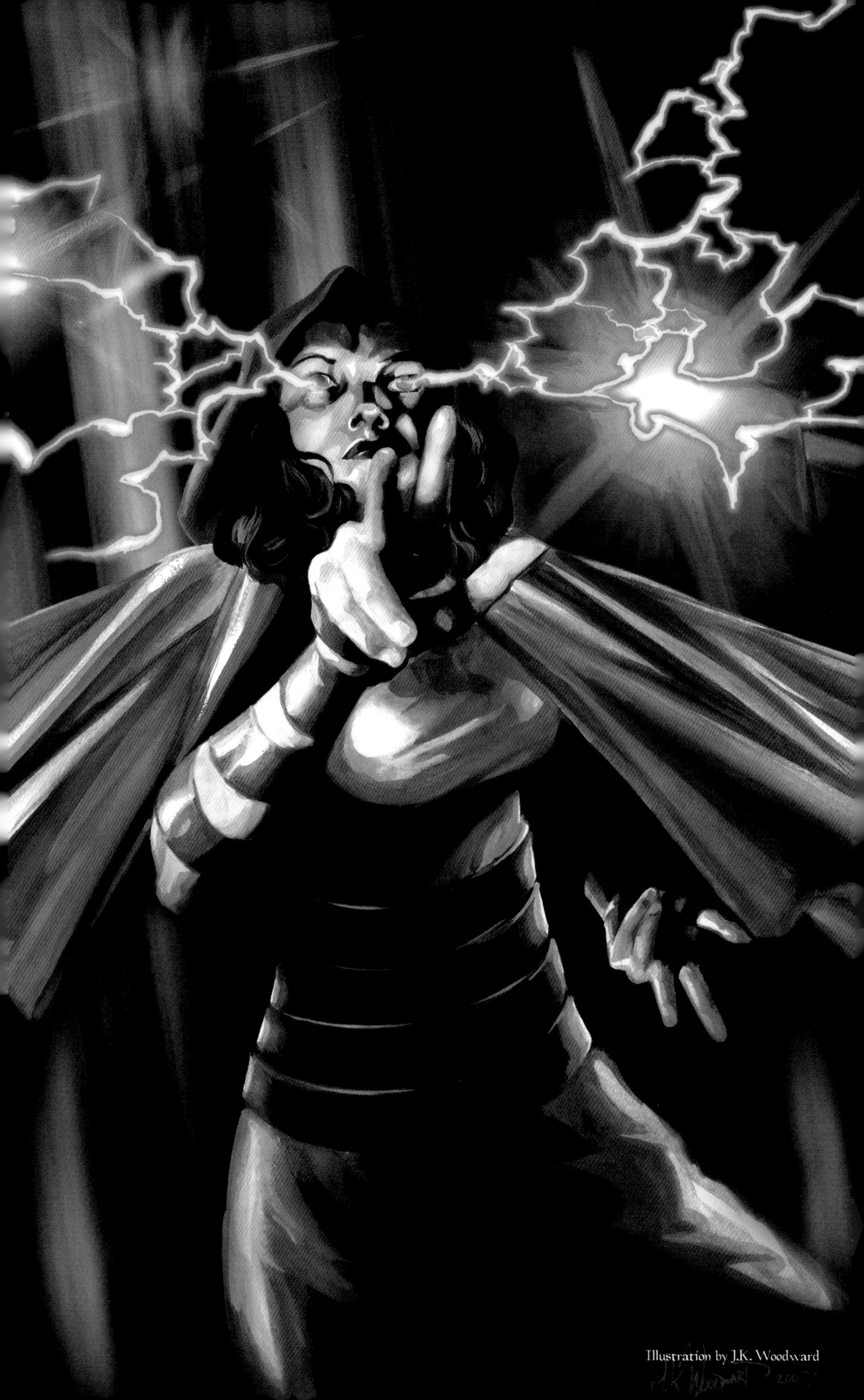

Illustration by J.K. Woodward

Chapter 4

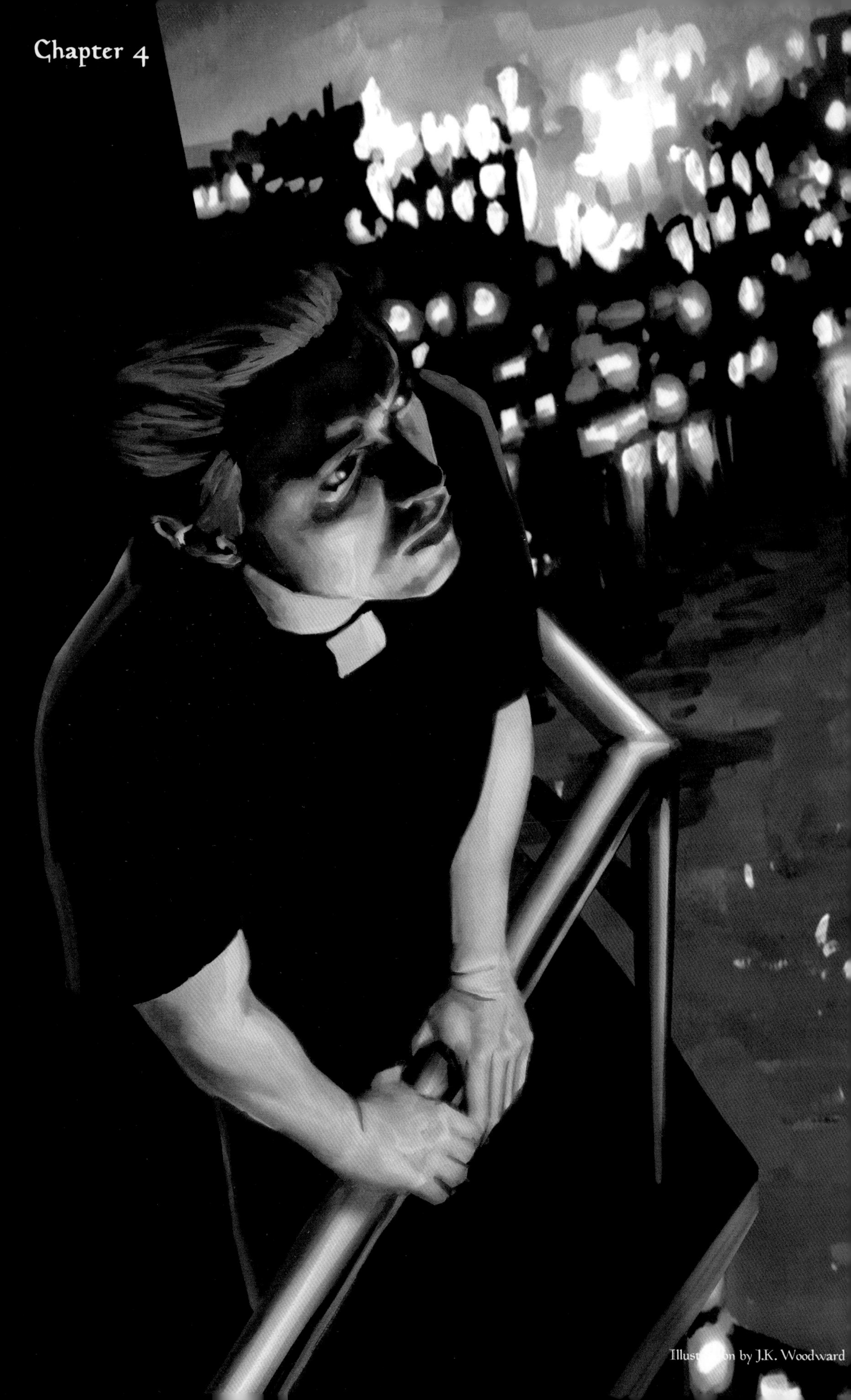

Illustration by J.K. Woodward

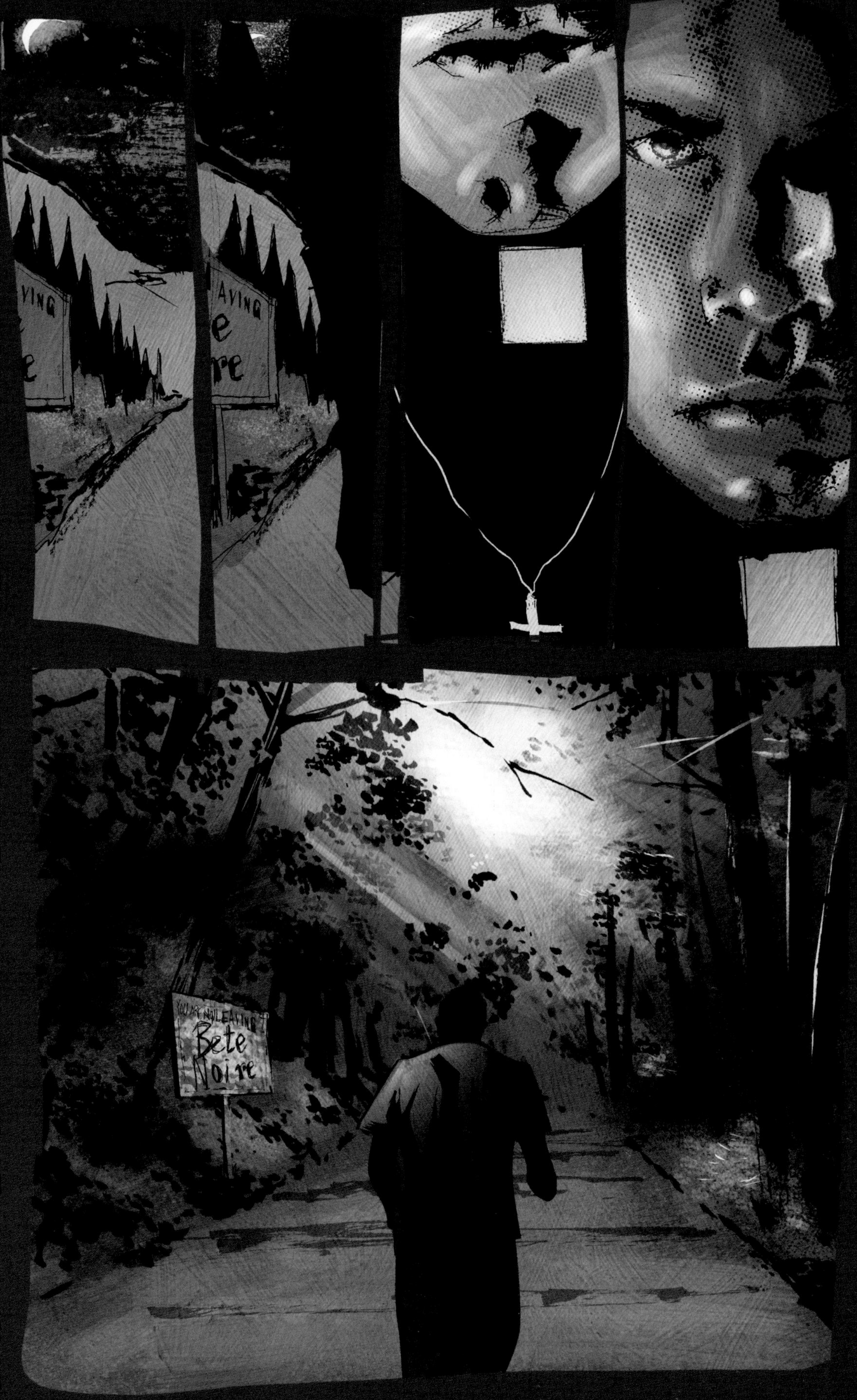
LEAVING
Bete Noire

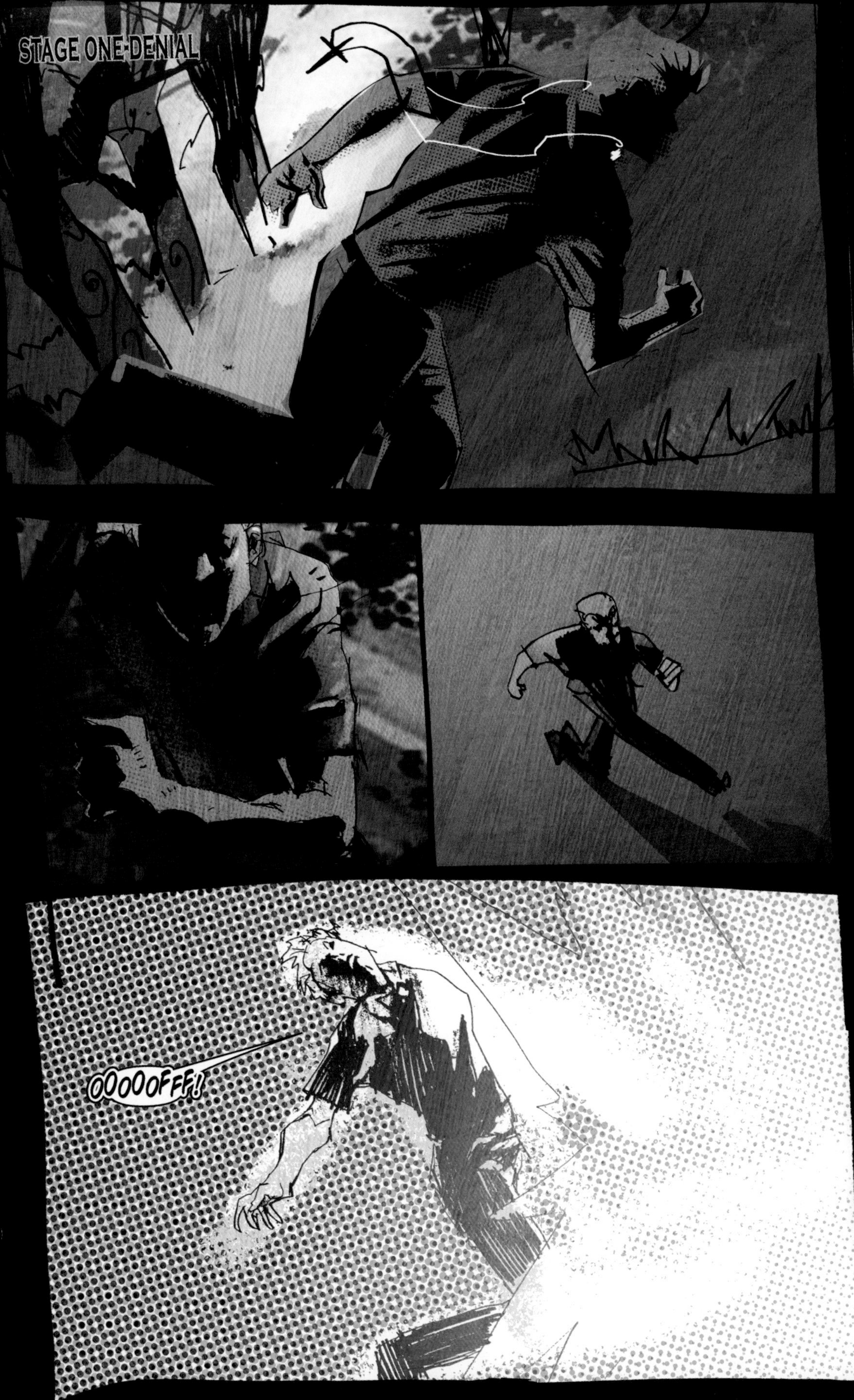
STAGE ONE-DENIAL
OOOOOFFF!

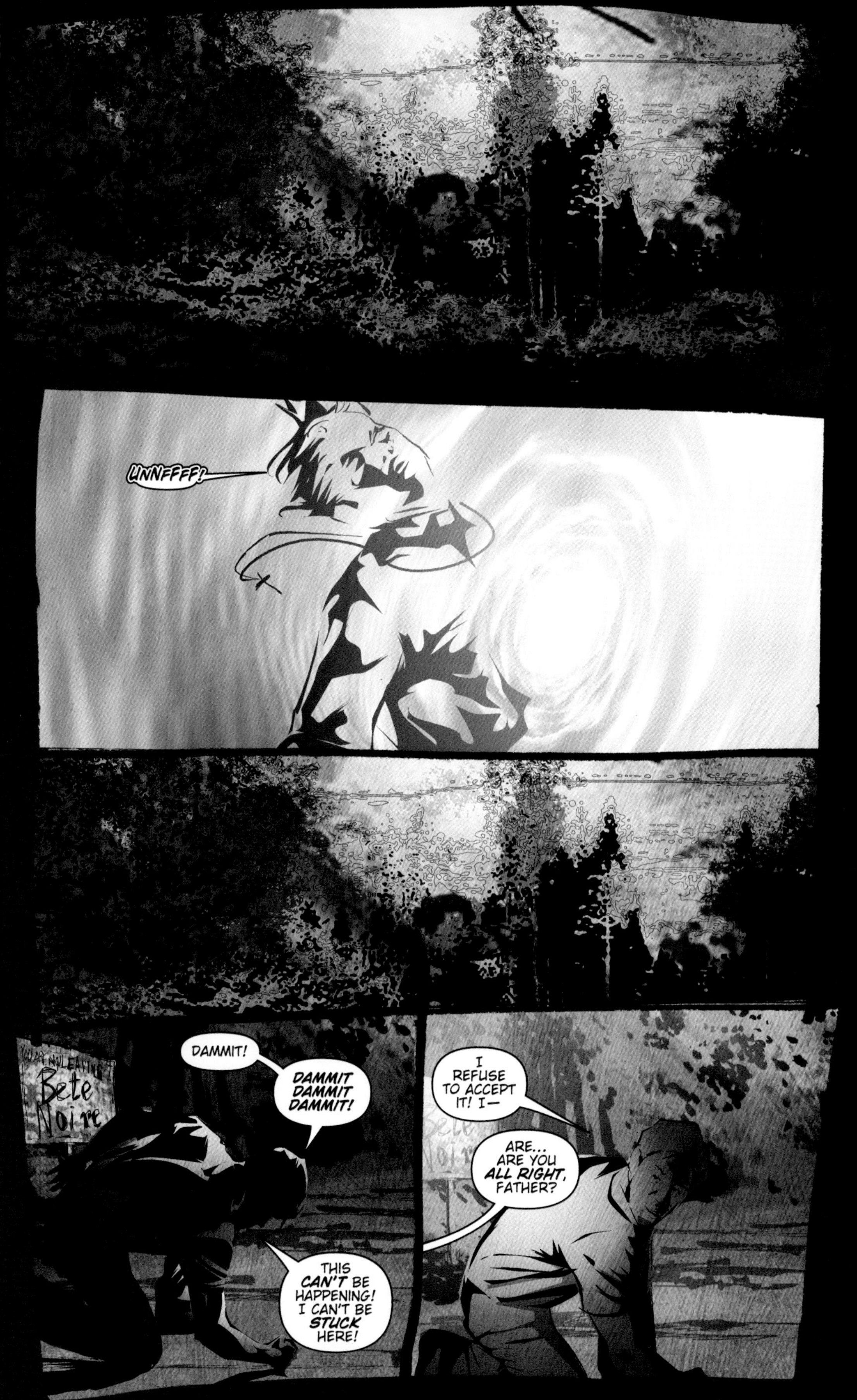
UNNFFFF!
Bete Noire
DAMMIT!
DAMMIT DAMMIT DAMMIT!
THIS CAN'T BE HAPPENING! I CAN'T BE STUCK HERE!
I REFUSE TO ACCEPT IT! I—
ARE... ARE YOU ALL RIGHT, FATHER?

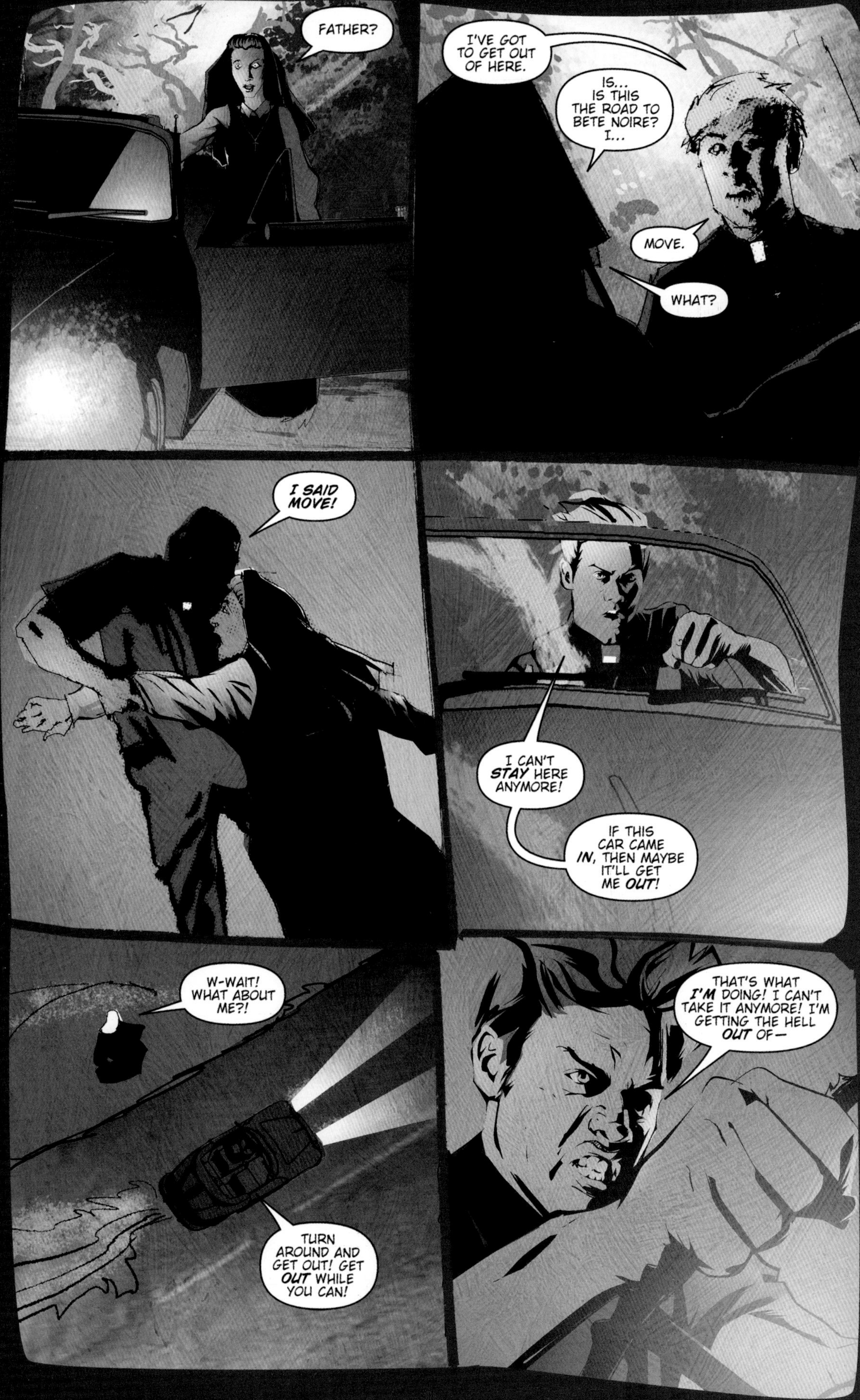
FATHER?
I'VE GOT TO GET OUT OF HERE.
IS... IS THIS THE ROAD TO BETE NOIRE? I...
MOVE.
WHAT?
I SAID MOVE!
I CAN'T STAY HERE ANYMORE!
IF THIS CAR CAME IN, THEN MAYBE IT'LL GET ME OUT!
W-WAIT! WHAT ABOUT ME?!
TURN AROUND AND GET OUT! GET OUT WHILE YOU CAN!
THAT'S WHAT I'M DOING! I CAN'T TAKE IT ANYMORE! I'M GETTING THE HELL OUT OF—

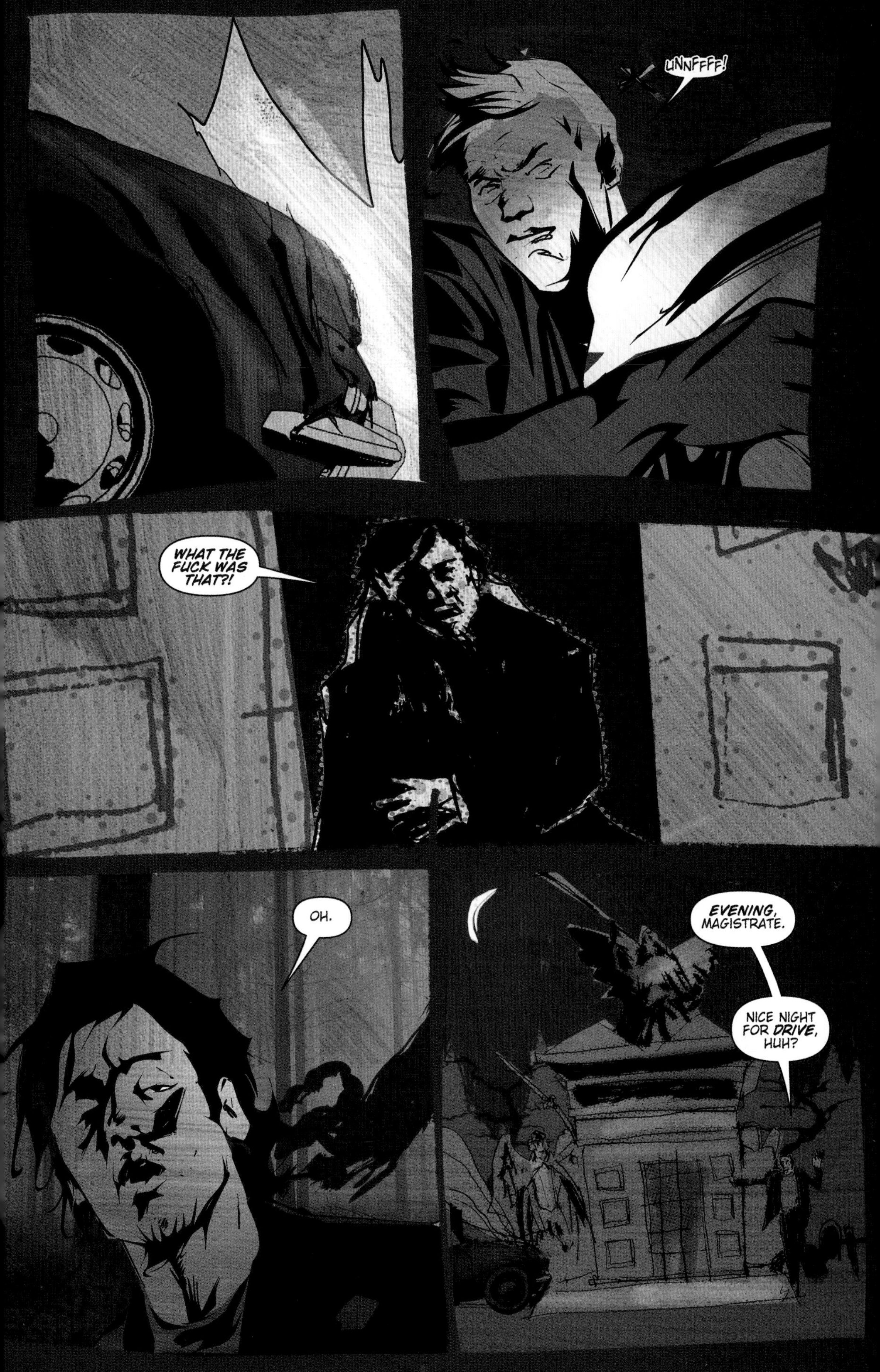
UNNFFFF!
WHAT THE FUCK WAS THAT?!
OH.
EVENING, MAGISTRATE.
NICE NIGHT FOR *DRIVE*, HUH?

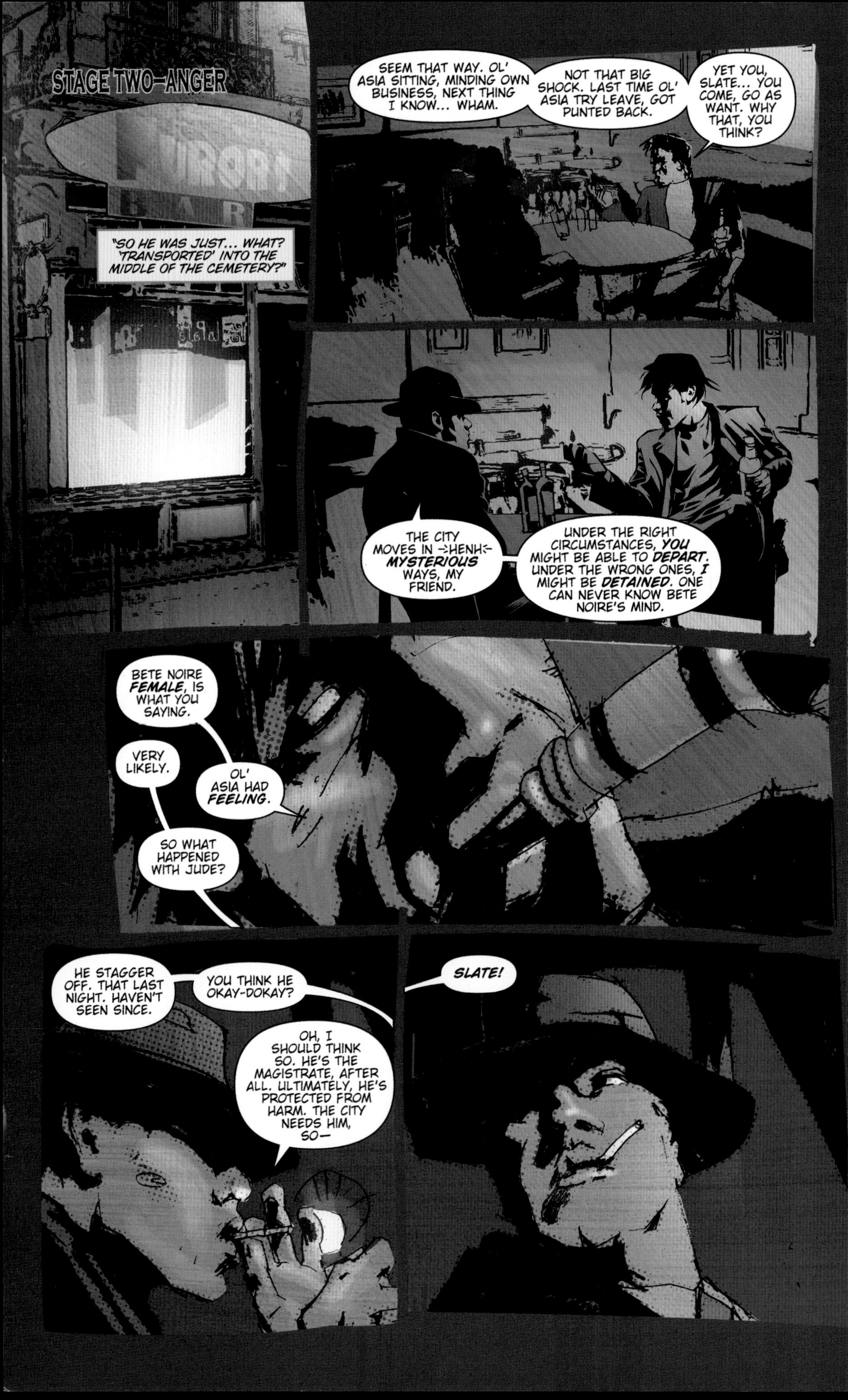

STAGE TWO—ANGER
EUROPE BAR
"SO HE WAS JUST... WHAT? 'TRANSPORTED' INTO THE MIDDLE OF THE CEMETERY?"
SEEM THAT WAY. OL' ASIA SITTING, MINDING OWN BUSINESS, NEXT THING I KNOW... WHAM.
NOT THAT BIG SHOCK. LAST TIME OL' ASIA TRY LEAVE, GOT PUNTED BACK.
YET YOU, SLATE... YOU COME, GO AS WANT. WHY THAT, YOU THINK?
THE CITY MOVES IN -HENH- *MYSTERIOUS* WAYS, MY FRIEND.
UNDER THE RIGHT CIRCUMSTANCES, *YOU* MIGHT BE ABLE TO *DEPART*. UNDER THE WRONG ONES, *I* MIGHT BE *DETAINED*. ONE CAN NEVER KNOW BETE NOIRE'S MIND.
BETE NOIRE *FEMALE*, IS WHAT YOU SAYING.
VERY LIKELY.
OL' ASIA HAD *FEELING*.
SO WHAT HAPPENED WITH JUDE?
HE STAGGER OFF. THAT LAST NIGHT. HAVEN'T SEEN SINCE.
YOU THINK HE OKAY-DOKAY?
OH, I SHOULD THINK SO. HE'S THE MAGISTRATE, AFTER ALL. ULTIMATELY, HE'S PROTECTED FROM HARM. THE CITY NEEDS HIM, SO—
SLATE!

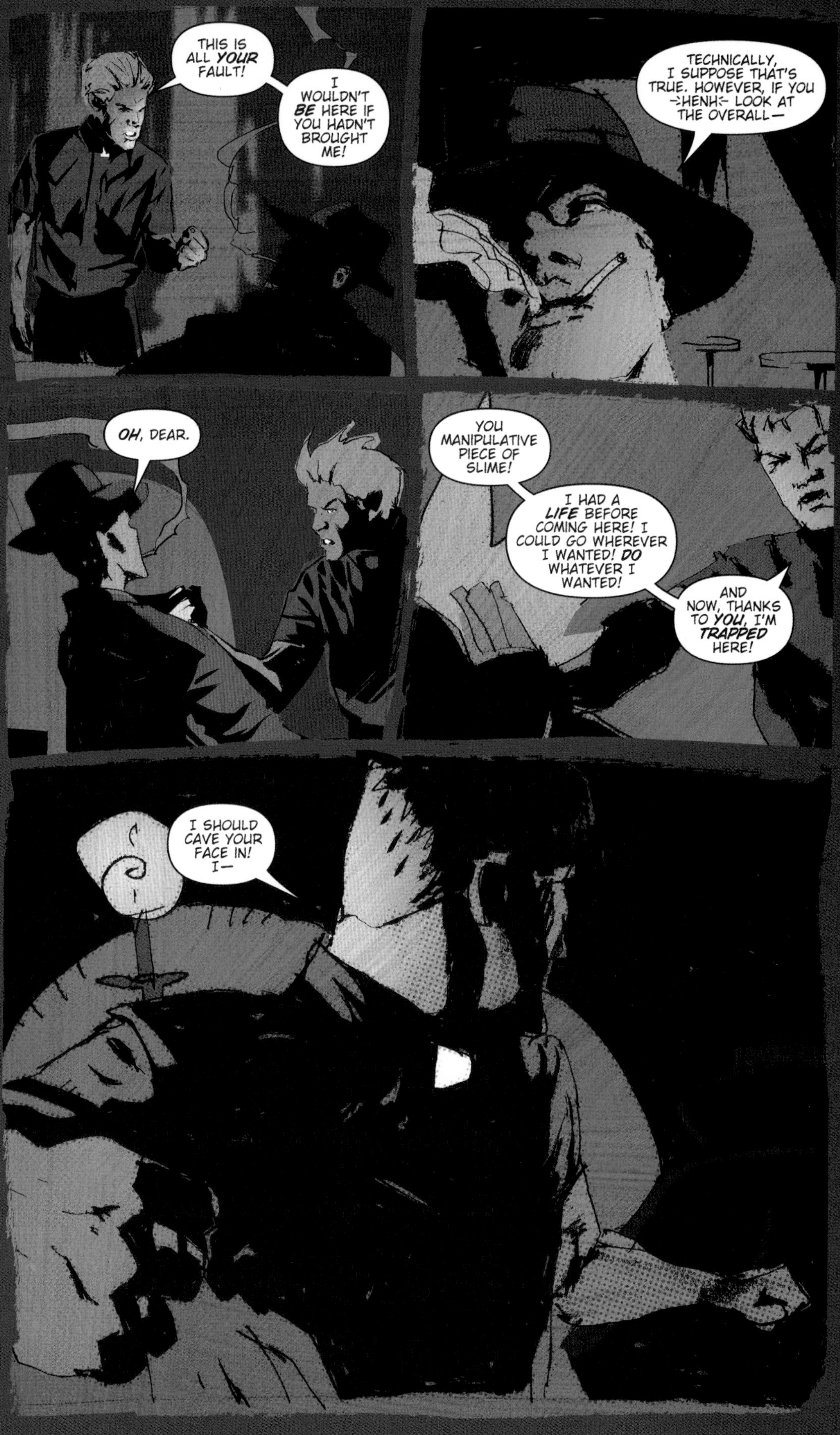
THIS IS ALL YOUR FAULT!
I WOULDN'T BE HERE IF YOU HADN'T BROUGHT ME!
TECHNICALLY, I SUPPOSE THAT'S TRUE. HOWEVER, IF YOU -HENH- LOOK AT THE OVERALL—
OH, DEAR.
YOU MANIPULATIVE PIECE OF SLIME!
I HAD A LIFE BEFORE COMING HERE! I COULD GO WHEREVER I WANTED! DO WHATEVER I WANTED!
AND NOW, THANKS TO YOU, I'M TRAPPED HERE!
I SHOULD CAVE YOUR FACE IN! I—

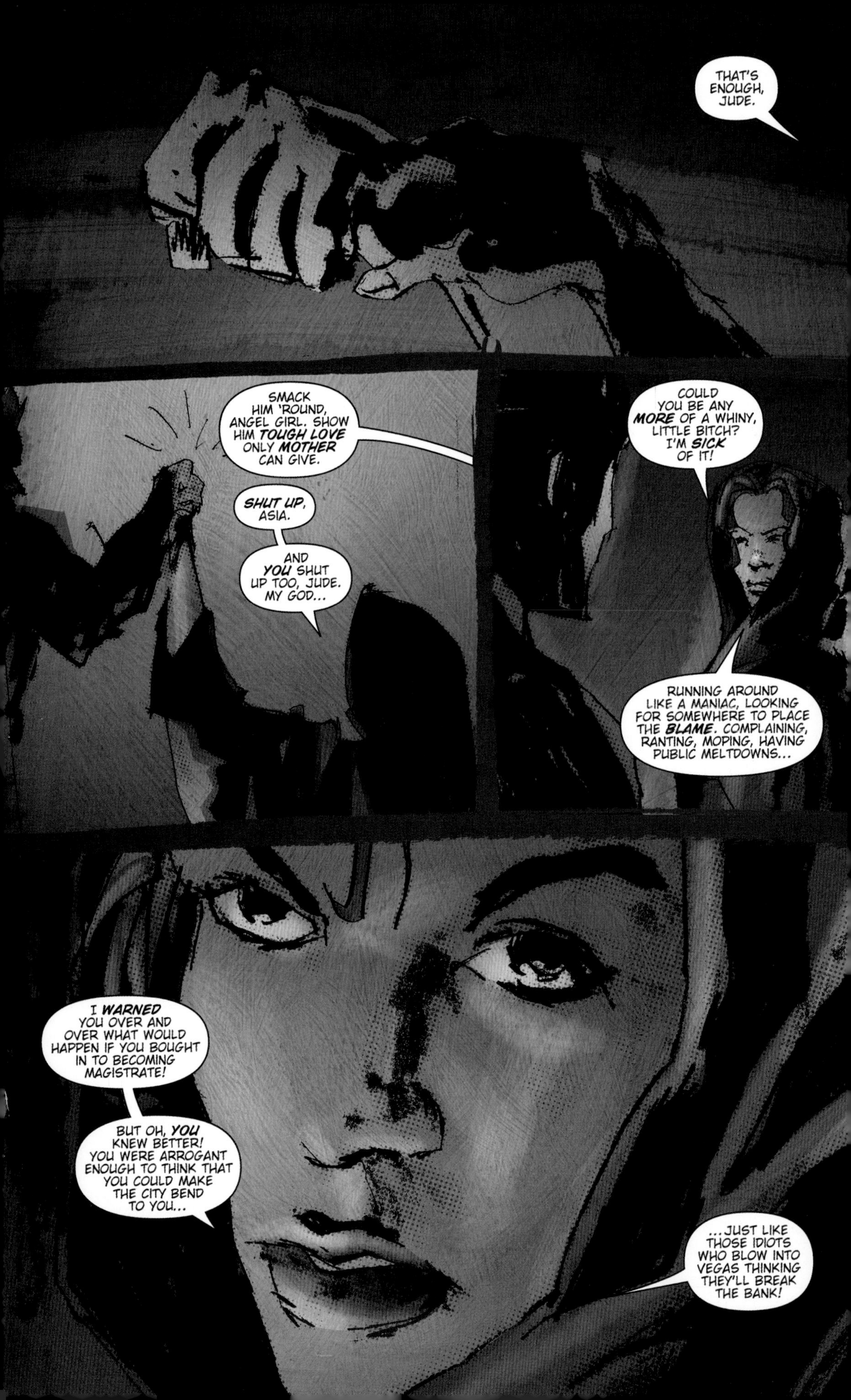
THAT'S ENOUGH, JUDE.
SMACK HIM 'ROUND, ANGEL GIRL. SHOW HIM TOUGH LOVE ONLY MOTHER CAN GIVE.
SHUT UP, ASIA.
AND YOU SHUT UP TOO, JUDE. MY GOD...
COULD YOU BE ANY MORE OF A WHINY, LITTLE BITCH? I'M SICK OF IT!
RUNNING AROUND LIKE A MANIAC, LOOKING FOR SOMEWHERE TO PLACE THE BLAME. COMPLAINING, RANTING, MOPING, HAVING PUBLIC MELTDOWNS...
I WARNED YOU OVER AND OVER WHAT WOULD HAPPEN IF YOU BOUGHT IN TO BECOMING MAGISTRATE!
BUT OH, YOU KNEW BETTER! YOU WERE ARROGANT ENOUGH TO THINK THAT YOU COULD MAKE THE CITY BEND TO YOU...
...JUST LIKE THOSE IDIOTS WHO BLOW INTO VEGAS THINKING THEY'LL BREAK THE BANK!

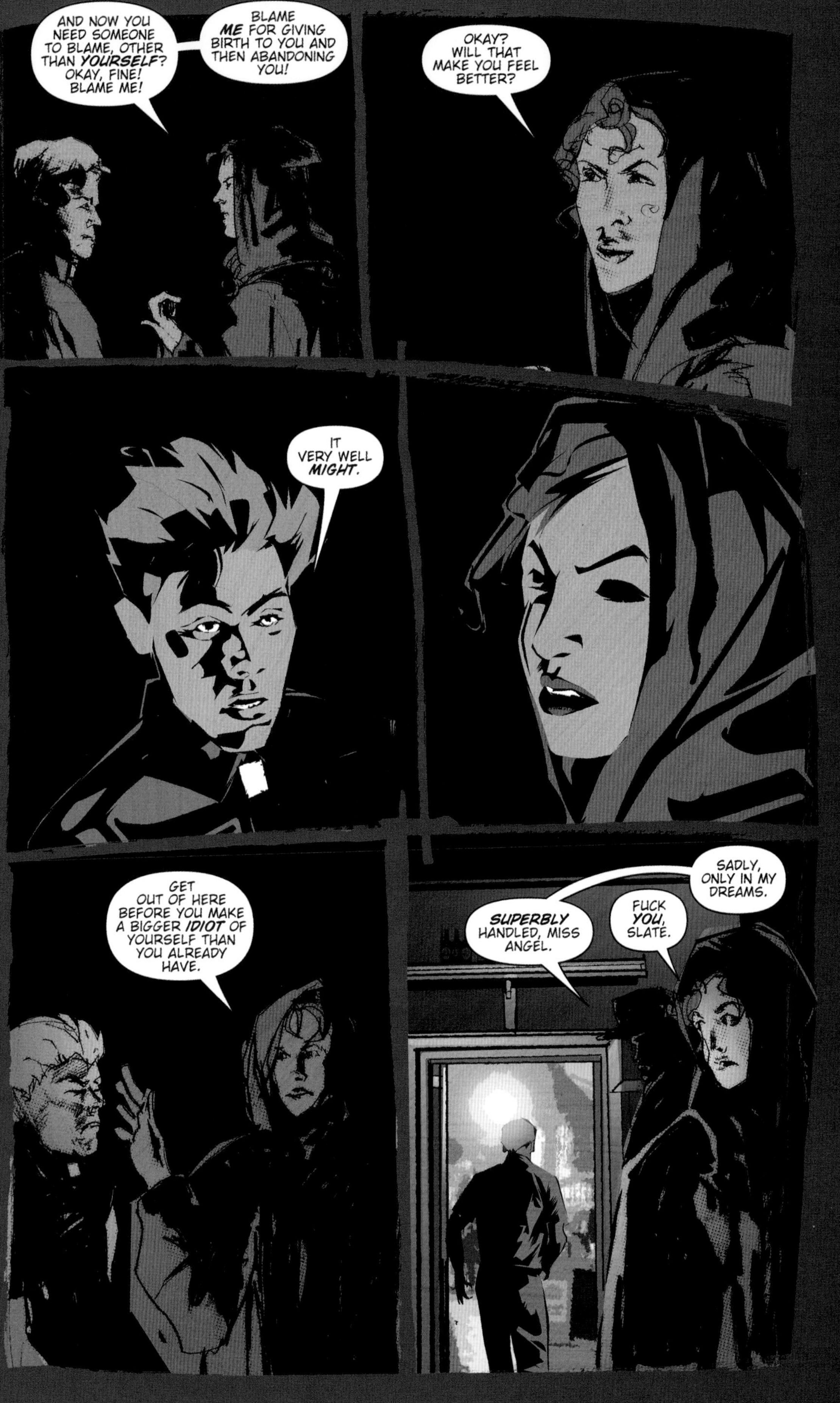
AND NOW YOU NEED SOMEONE TO BLAME, OTHER THAN YOURSELF? OKAY, FINE! BLAME ME!
BLAME ME FOR GIVING BIRTH TO YOU AND THEN ABANDONING YOU!
OKAY? WILL THAT MAKE YOU FEEL BETTER?
IT VERY WELL MIGHT.
GET OUT OF HERE BEFORE YOU MAKE A BIGGER IDIOT OF YOURSELF THAN YOU ALREADY HAVE.
SUPERBLY HANDLED, MISS ANGEL.
FUCK YOU, SLATE.
SADLY, ONLY IN MY DREAMS.

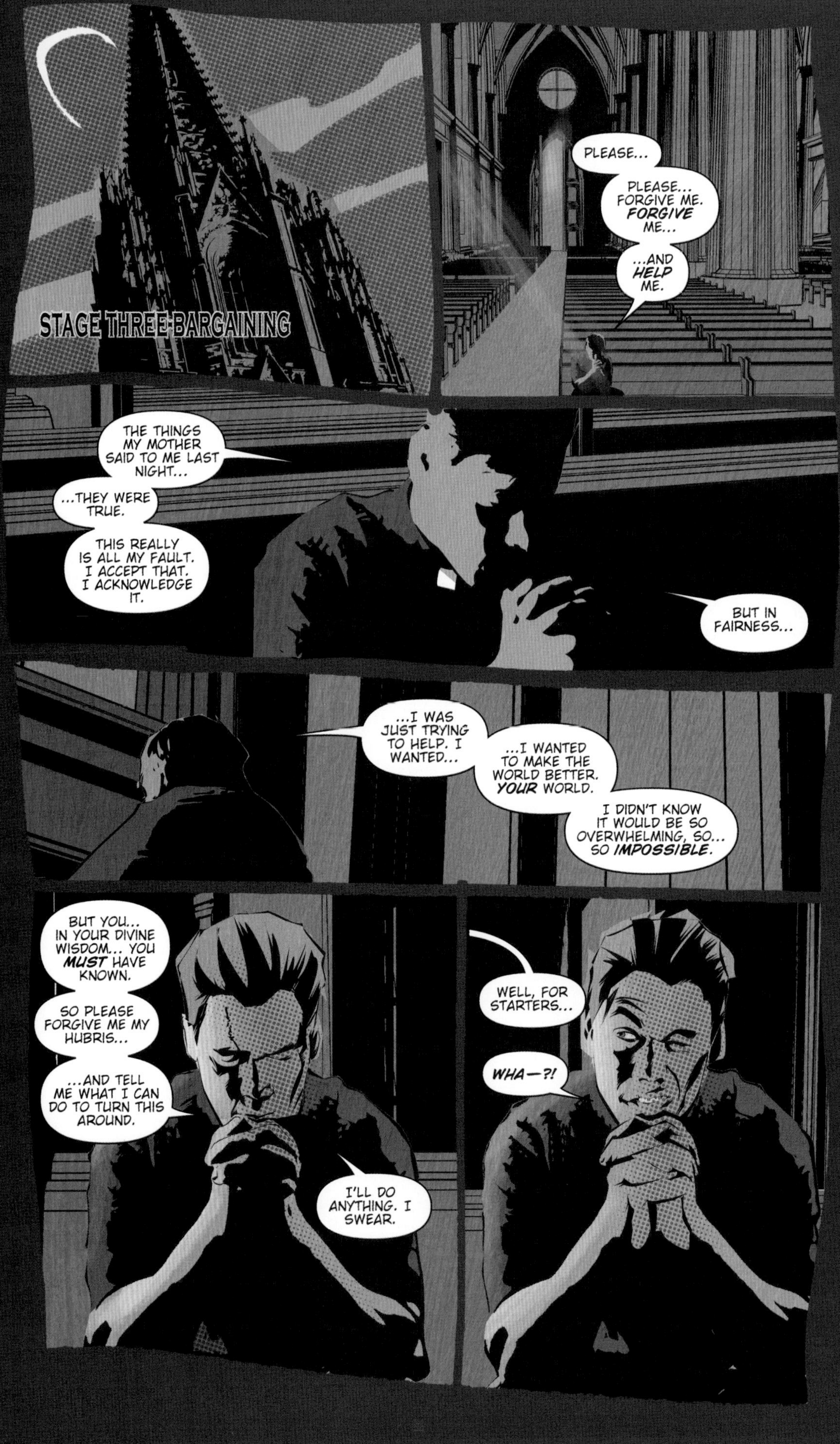
STAGE THREE-BARGAINING
PLEASE...
PLEASE... FORGIVE ME. FORGIVE ME...
...AND HELP ME.
THE THINGS MY MOTHER SAID TO ME LAST NIGHT...
...THEY WERE TRUE.
THIS REALLY IS ALL MY FAULT. I ACCEPT THAT. I ACKNOWLEDGE IT.
BUT IN FAIRNESS...
...I WAS JUST TRYING TO HELP. I WANTED...
...I WANTED TO MAKE THE WORLD BETTER. YOUR WORLD.
I DIDN'T KNOW IT WOULD BE SO OVERWHELMING, SO... SO IMPOSSIBLE.
BUT YOU... IN YOUR DIVINE WISDOM... YOU MUST HAVE KNOWN.
SO PLEASE FORGIVE ME MY HUBRIS...
...AND TELL ME WHAT I CAN DO TO TURN THIS AROUND.
I'LL DO ANYTHING. I SWEAR.
WELL, FOR STARTERS...
WHA—?!

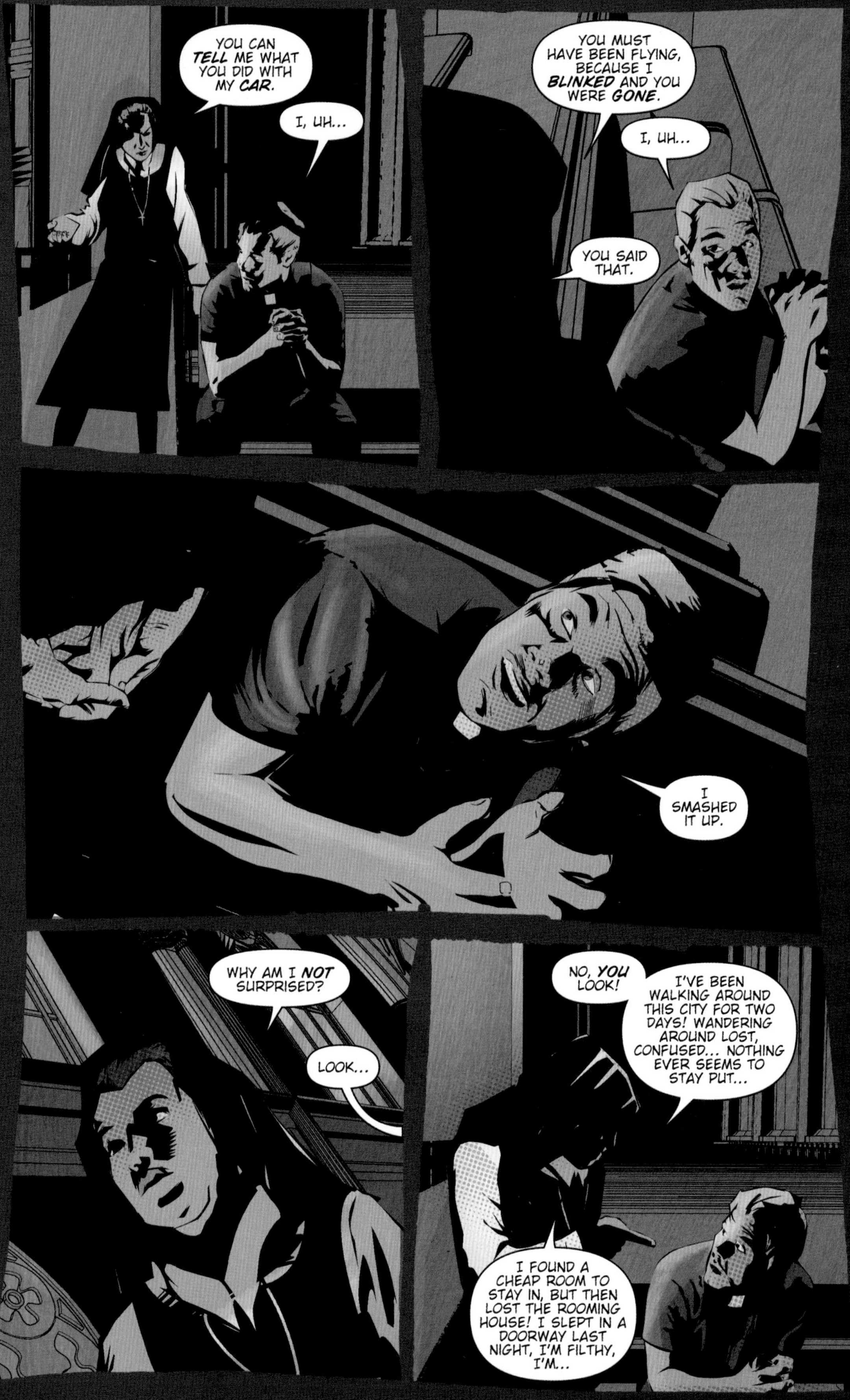
YOU CAN TELL ME WHAT YOU DID WITH MY CAR.
I, UH...
YOU MUST HAVE BEEN FLYING, BECAUSE I BLINKED AND YOU WERE GONE.
I, UH...
YOU SAID THAT.
I SMASHED IT UP.
WHY AM I NOT SURPRISED?
LOOK...
NO, YOU LOOK!
I'VE BEEN WALKING AROUND THIS CITY FOR TWO DAYS! WANDERING AROUND LOST, CONFUSED... NOTHING EVER SEEMS TO STAY PUT...
I FOUND A CHEAP ROOM TO STAY IN, BUT THEN LOST THE ROOMING HOUSE! I SLEPT IN A DOORWAY LAST NIGHT, I'M FILTHY, I'M...

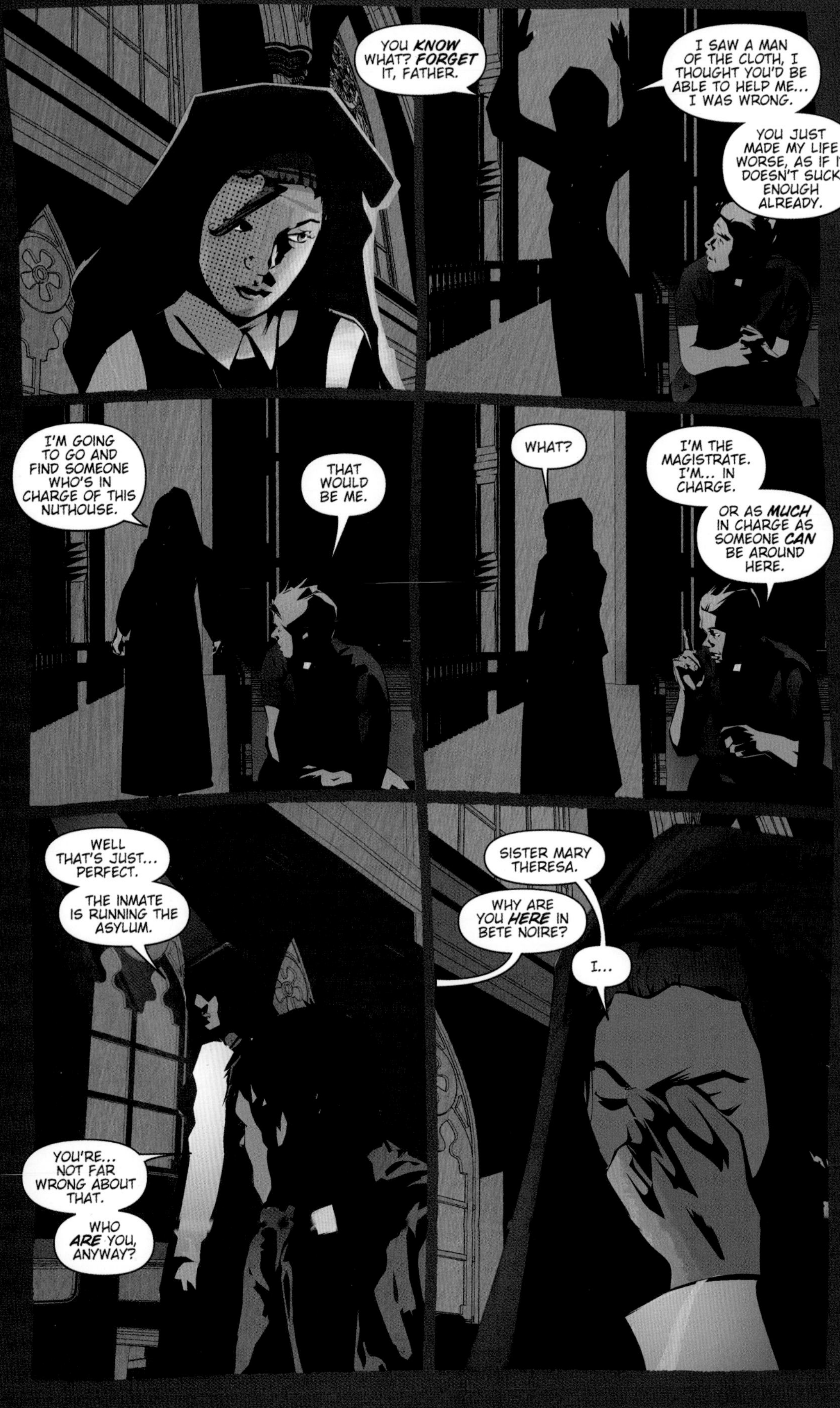

YOU KNOW WHAT? FORGET IT, FATHER.
I SAW A MAN OF THE CLOTH, I THOUGHT YOU'D BE ABLE TO HELP ME... I WAS WRONG.
YOU JUST MADE MY LIFE WORSE, AS IF IT DOESN'T SUCK ENOUGH ALREADY.
I'M GOING TO GO AND FIND SOMEONE WHO'S IN CHARGE OF THIS NUTHOUSE.
THAT WOULD BE ME.
WHAT?
I'M THE MAGISTRATE. I'M... IN CHARGE.
OR AS MUCH IN CHARGE AS SOMEONE CAN BE AROUND HERE.
WELL THAT'S JUST... PERFECT.
THE INMATE IS RUNNING THE ASYLUM.
YOU'RE... NOT FAR WRONG ABOUT THAT.
WHO ARE YOU, ANYWAY?
SISTER MARY THERESA.
WHY ARE YOU HERE IN BETE NOIRE?
I...

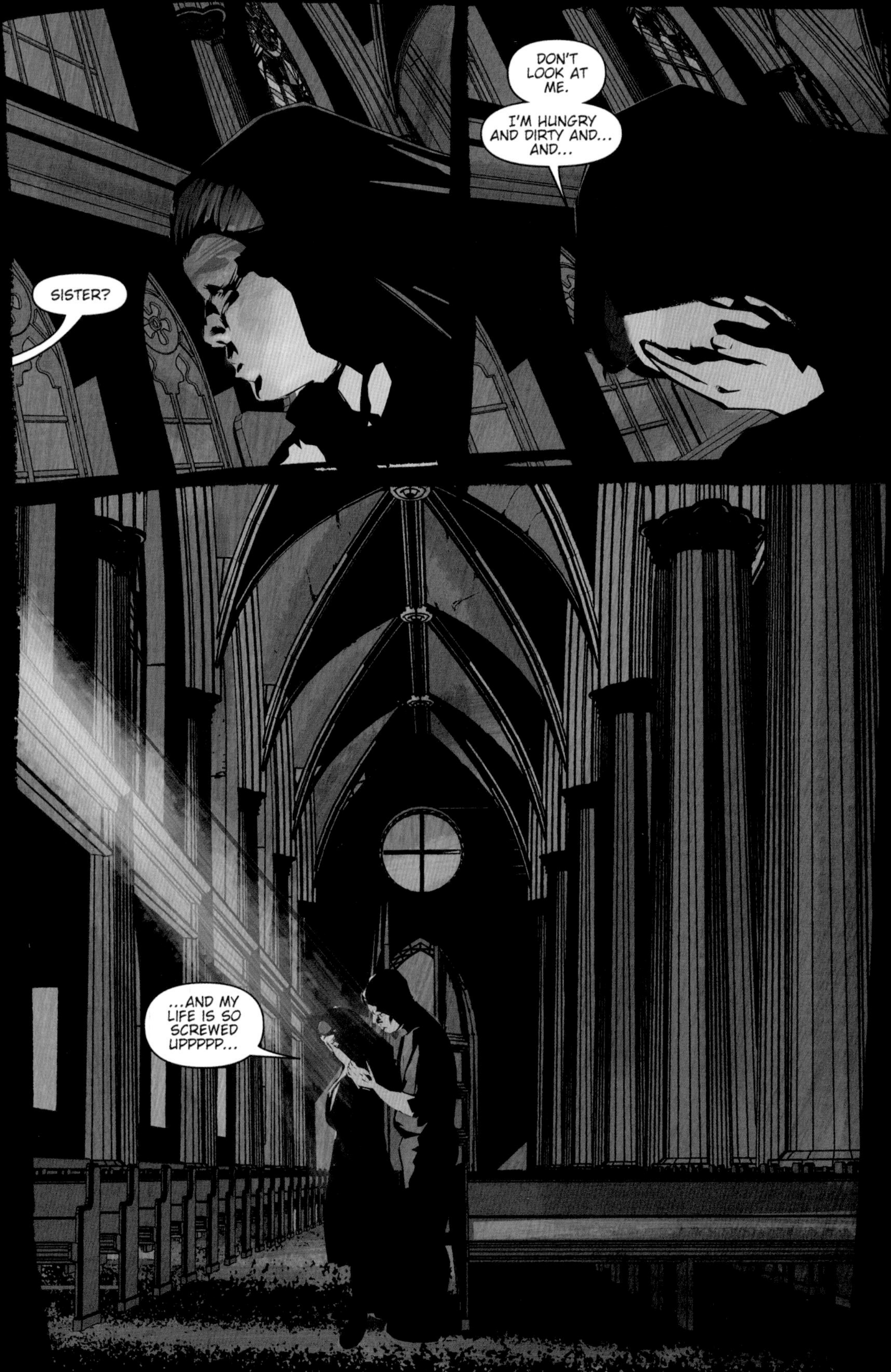
SISTER?
DON'T LOOK AT ME.
I'M HUNGRY AND DIRTY AND... AND...
...AND MY LIFE IS SO SCREWED UPPPPP...

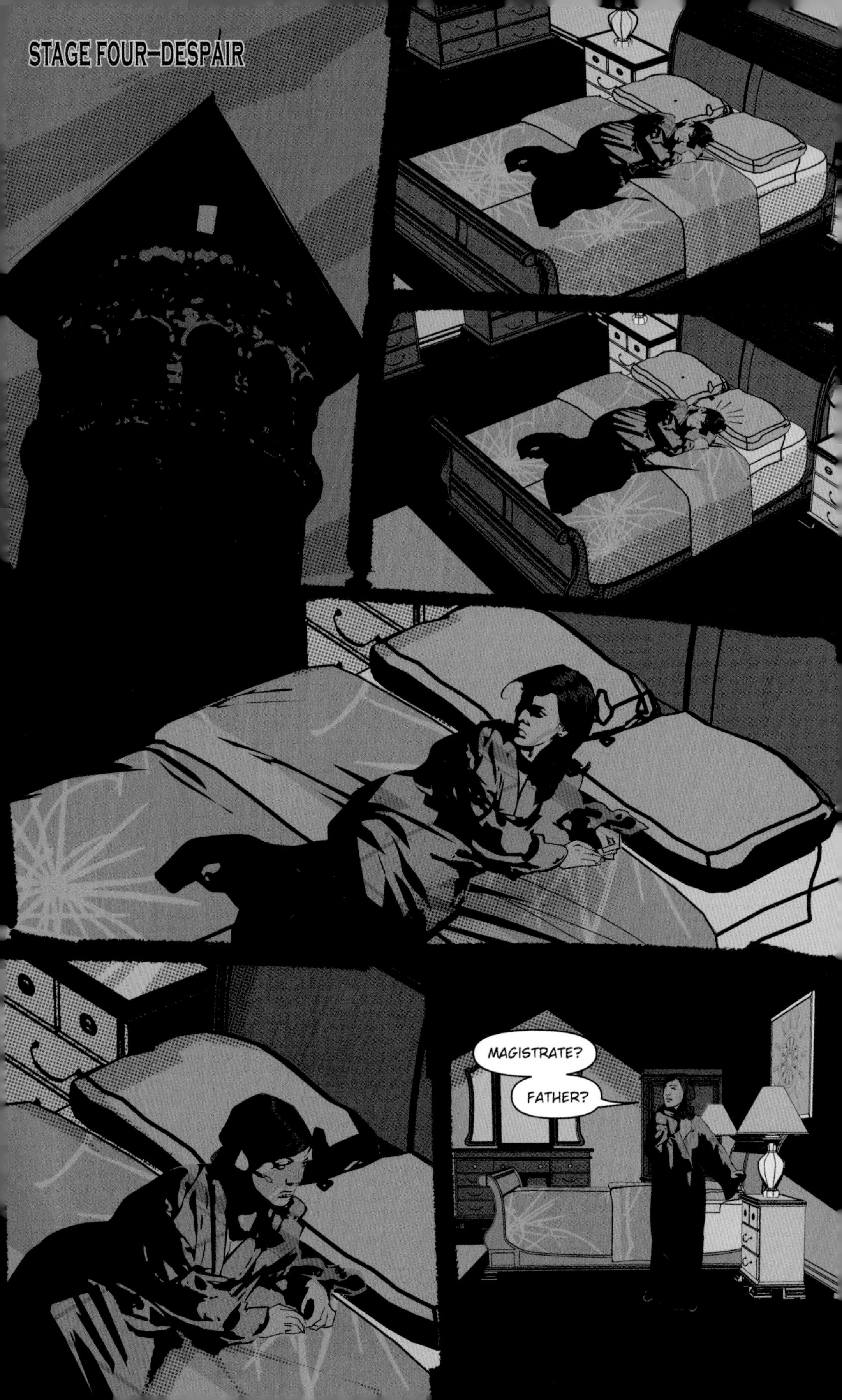
STAGE FOUR—DESPAIR
MAGISTRATE?
FATHER?

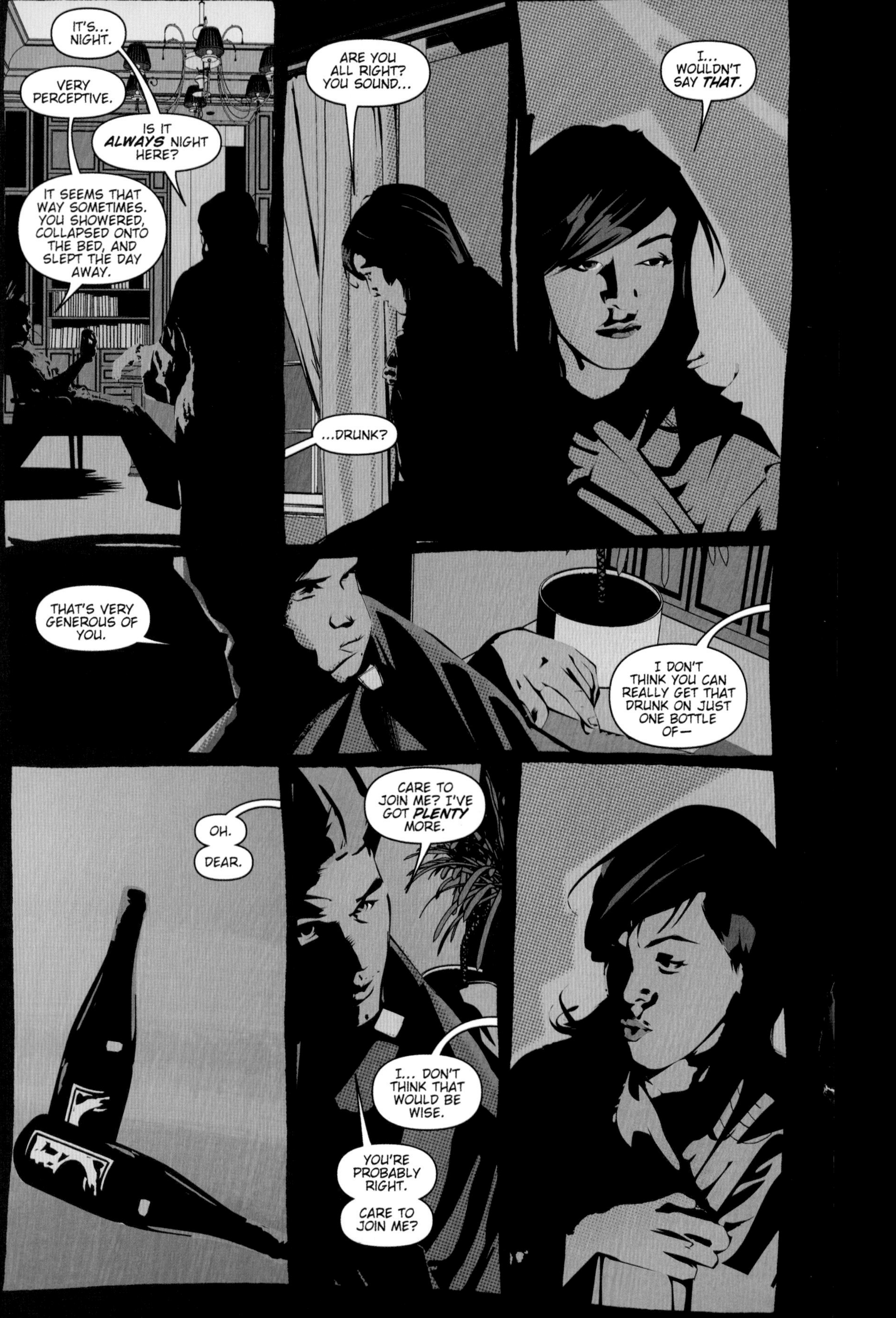
IT'S... NIGHT.
VERY PERCEPTIVE.
IS IT ALWAYS NIGHT HERE?
IT SEEMS THAT WAY SOMETIMES. YOU SHOWERED, COLLAPSED ONTO THE BED, AND SLEPT THE DAY AWAY.
ARE YOU ALL RIGHT? YOU SOUND...
...DRUNK?
I... WOULDN'T SAY THAT.
THAT'S VERY GENEROUS OF YOU.
I DON'T THINK YOU CAN REALLY GET THAT DRUNK ON JUST ONE BOTTLE OF—
OH.
DEAR.
CARE TO JOIN ME? I'VE GOT PLENTY MORE.
I... DON'T THINK THAT WOULD BE WISE.
YOU'RE PROBABLY RIGHT.
CARE TO JOIN ME?

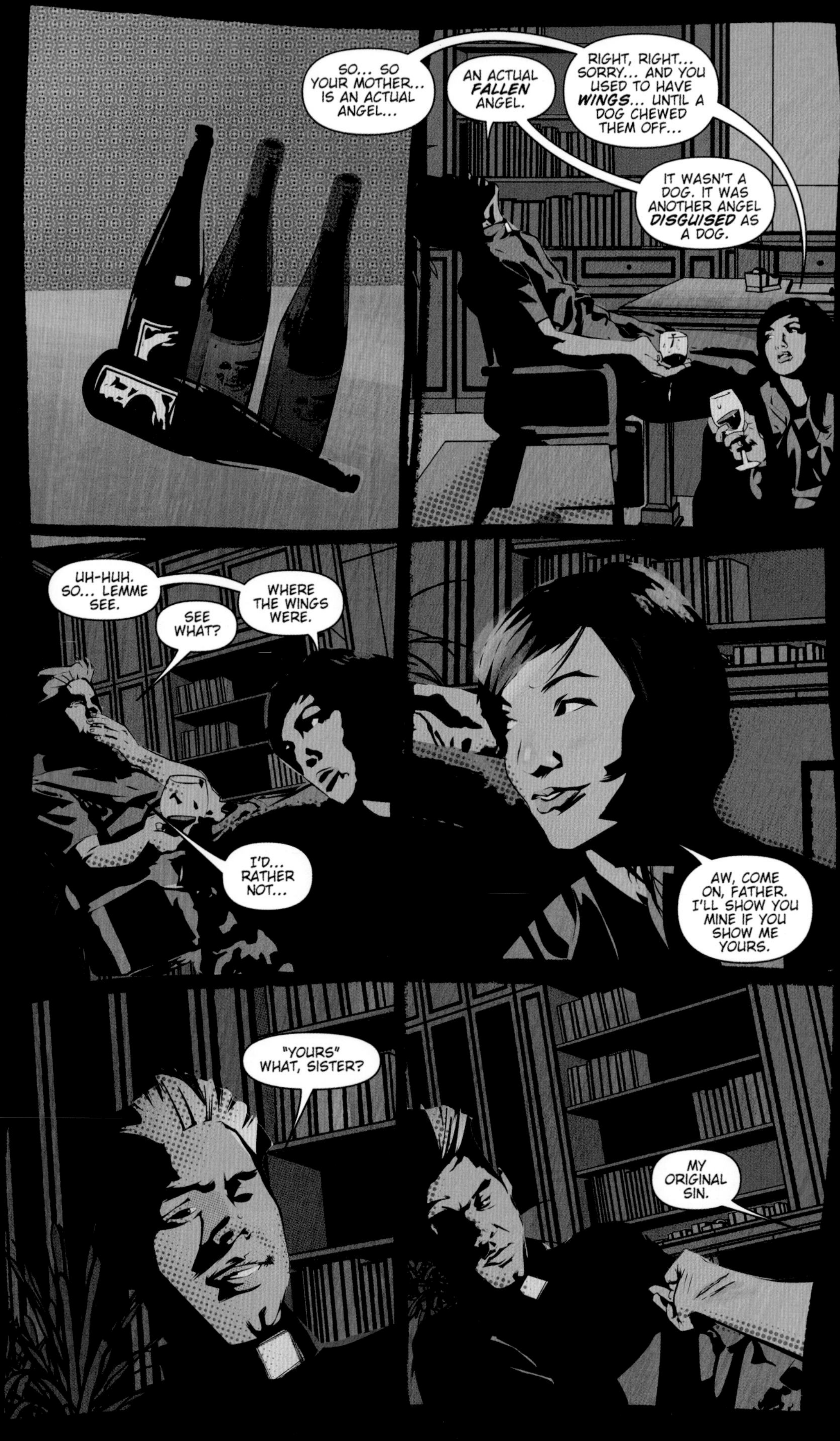
SO... SO YOUR MOTHER... IS AN ACTUAL ANGEL...
AN ACTUAL FALLEN ANGEL.
RIGHT, RIGHT... SORRY... AND YOU USED TO HAVE WINGS... UNTIL A DOG CHEWED THEM OFF...
IT WASN'T A DOG. IT WAS ANOTHER ANGEL DISGUISED AS A DOG.
UH-HUH. SO... LEMME SEE.
SEE WHAT?
WHERE THE WINGS WERE.
I'D... RATHER NOT...
AW, COME ON, FATHER. I'LL SHOW YOU MINE IF YOU SHOW ME YOURS.
"YOURS" WHAT, SISTER?
MY ORIGINAL SIN.

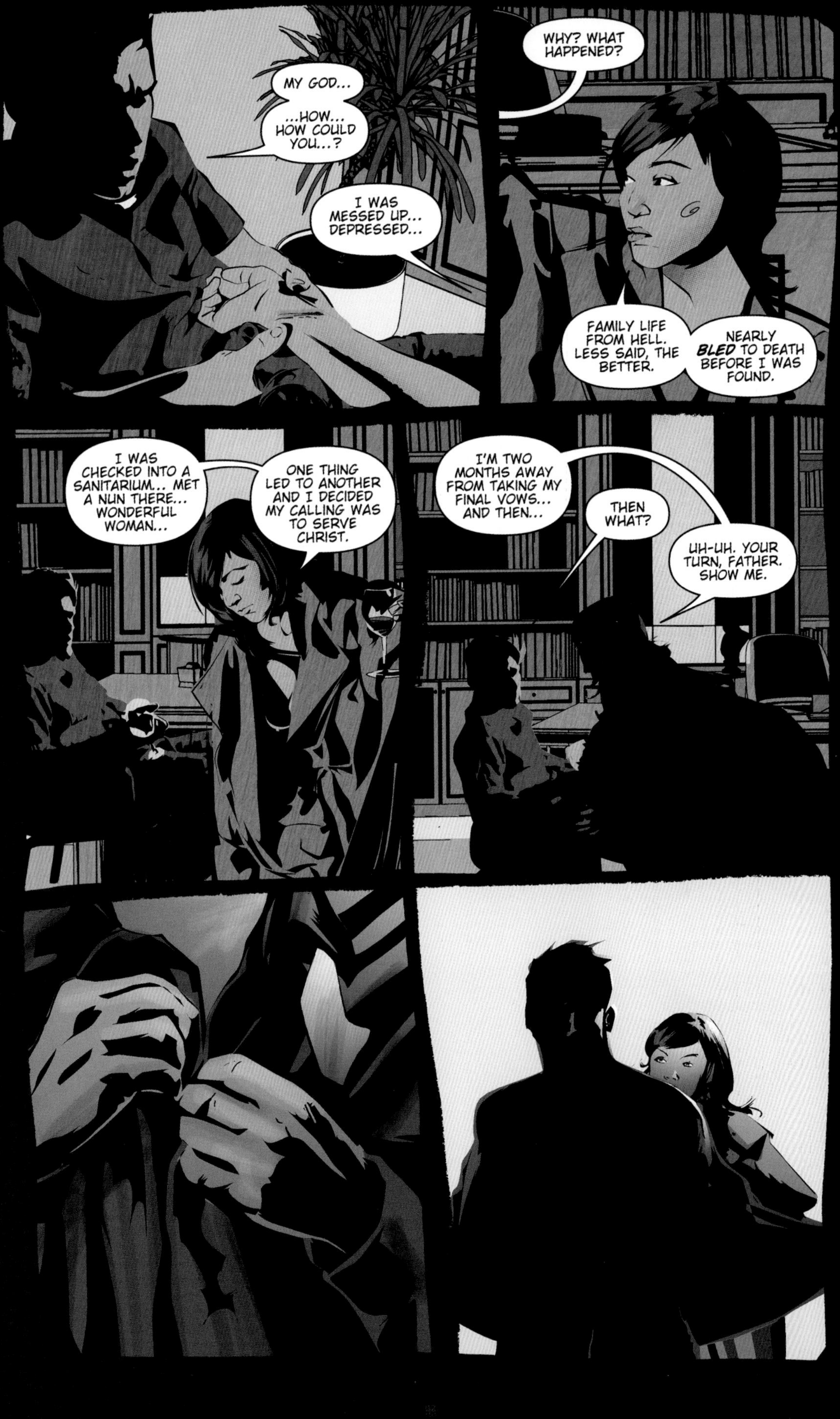
MY GOD...
...HOW... HOW COULD YOU...?
I WAS MESSED UP... DEPRESSED...
WHY? WHAT HAPPENED?
FAMILY LIFE FROM HELL. LESS SAID, THE BETTER.
NEARLY BLED TO DEATH BEFORE I WAS FOUND.
I WAS CHECKED INTO A SANITARIUM... MET A NUN THERE... WONDERFUL WOMAN...
ONE THING LED TO ANOTHER AND I DECIDED MY CALLING WAS TO SERVE CHRIST.
I'M TWO MONTHS AWAY FROM TAKING MY FINAL VOWS... AND THEN...
THEN WHAT?
UH-UH. YOUR TURN, FATHER. SHOW ME.

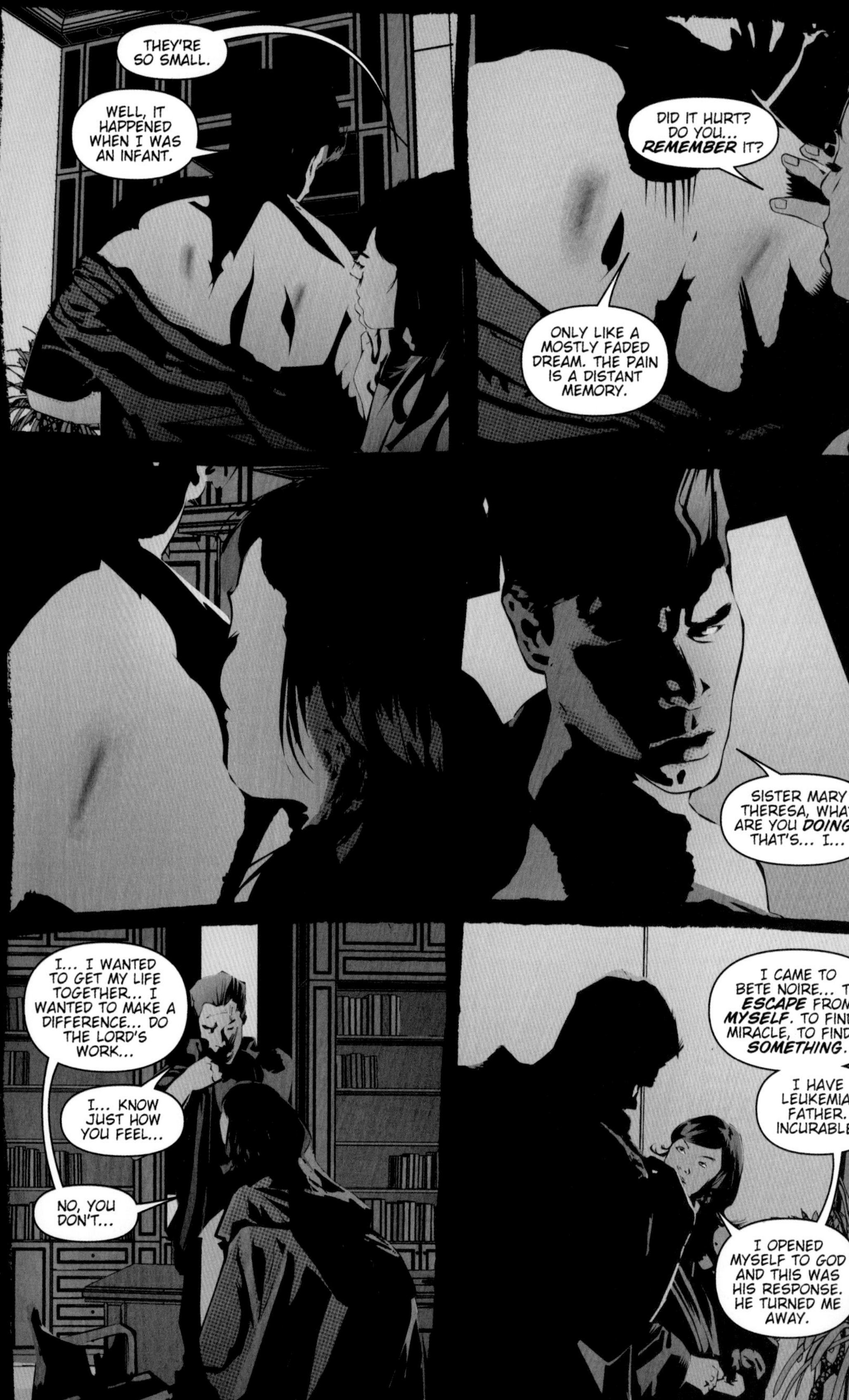
THEY'RE SO SMALL.
WELL, IT HAPPENED WHEN I WAS AN INFANT.
DID IT HURT? DO YOU... REMEMBER IT?
ONLY LIKE A MOSTLY FADED DREAM. THE PAIN IS A DISTANT MEMORY.
SISTER MARY THERESA, WHAT ARE YOU DOING? THAT'S... I...
I... I WANTED TO GET MY LIFE TOGETHER... I WANTED TO MAKE A DIFFERENCE... DO THE LORD'S WORK...
I... KNOW JUST HOW YOU FEEL...
NO, YOU DON'T...
I CAME TO BETE NOIRE... TO ESCAPE FROM MYSELF. TO FIND A MIRACLE, TO FIND... SOMETHING.
I HAVE LEUKEMIA, FATHER. INCURABLE.
I OPENED MYSELF TO GOD AND THIS WAS HIS RESPONSE. HE TURNED ME AWAY.

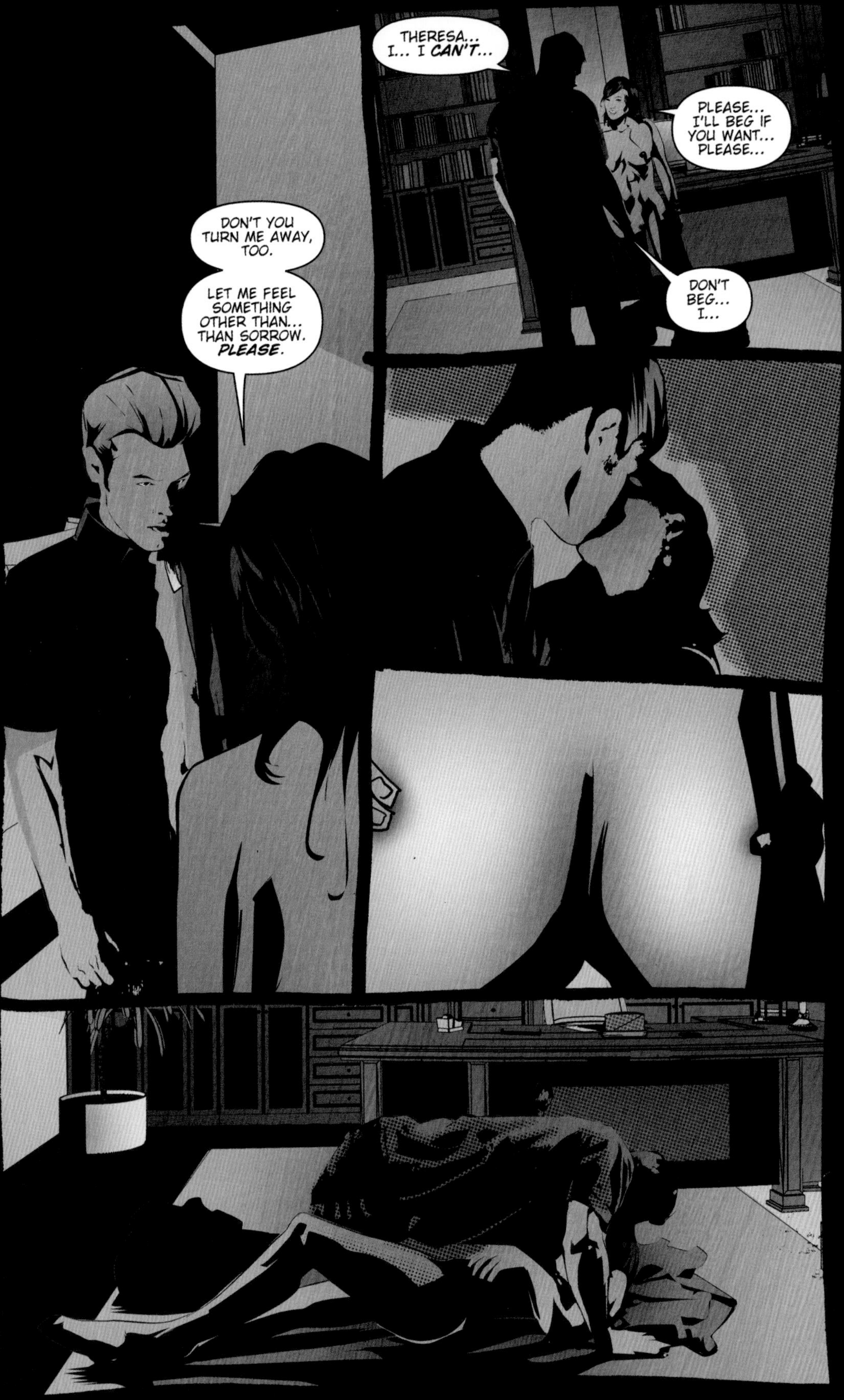
THERESA... I... I CAN'T...
PLEASE... I'LL BEG IF YOU WANT... PLEASE...
DON'T BEG... I...
DON'T YOU TURN ME AWAY, TOO.
LET ME FEEL SOMETHING OTHER THAN... THAN SORROW. PLEASE.

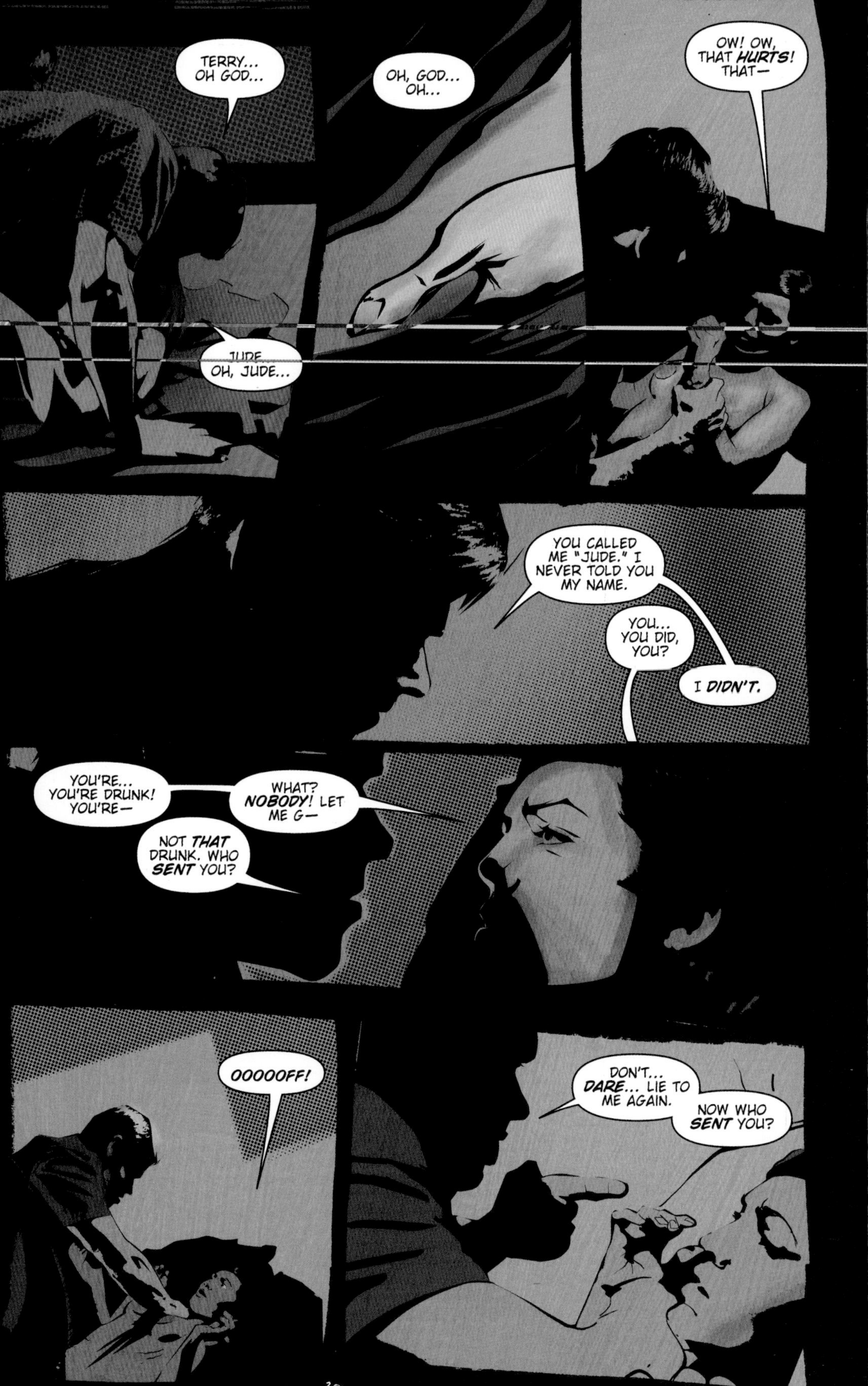
TERRY... OH GOD...
JUDE. OH, JUDE...
OH, GOD... OH...
OW! OW, THAT HURTS! THAT—
YOU CALLED ME "JUDE." I NEVER TOLD YOU MY NAME.
YOU... YOU DID, YOU?
I DIDN'T.
YOU'RE... YOU'RE DRUNK! YOU'RE—
NOT THAT DRUNK. WHO SENT YOU?
WHAT? NOBODY! LET ME G—
OOOOOFF!
DON'T... DARE... LIE TO ME AGAIN.
NOW WHO SENT YOU?

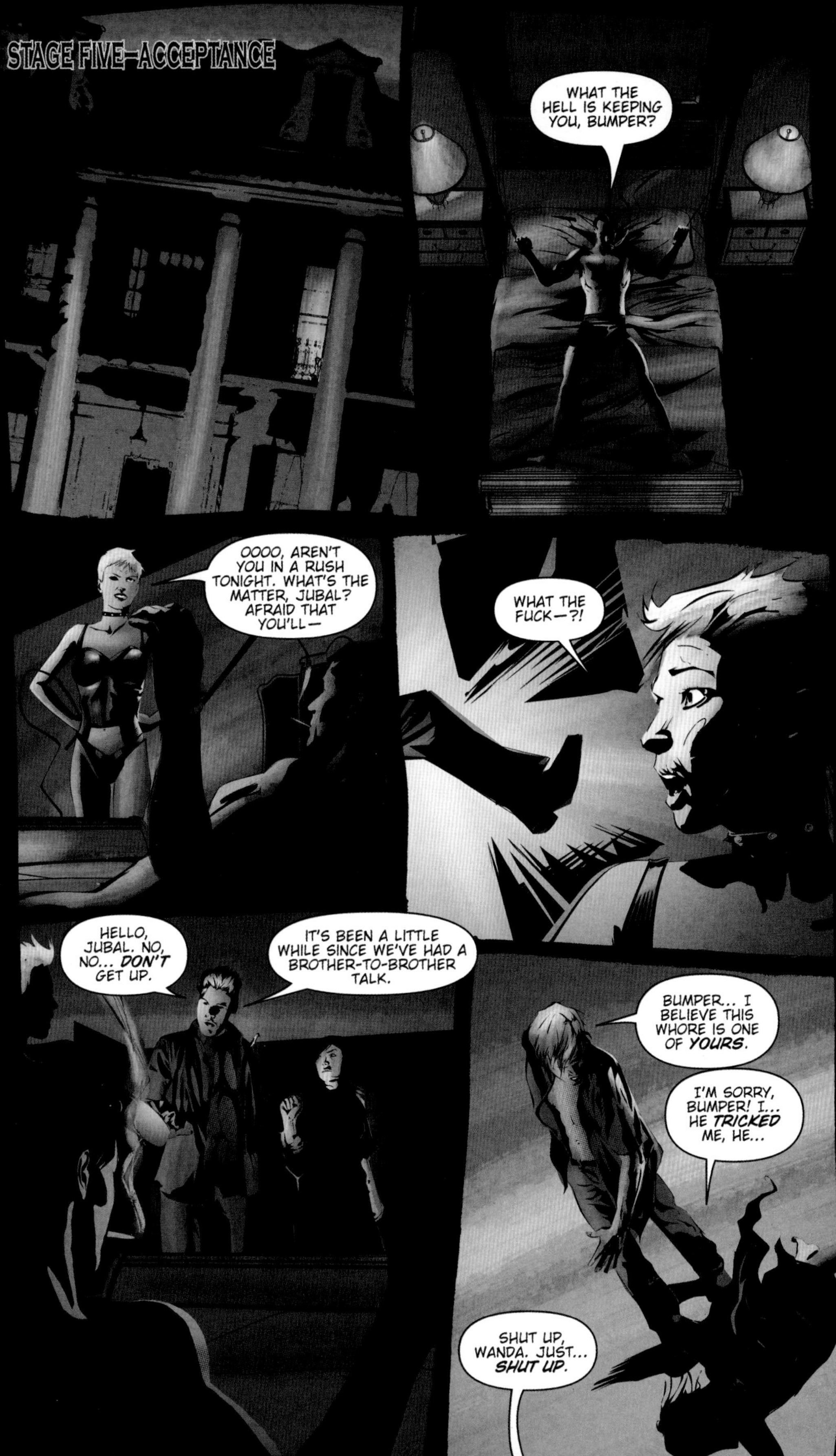
STAGE FIVE—ACCEPTANCE
WHAT THE HELL IS KEEPING YOU, BUMPER?
OOOO, AREN'T YOU IN A RUSH TONIGHT. WHAT'S THE MATTER, JUBAL? AFRAID THAT YOU'LL—
WHAT THE FUCK—?!
HELLO, JUBAL. NO, NO... DON'T GET UP.
IT'S BEEN A LITTLE WHILE SINCE WE'VE HAD A BROTHER-TO-BROTHER TALK.
BUMPER... I BELIEVE THIS WHORE IS ONE OF YOURS.
I'M SORRY, BUMPER! I... HE TRICKED ME, HE...
SHUT UP, WANDA. JUST... SHUT UP.

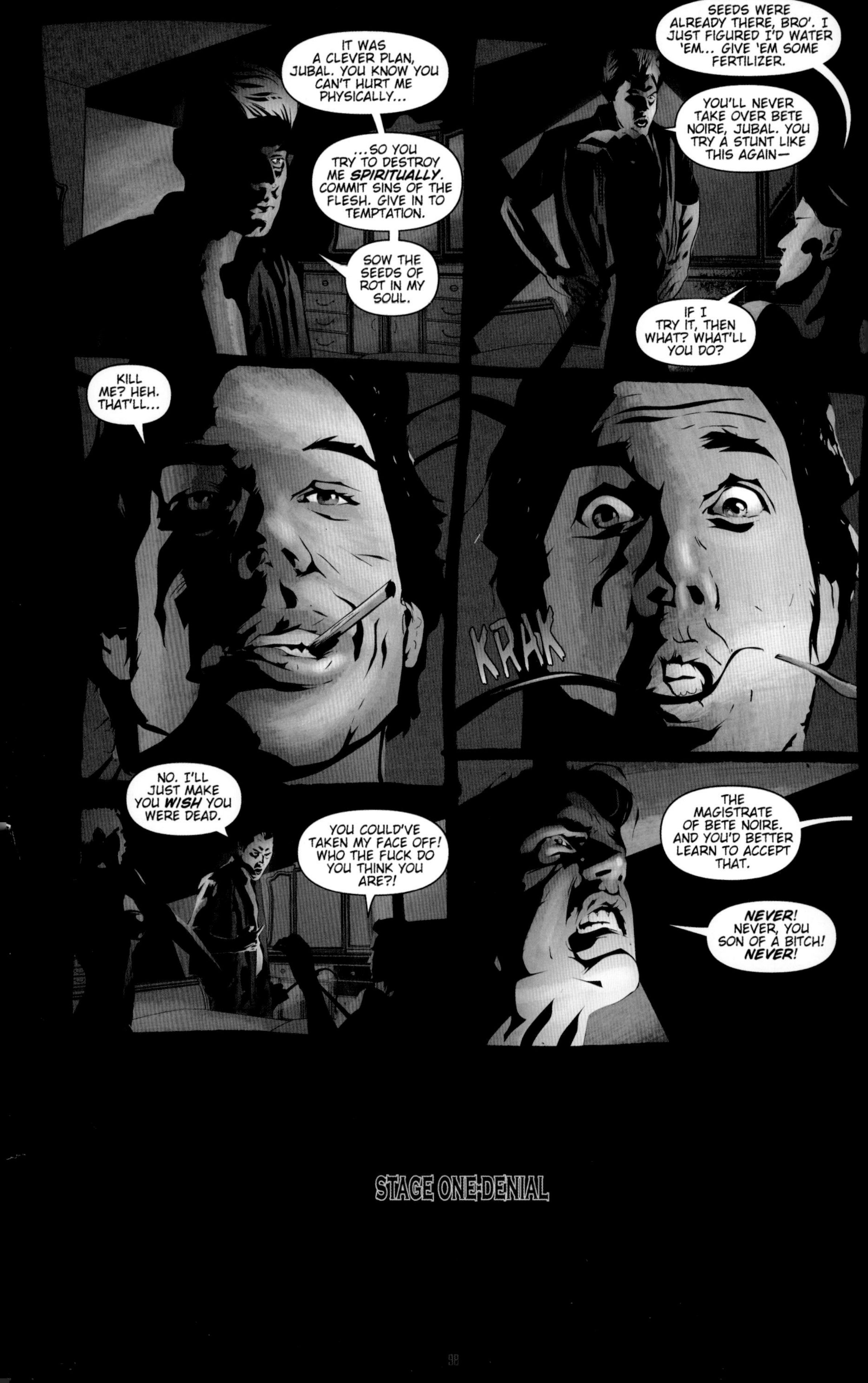
IT WAS A CLEVER PLAN, JUBAL. YOU KNOW YOU CAN'T HURT ME PHYSICALLY...
...SO YOU TRY TO DESTROY ME **SPIRITUALLY**. COMMIT SINS OF THE FLESH. GIVE IN TO TEMPTATION.
SOW THE SEEDS OF ROT IN MY SOUL.
SEEDS WERE ALREADY THERE, BRO'. I JUST FIGURED I'D WATER 'EM... GIVE 'EM SOME FERTILIZER.
YOU'LL NEVER TAKE OVER BETE NOIRE, JUBAL. YOU TRY A STUNT LIKE THIS AGAIN—
IF I TRY IT, THEN WHAT? WHAT'LL YOU DO?
KILL ME? HEH. THAT'LL...
KRAK
NO. I'LL JUST MAKE YOU ***WISH*** YOU WERE DEAD.
YOU COULD'VE TAKEN MY FACE OFF! WHO THE FUCK DO YOU THINK YOU ARE?!
THE MAGISTRATE OF BETE NOIRE. AND YOU'D BETTER LEARN TO ACCEPT THAT.
NEVER! NEVER, YOU SON OF A BITCH! ***NEVER!***

STAGE ONE: DENIAL

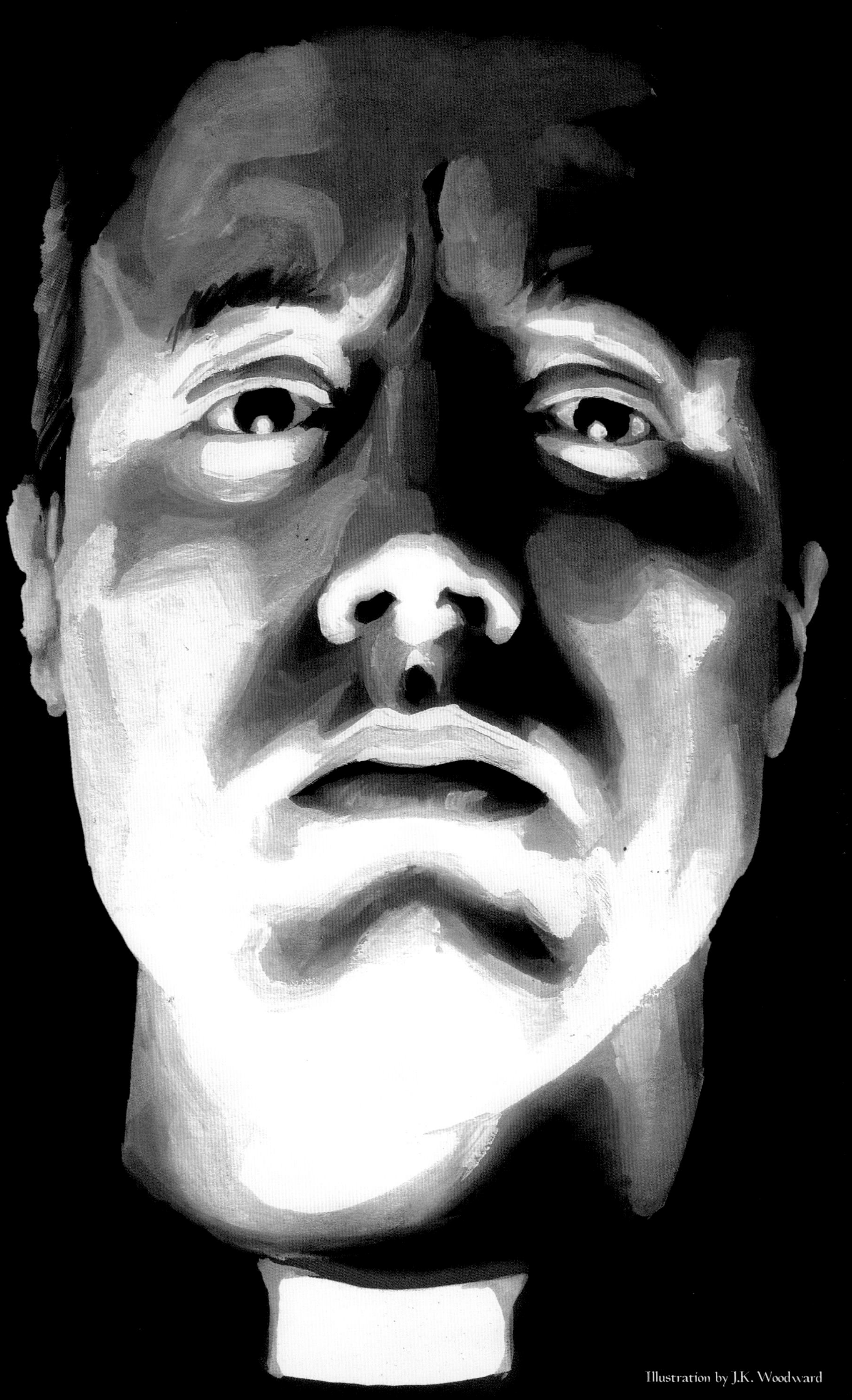

Illustration by J.K. Woodward

Chapter 5

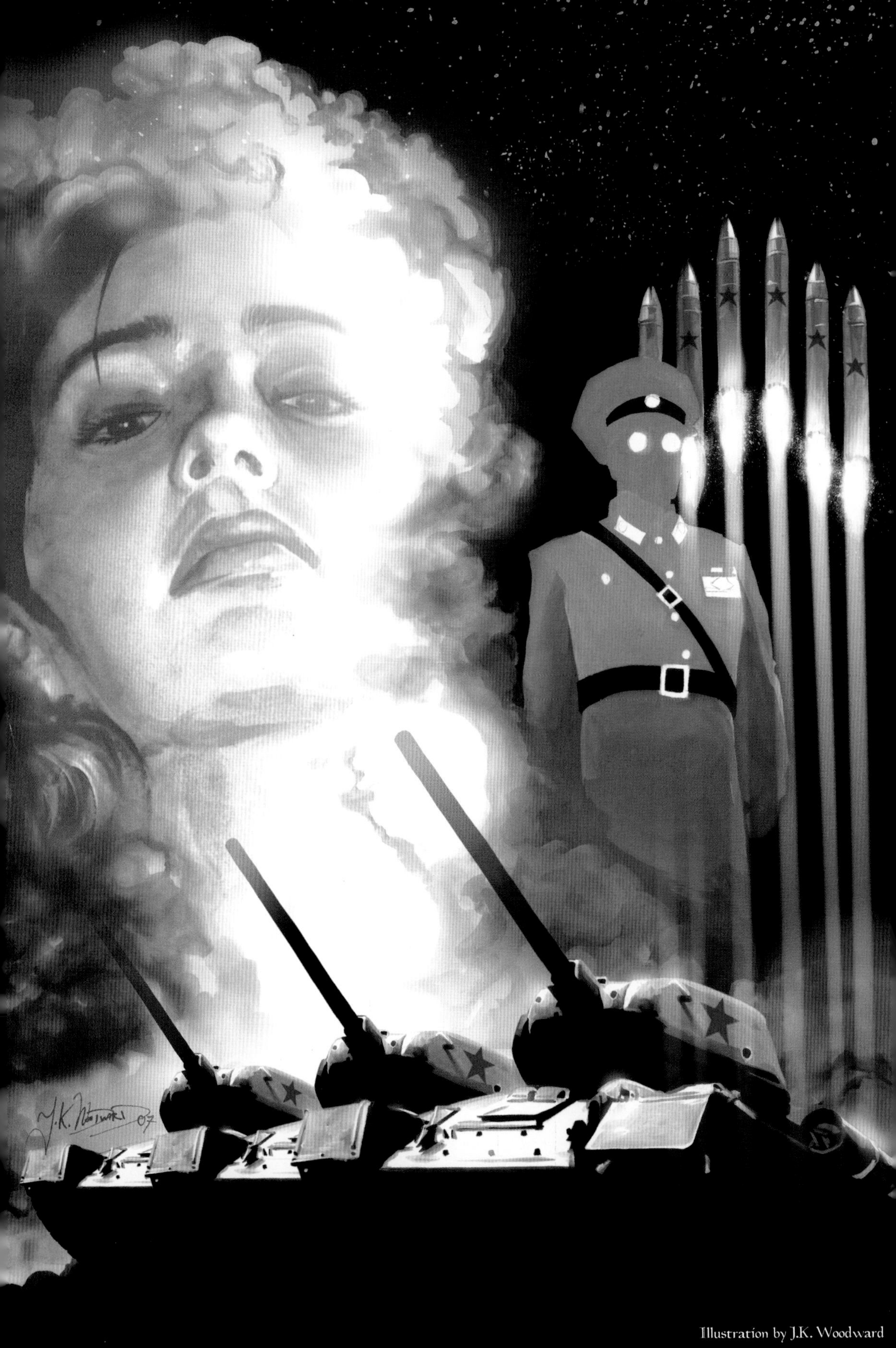
J.K. Woodward 07

Illustration by J.K. Woodward

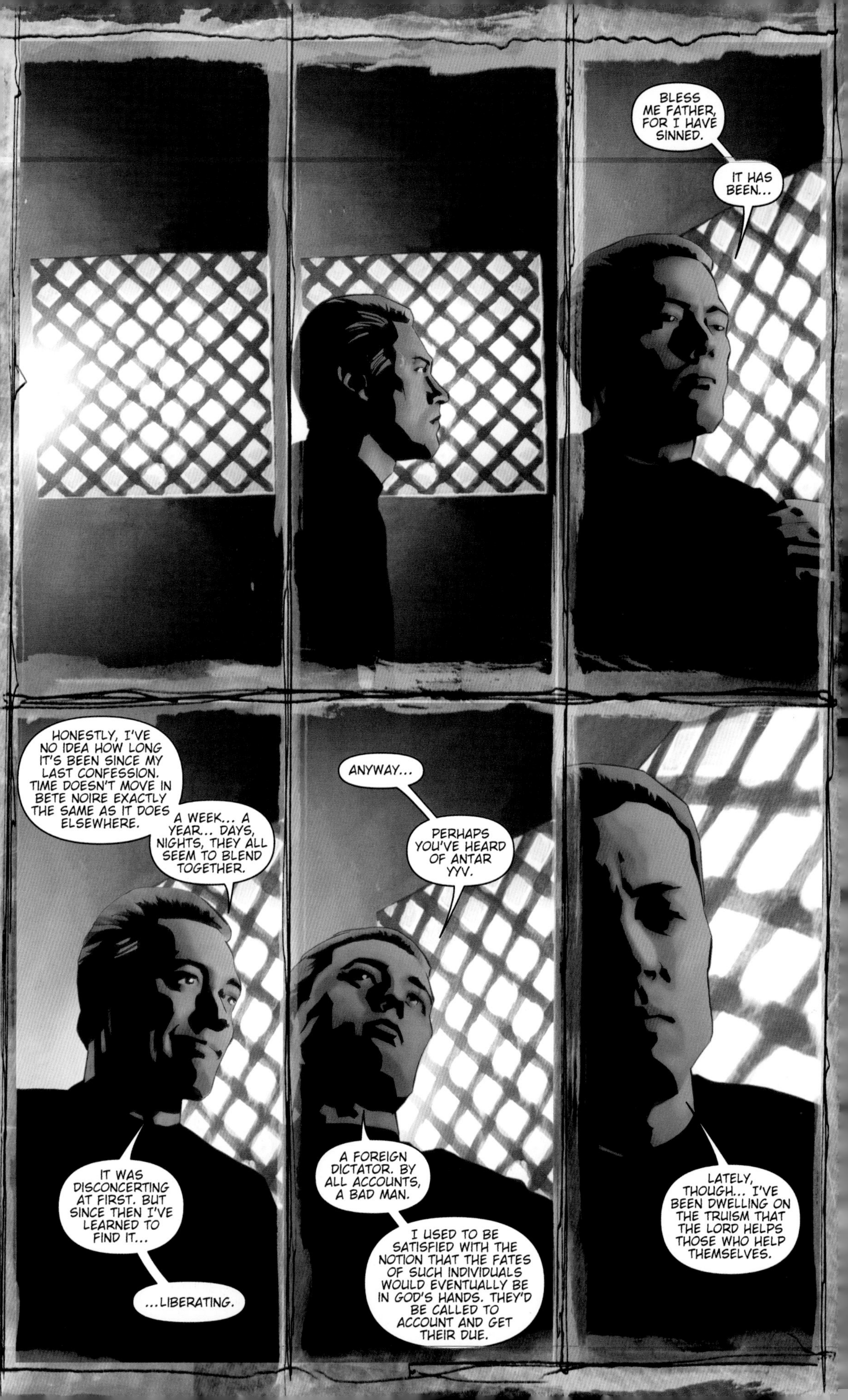
BLESS ME FATHER, FOR I HAVE SINNED.
IT HAS BEEN...
HONESTLY, I'VE NO IDEA HOW LONG IT'S BEEN SINCE MY LAST CONFESSION. TIME DOESN'T MOVE IN BETE NOIRE EXACTLY THE SAME AS IT DOES ELSEWHERE.
A WEEK... A YEAR... DAYS, NIGHTS, THEY ALL SEEM TO BLEND TOGETHER.
IT WAS DISCONCERTING AT FIRST. BUT SINCE THEN I'VE LEARNED TO FIND IT...
...LIBERATING.
ANYWAY...
PERHAPS YOU'VE HEARD OF ANTAR YYV.
A FOREIGN DICTATOR. BY ALL ACCOUNTS, A BAD MAN.
I USED TO BE SATISFIED WITH THE NOTION THAT THE FATES OF SUCH INDIVIDUALS WOULD EVENTUALLY BE IN GOD'S HANDS. THEY'D BE CALLED TO ACCOUNT AND GET THEIR DUE.
LATELY, THOUGH... I'VE BEEN DWELLING ON THE TRUISM THAT THE LORD HELPS THOSE WHO HELP THEMSELVES.

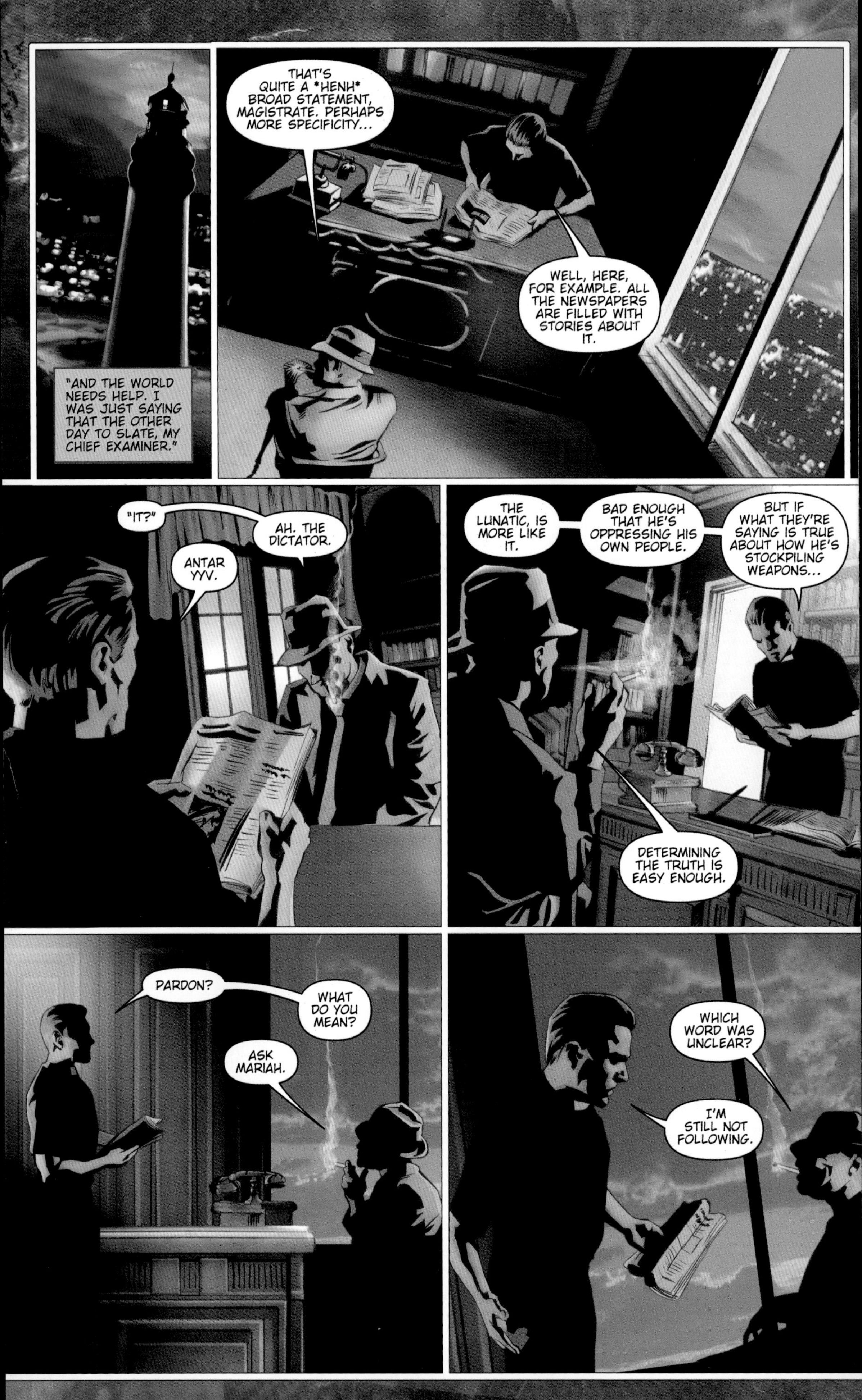
"AND THE WORLD NEEDS HELP. I WAS JUST SAYING THAT THE OTHER DAY TO SLATE, MY CHIEF EXAMINER."
THAT'S QUITE A *HENH* BROAD STATEMENT, MAGISTRATE. PERHAPS MORE SPECIFICITY...
WELL, HERE, FOR EXAMPLE. ALL THE NEWSPAPERS ARE FILLED WITH STORIES ABOUT IT.
"IT?"
AH. THE DICTATOR.
ANTAR YYV.
THE LUNATIC, IS MORE LIKE IT.
BAD ENOUGH THAT HE'S OPPRESSING HIS OWN PEOPLE.
BUT IF WHAT THEY'RE SAYING IS TRUE ABOUT HOW HE'S STOCKPILING WEAPONS...
DETERMINING THE TRUTH IS EASY ENOUGH.
PARDON?
WHAT DO YOU MEAN?
ASK MARIAH.
WHICH WORD WAS UNCLEAR?
I'M STILL NOT FOLLOWING.

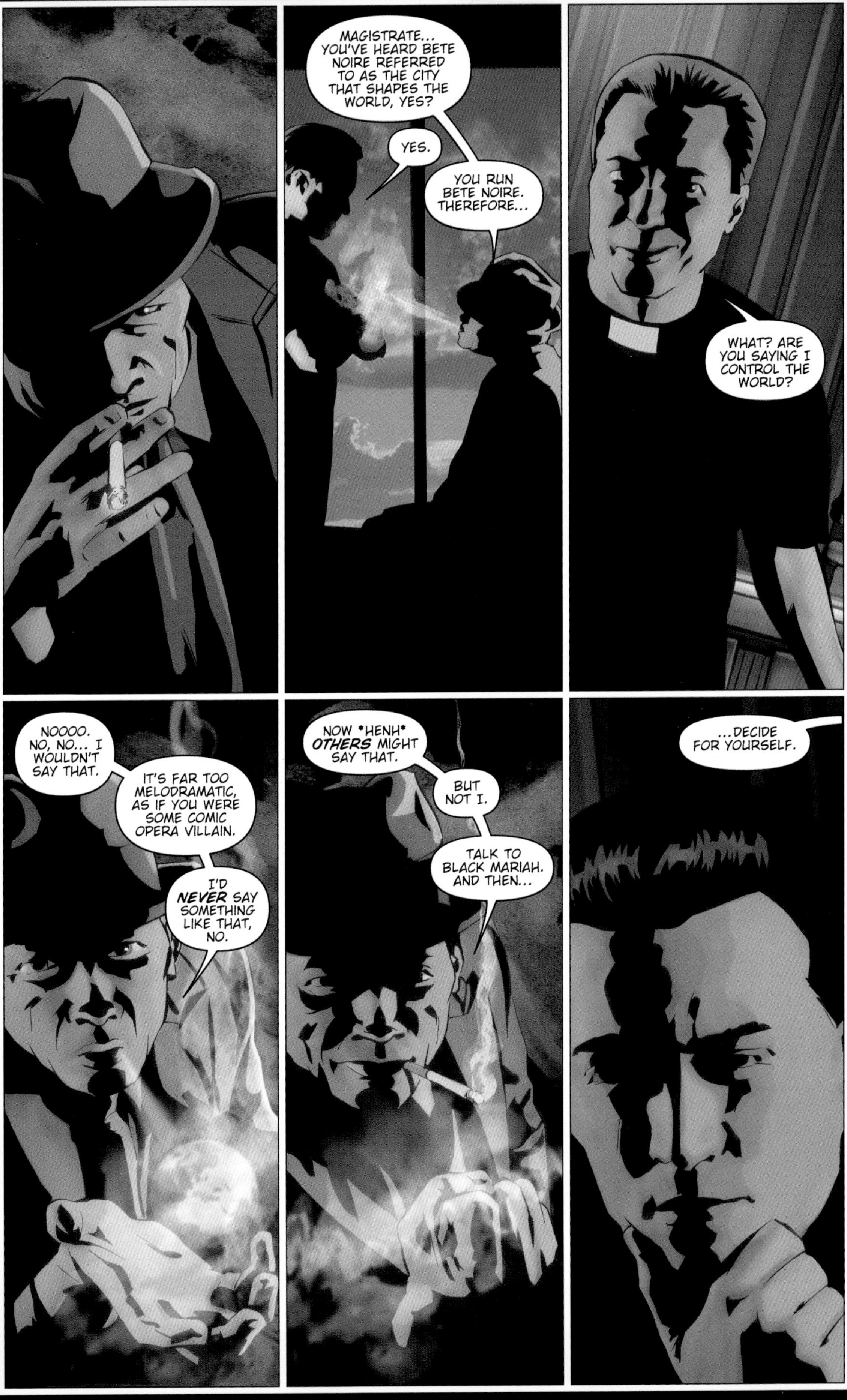
MAGISTRATE... YOU'VE HEARD BETE NOIRE REFERRED TO AS THE CITY THAT SHAPES THE WORLD, YES?
YES.
YOU RUN BETE NOIRE. THEREFORE...
WHAT? ARE YOU SAYING I CONTROL THE WORLD?
NOOOO. NO, NO... I WOULDN'T SAY THAT.
IT'S FAR TOO MELODRAMATIC, AS IF YOU WERE SOME COMIC OPERA VILLAIN.
I'D NEVER SAY SOMETHING LIKE THAT, NO.
NOW *HENH* OTHERS MIGHT SAY THAT.
BUT NOT I.
TALK TO BLACK MARIAH. AND THEN...
...DECIDE FOR YOURSELF.

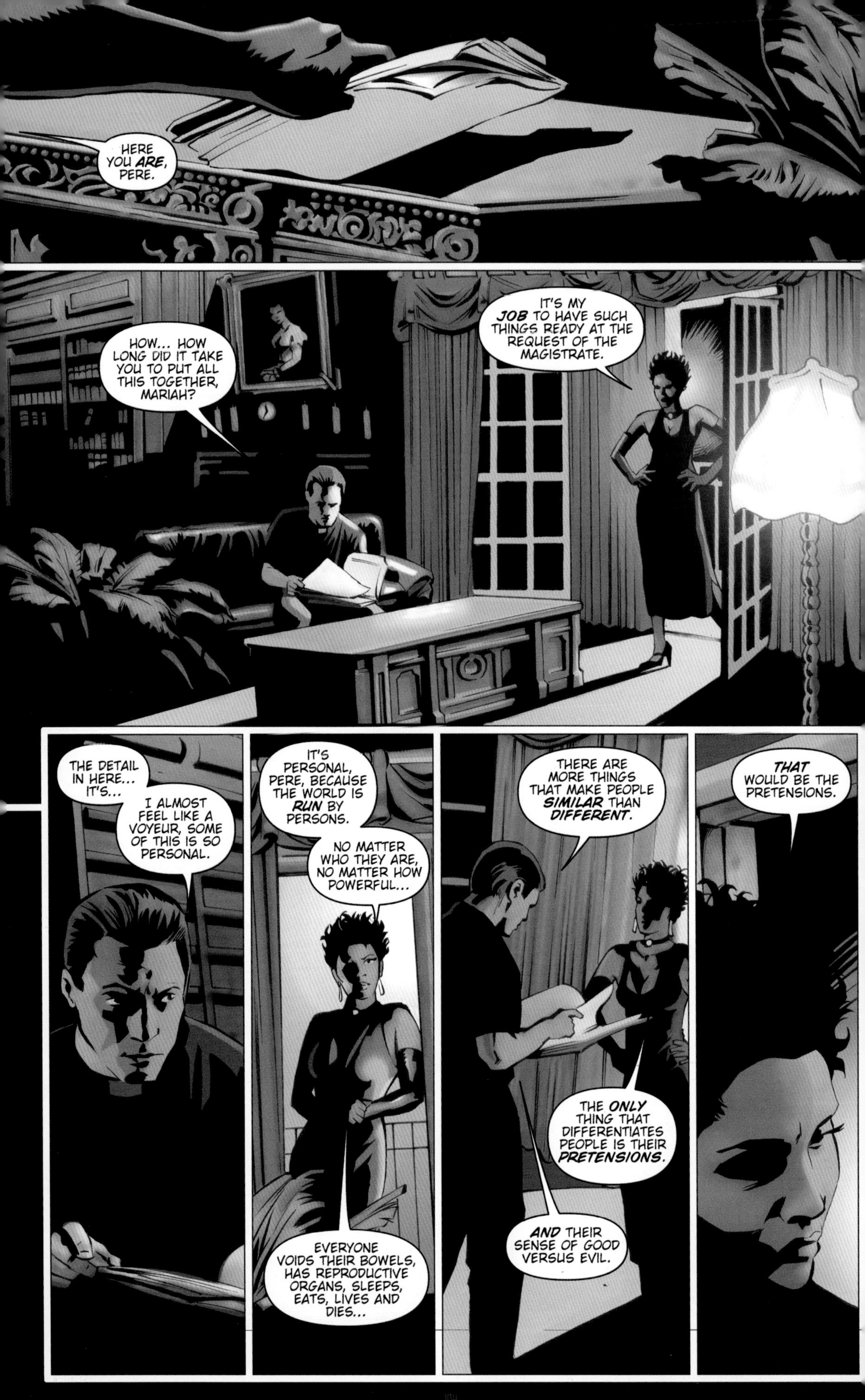
HERE YOU ARE, PERE.
HOW... HOW LONG DID IT TAKE YOU TO PUT ALL THIS TOGETHER, MARIAH?
IT'S MY JOB TO HAVE SUCH THINGS READY AT THE REQUEST OF THE MAGISTRATE.
THE DETAIL IN HERE... IT'S...
I ALMOST FEEL LIKE A VOYEUR, SOME OF THIS IS SO PERSONAL.
IT'S PERSONAL, PERE, BECAUSE THE WORLD IS RUN BY PERSONS.
NO MATTER WHO THEY ARE, NO MATTER HOW POWERFUL...
EVERYONE VOIDS THEIR BOWELS, HAS REPRODUCTIVE ORGANS, SLEEPS, EATS, LIVES AND DIES...
THERE ARE MORE THINGS THAT MAKE PEOPLE SIMILAR THAN DIFFERENT.
THE ONLY THING THAT DIFFERENTIATES PEOPLE IS THEIR PRETENSIONS.
AND THEIR SENSE OF GOOD VERSUS EVIL.
THAT WOULD BE THE PRETENSIONS.

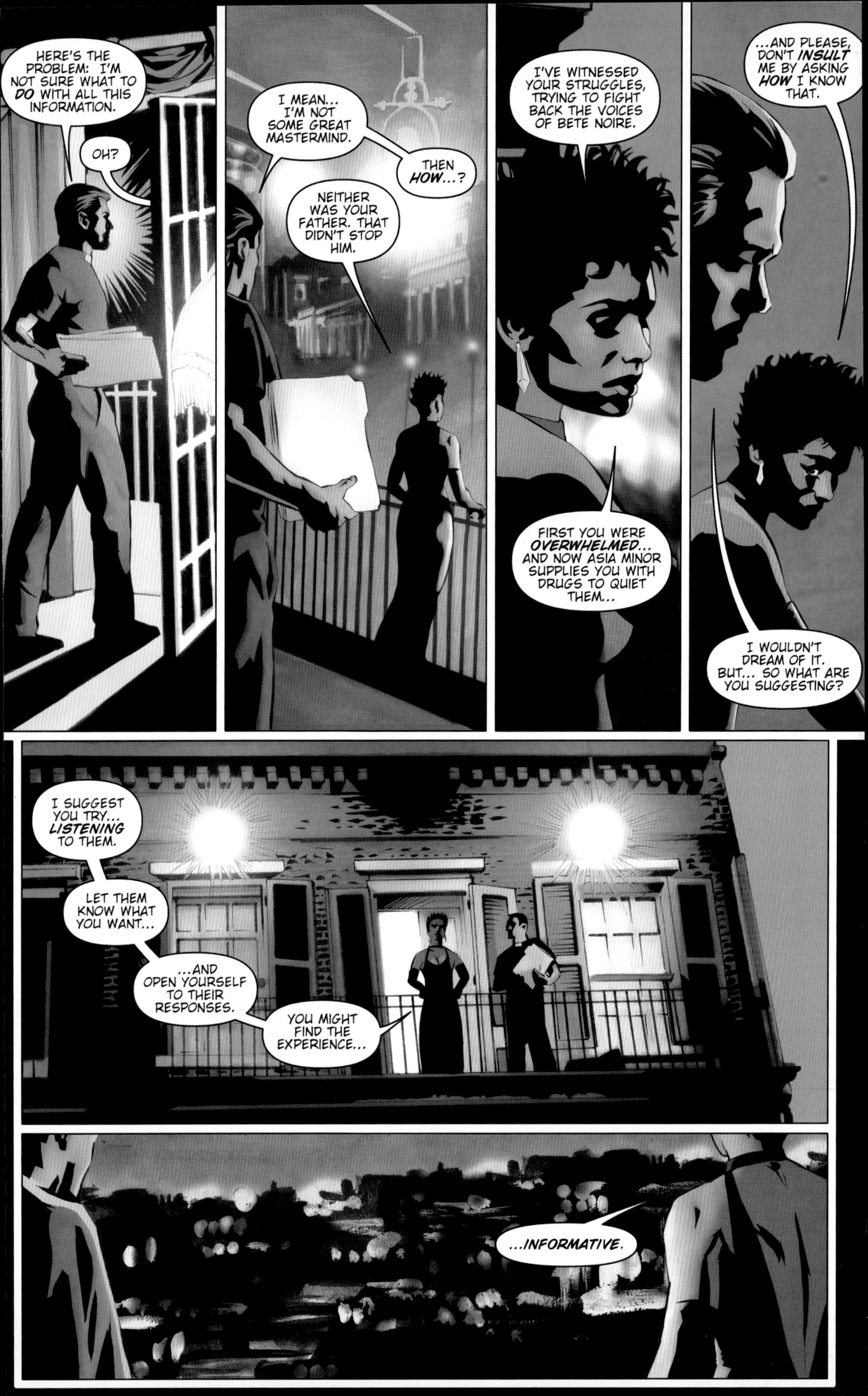
HERE'S THE PROBLEM: I'M NOT SURE WHAT TO DO WITH ALL THIS INFORMATION.
OH?
I MEAN... I'M NOT SOME GREAT MASTERMIND.
THEN HOW...?
NEITHER WAS YOUR FATHER. THAT DIDN'T STOP HIM.
I'VE WITNESSED YOUR STRUGGLES, TRYING TO FIGHT BACK THE VOICES OF BETE NOIRE.
FIRST YOU WERE OVERWHELMED... AND NOW ASIA MINOR SUPPLIES YOU WITH DRUGS TO QUIET THEM...
...AND PLEASE, DON'T INSULT ME BY ASKING HOW I KNOW THAT.
I WOULDN'T DREAM OF IT. BUT... SO WHAT ARE YOU SUGGESTING?
I SUGGEST YOU TRY... LISTENING TO THEM.
LET THEM KNOW WHAT YOU WANT...
...AND OPEN YOURSELF TO THEIR RESPONSES.
YOU MIGHT FIND THE EXPERIENCE...
...INFORMATIVE.

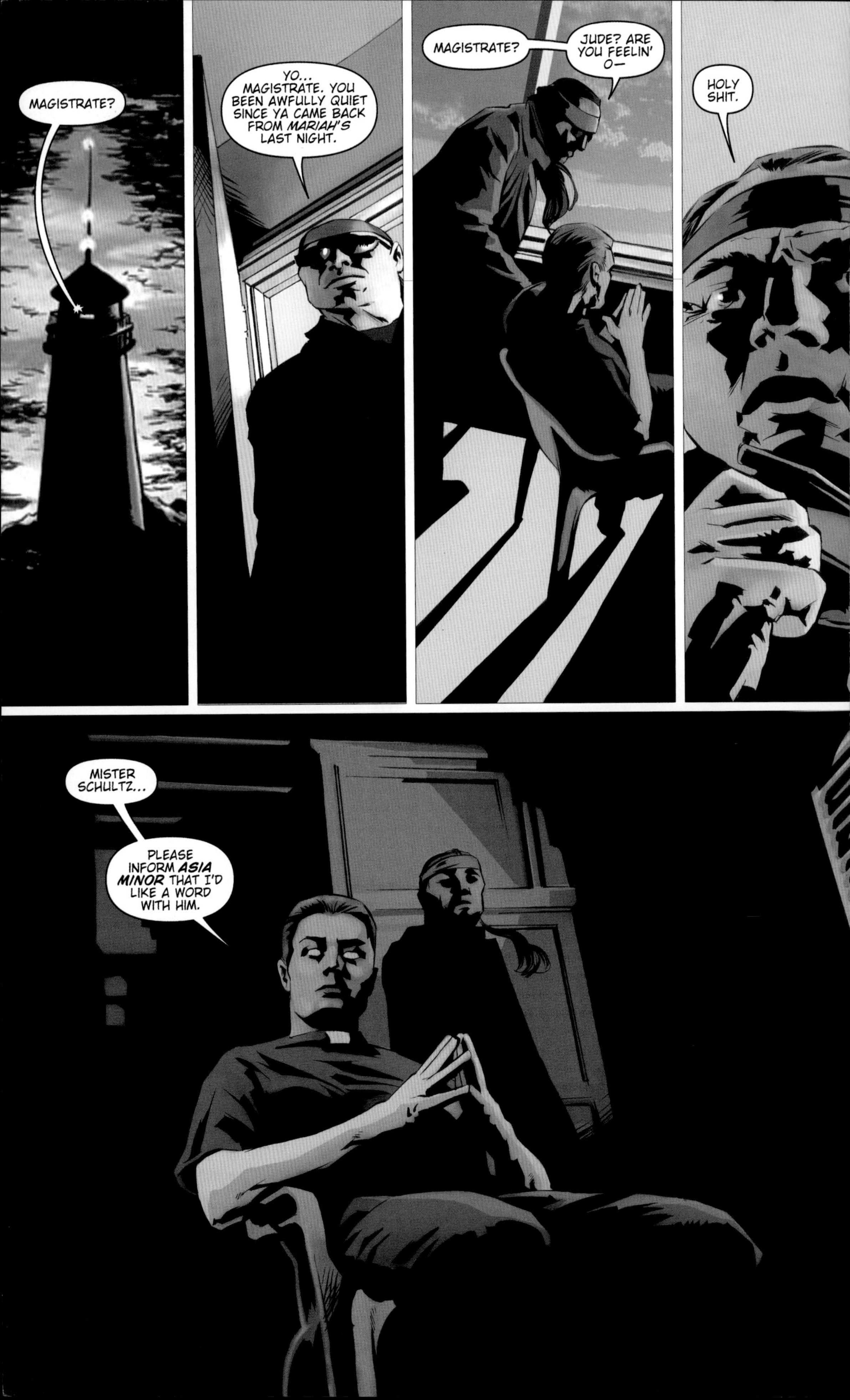
MAGISTRATE?
YO... MAGISTRATE. YOU BEEN AWFULLY QUIET SINCE YA CAME BACK FROM MARIAH'S LAST NIGHT.
MAGISTRATE?
JUDE? ARE YOU FEELIN' O—
HOLY SHIT.
MISTER SCHULTZ...
PLEASE INFORM ASIA MINOR THAT I'D LIKE A WORD WITH HIM.

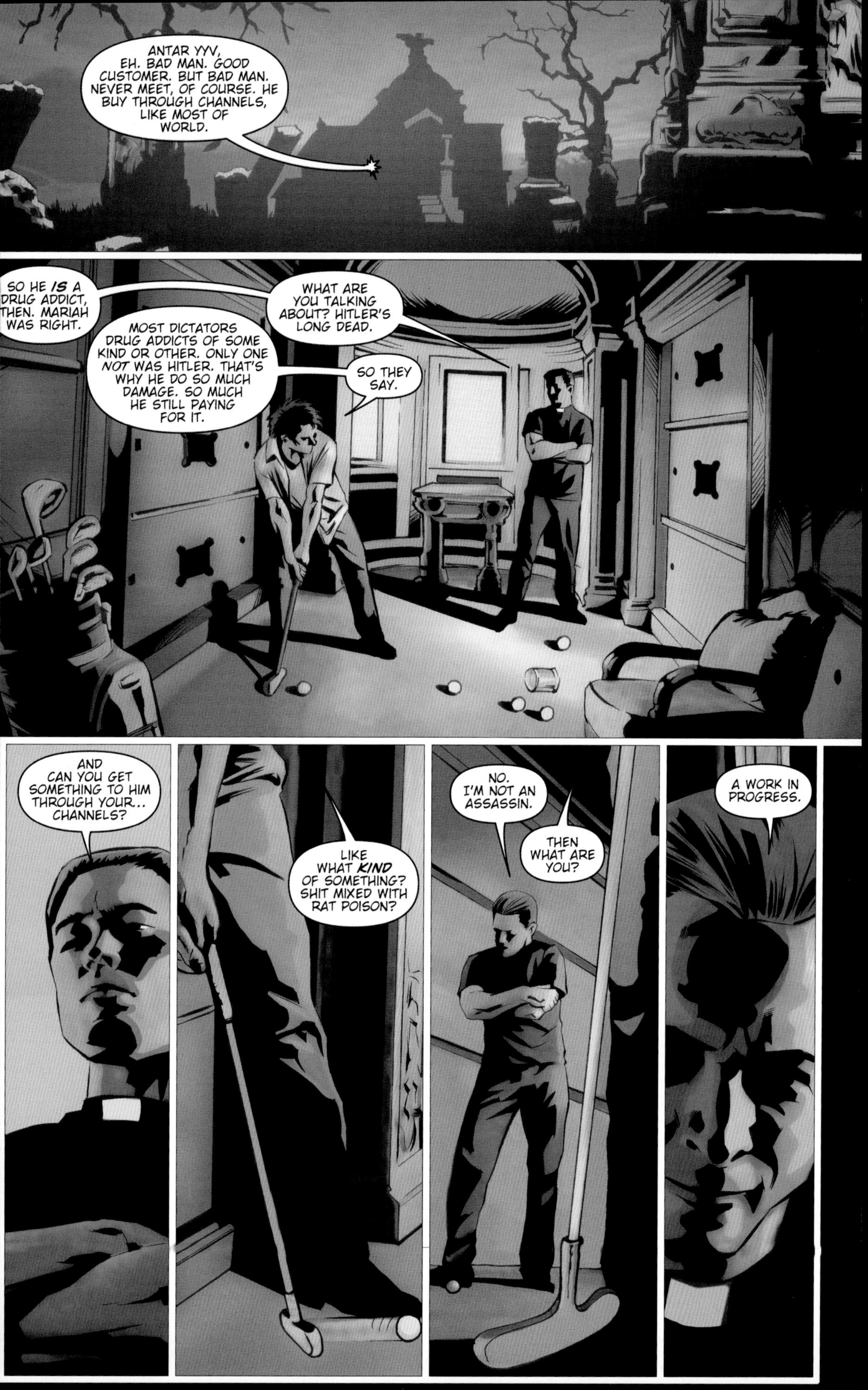
ANTAR YYV, EH. BAD MAN. GOOD CUSTOMER. BUT BAD MAN. NEVER MEET, OF COURSE. HE BUY THROUGH CHANNELS, LIKE MOST OF WORLD.
SO HE *IS* A DRUG ADDICT, THEN. MARIAH WAS RIGHT.
MOST DICTATORS DRUG ADDICTS OF SOME KIND OR OTHER. ONLY ONE *NOT* WAS HITLER. THAT'S WHY HE DO SO MUCH DAMAGE. SO MUCH HE STILL PAYING FOR IT.
WHAT ARE YOU TALKING ABOUT? HITLER'S LONG DEAD.
SO THEY SAY.
AND CAN YOU GET SOMETHING TO HIM THROUGH YOUR... CHANNELS?
LIKE WHAT *KIND* OF SOMETHING? SHIT MIXED WITH RAT POISON?
NO. I'M NOT AN ASSASSIN.
THEN WHAT ARE YOU?
A WORK IN PROGRESS.

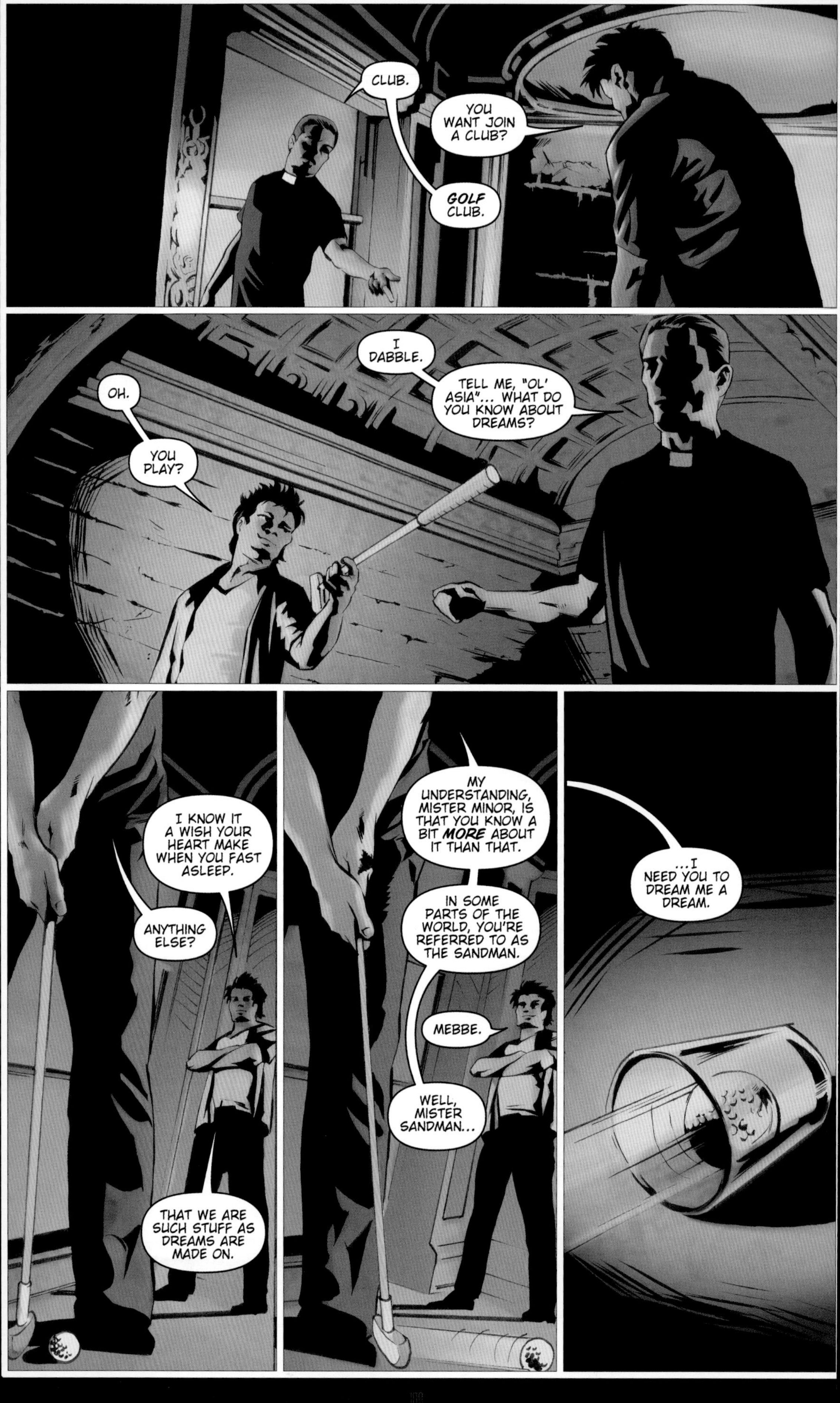
CLUB.
YOU WANT JOIN A CLUB?
GOLF CLUB.
OH.
YOU PLAY?
I DABBLE.
TELL ME, "OL' ASIA"... WHAT DO YOU KNOW ABOUT DREAMS?
I KNOW IT A WISH YOUR HEART MAKE WHEN YOU FAST ASLEEP.
ANYTHING ELSE?
THAT WE ARE SUCH STUFF AS DREAMS ARE MADE ON.
MY UNDERSTANDING, MISTER MINOR, IS THAT YOU KNOW A BIT MORE ABOUT IT THAN THAT.
IN SOME PARTS OF THE WORLD, YOU'RE REFERRED TO AS THE SANDMAN.
MEBBE.
WELL, MISTER SANDMAN...
...I NEED YOU TO DREAM ME A DREAM.

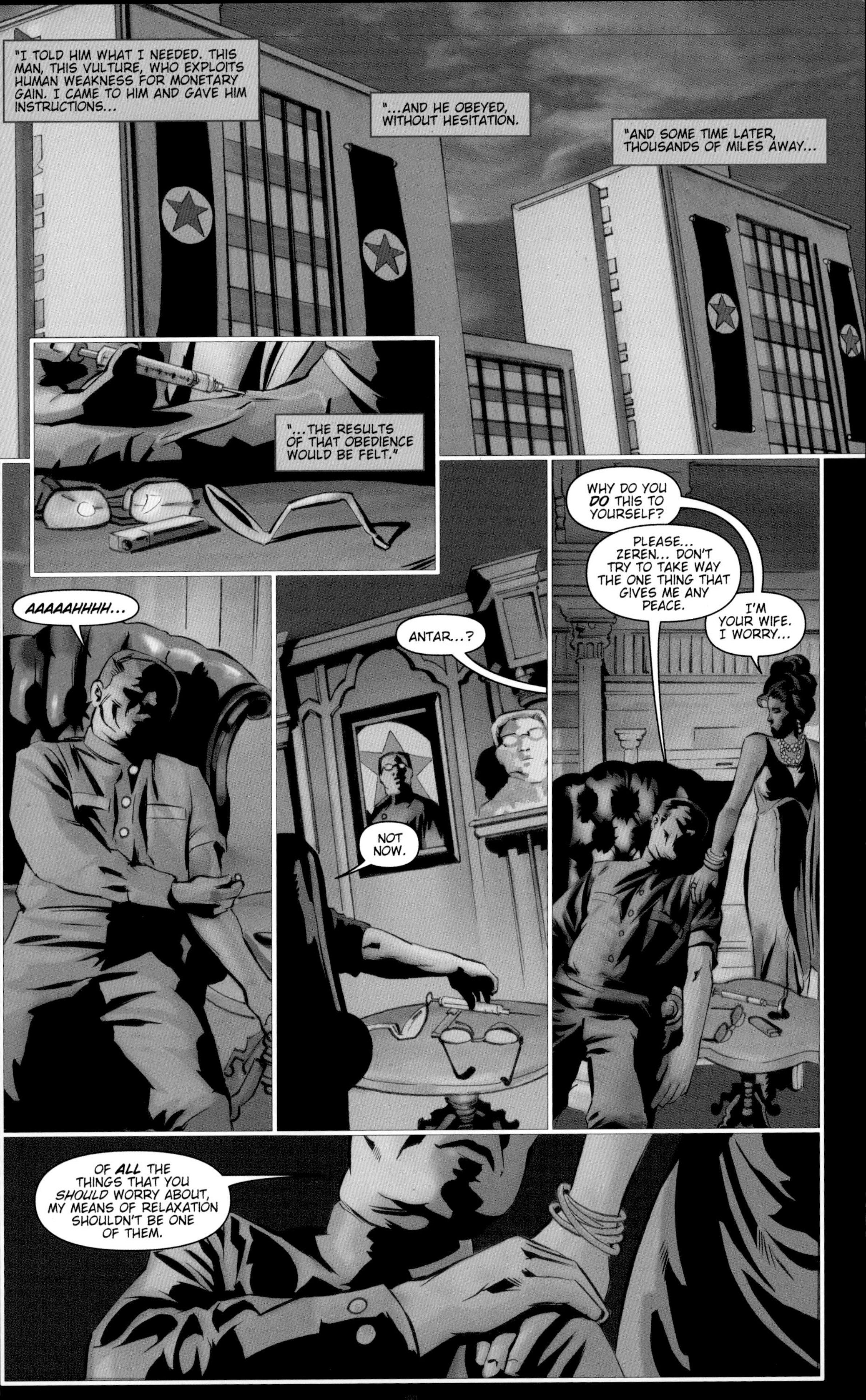
"I TOLD HIM WHAT I NEEDED. THIS MAN, THIS VULTURE, WHO EXPLOITS HUMAN WEAKNESS FOR MONETARY GAIN. I CAME TO HIM AND GAVE HIM INSTRUCTIONS...
"...AND HE OBEYED, WITHOUT HESITATION.
"AND SOME TIME LATER, THOUSANDS OF MILES AWAY...
"...THE RESULTS OF THAT OBEDIENCE WOULD BE FELT."
AAAAAHHHH...
ANTAR...?
NOT NOW.
WHY DO YOU DO THIS TO YOURSELF?
PLEASE... ZEREN... DON'T TRY TO TAKE WAY THE ONE THING THAT GIVES ME ANY PEACE.
I'M YOUR WIFE. I WORRY...
OF ALL THE THINGS THAT YOU SHOULD WORRY ABOUT, MY MEANS OF RELAXATION SHOULDN'T BE ONE OF THEM.

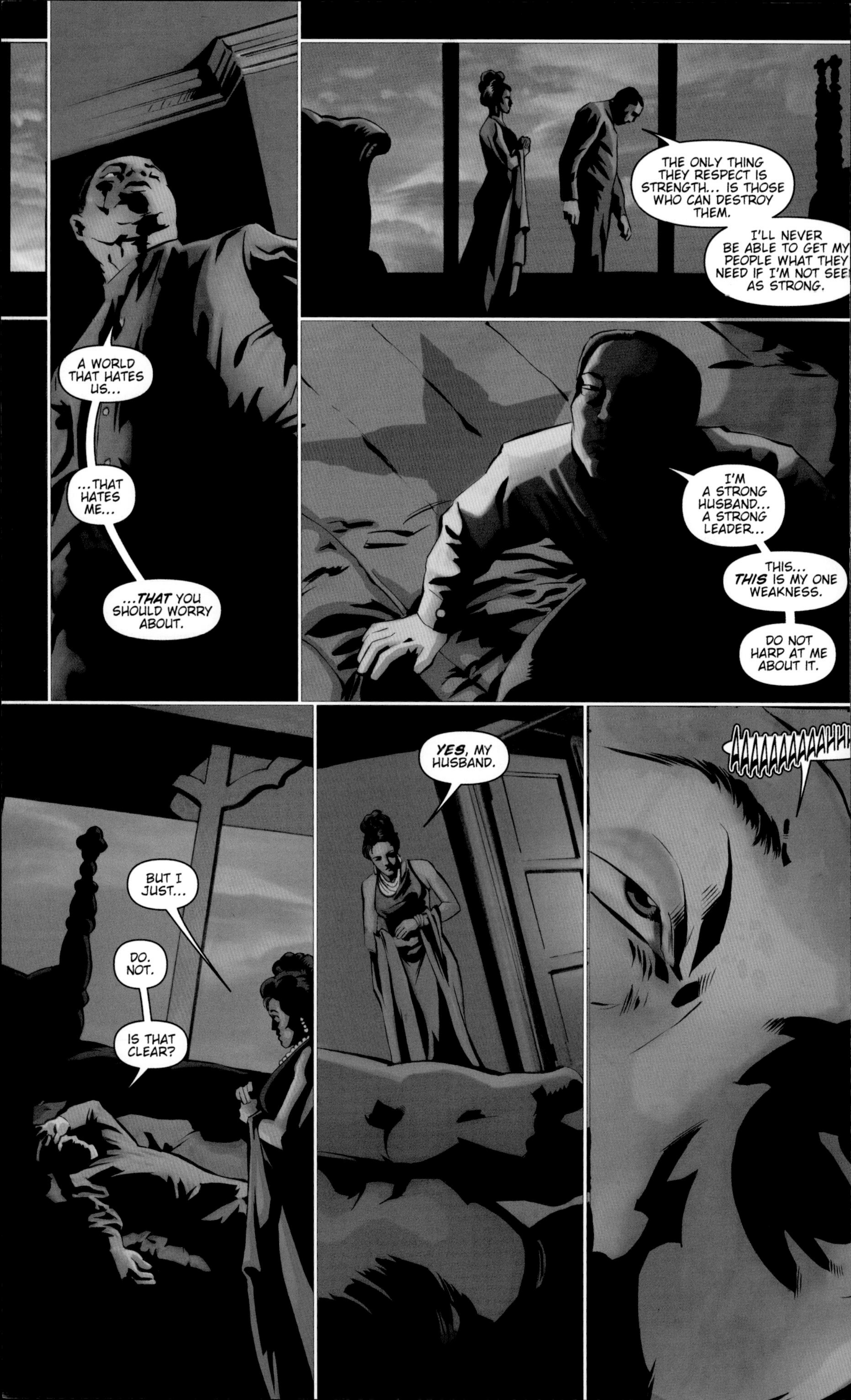
A WORLD THAT HATES US...
...THAT HATES ME...
...THAT YOU SHOULD WORRY ABOUT.
THE ONLY THING THEY RESPECT IS STRENGTH... IS THOSE WHO CAN DESTROY THEM.
I'LL NEVER BE ABLE TO GET MY PEOPLE WHAT THEY NEED IF I'M NOT SEE AS STRONG.
I'M A STRONG HUSBAND... A STRONG LEADER...
THIS... THIS IS MY ONE WEAKNESS.
DO NOT HARP AT ME ABOUT IT.
BUT I JUST...
DO. NOT.
IS THAT CLEAR?
YES, MY HUSBAND.
AAAAAAAAAAHH

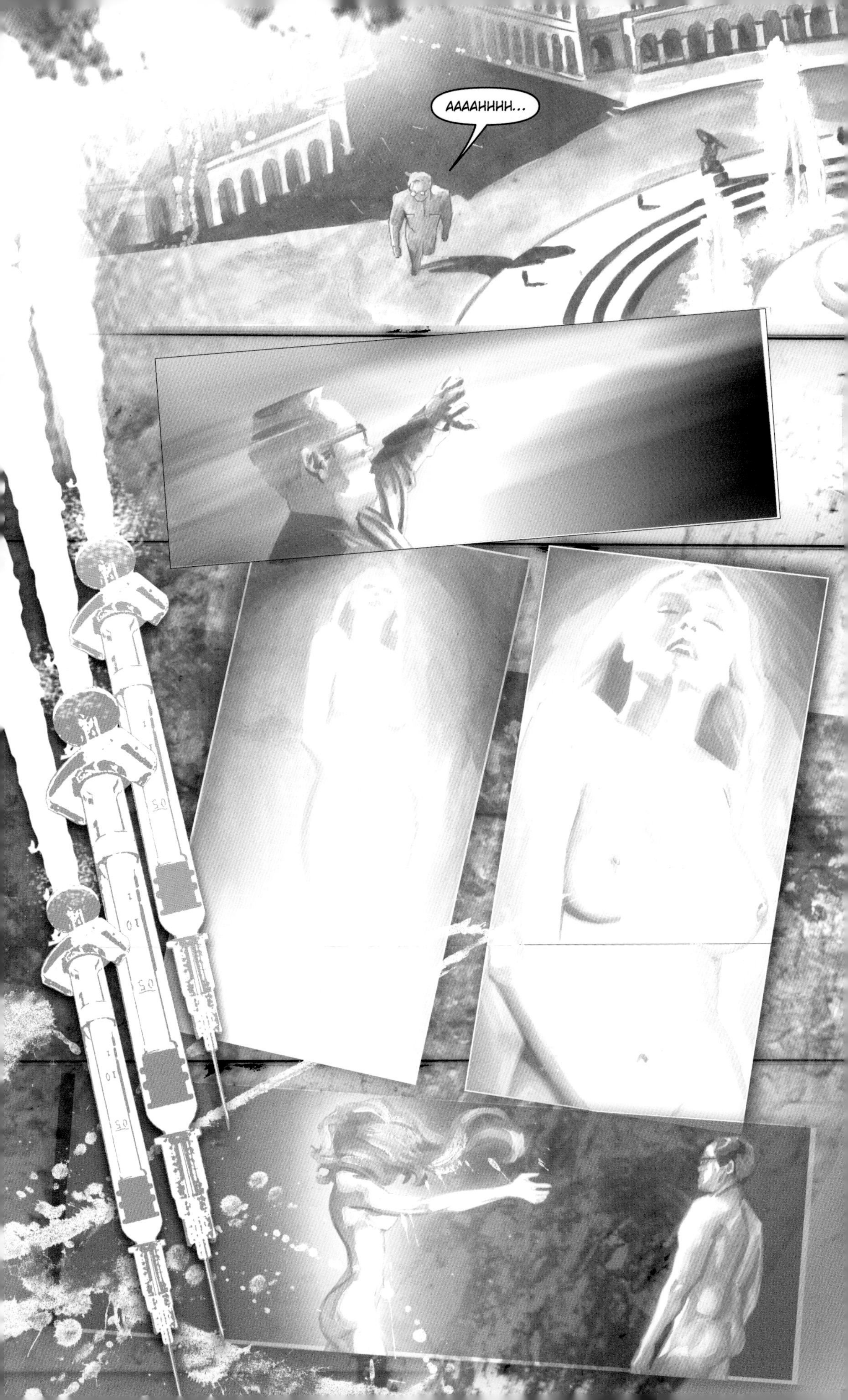
AAAAHHHH...

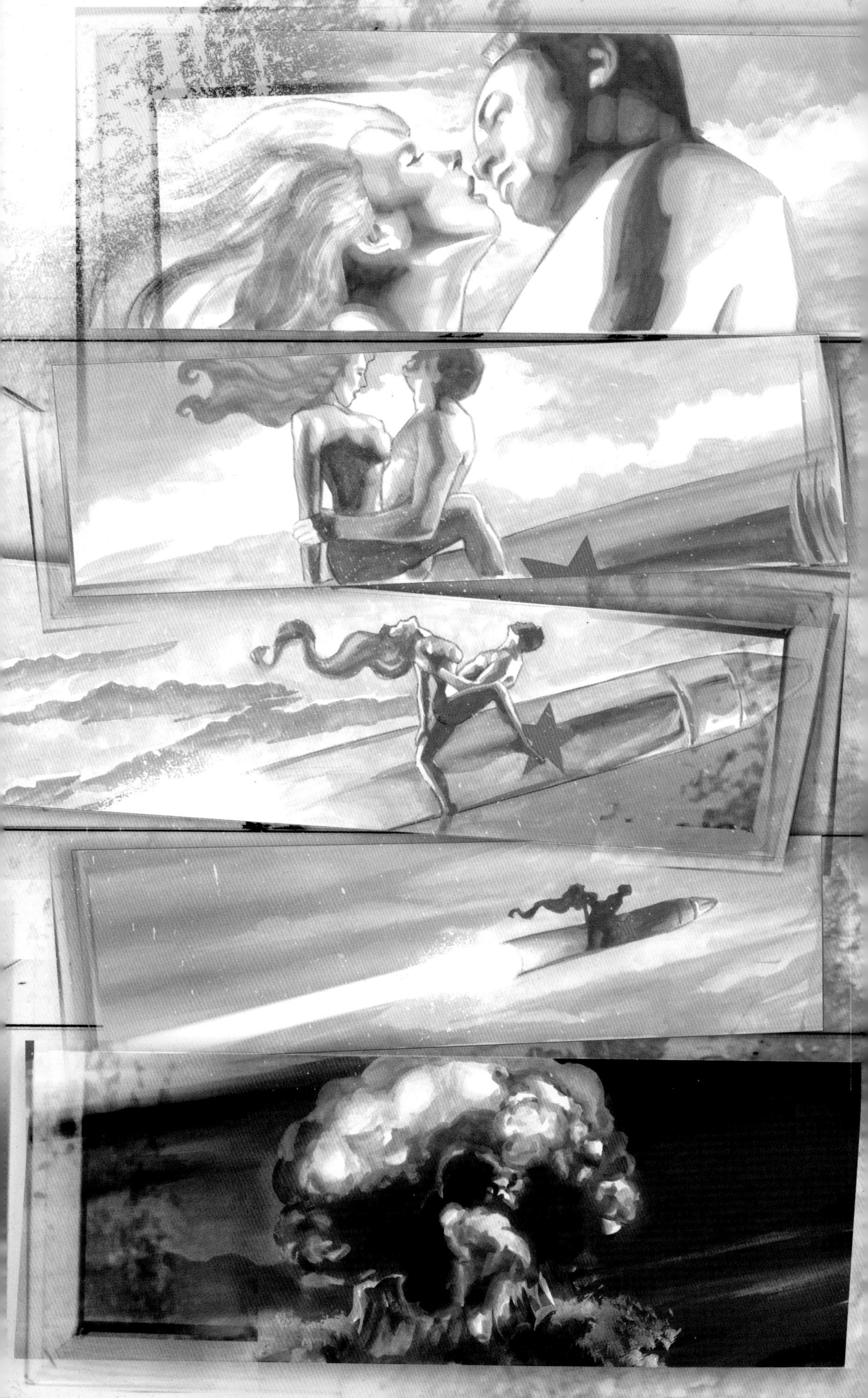

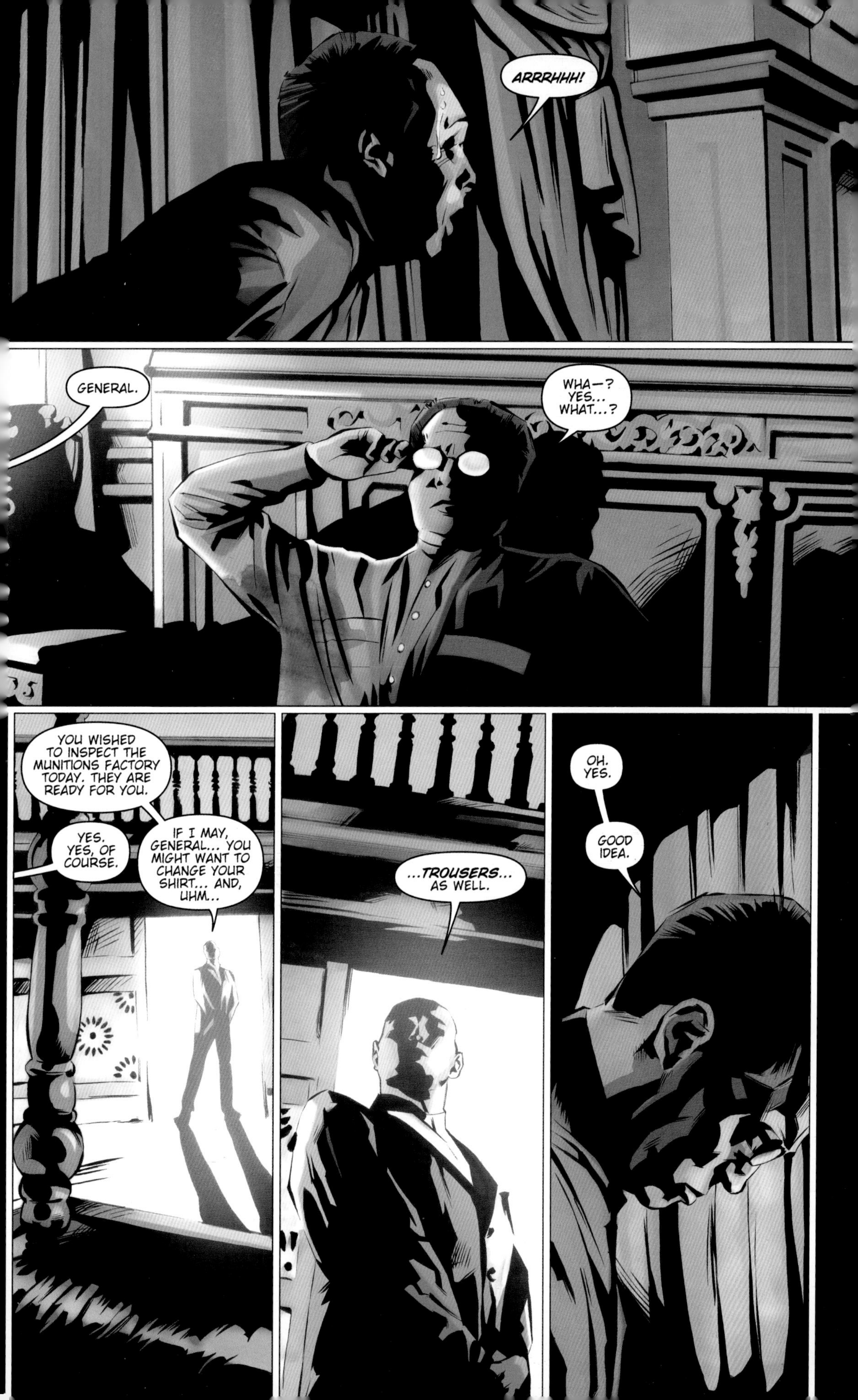
ARRRHHH!
GENERAL.
WHA—? YES... WHAT...?
YOU WISHED TO INSPECT THE MUNITIONS FACTORY TODAY. THEY ARE READY FOR YOU.
YES. YES, OF COURSE.
IF I MAY, GENERAL... YOU MIGHT WANT TO CHANGE YOUR SHIRT... AND, UHM...
...TROUSERS... AS WELL.
OH. YES.
GOOD IDEA.

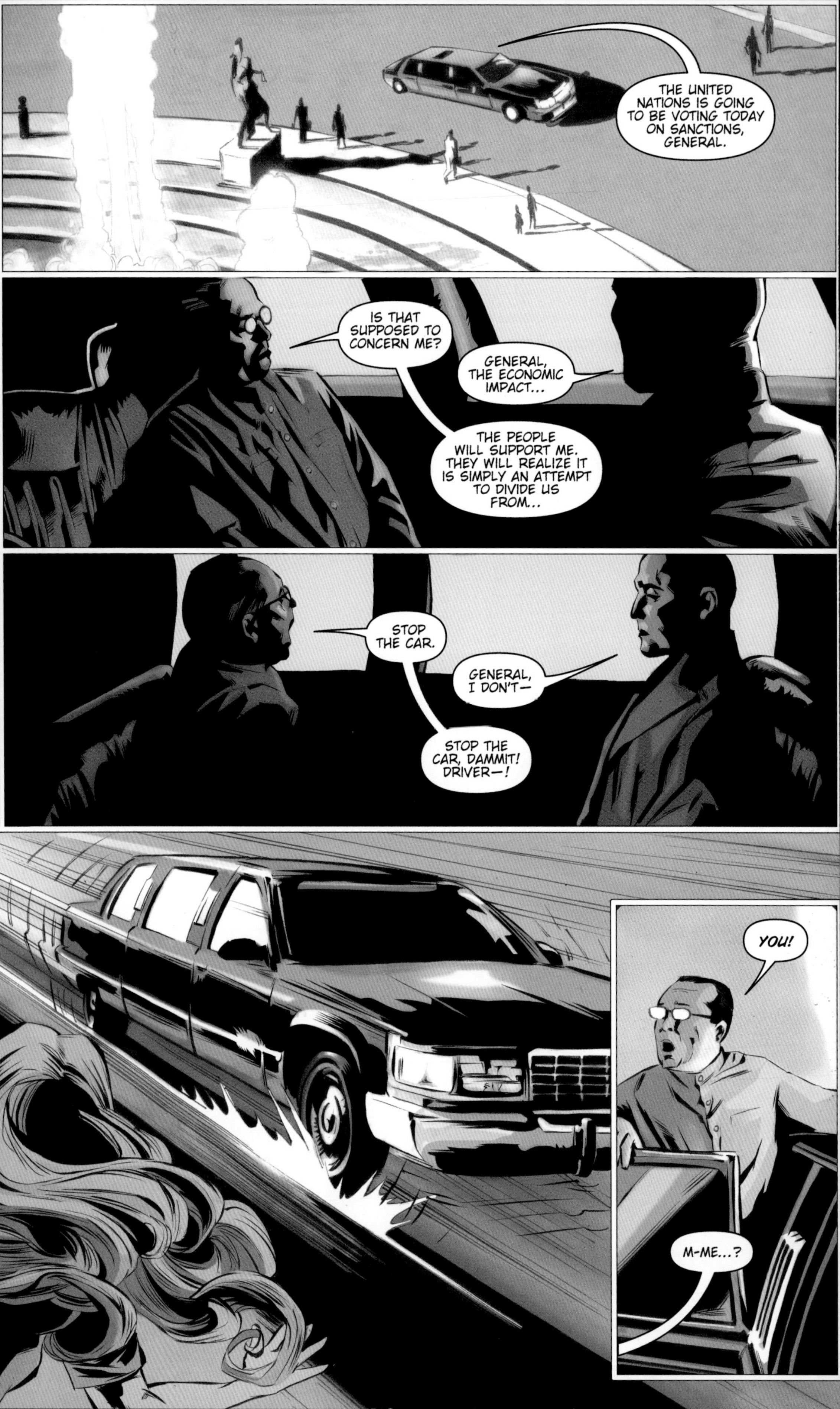
THE UNITED NATIONS IS GOING TO BE VOTING TODAY ON SANCTIONS, GENERAL.
IS THAT SUPPOSED TO CONCERN ME?
GENERAL, THE ECONOMIC IMPACT...
THE PEOPLE WILL SUPPORT ME. THEY WILL REALIZE IT IS SIMPLY AN ATTEMPT TO DIVIDE US FROM...
STOP THE CAR.
GENERAL, I DON'T—
STOP THE CAR, DAMMIT! DRIVER—!
YOU!
M-ME...?

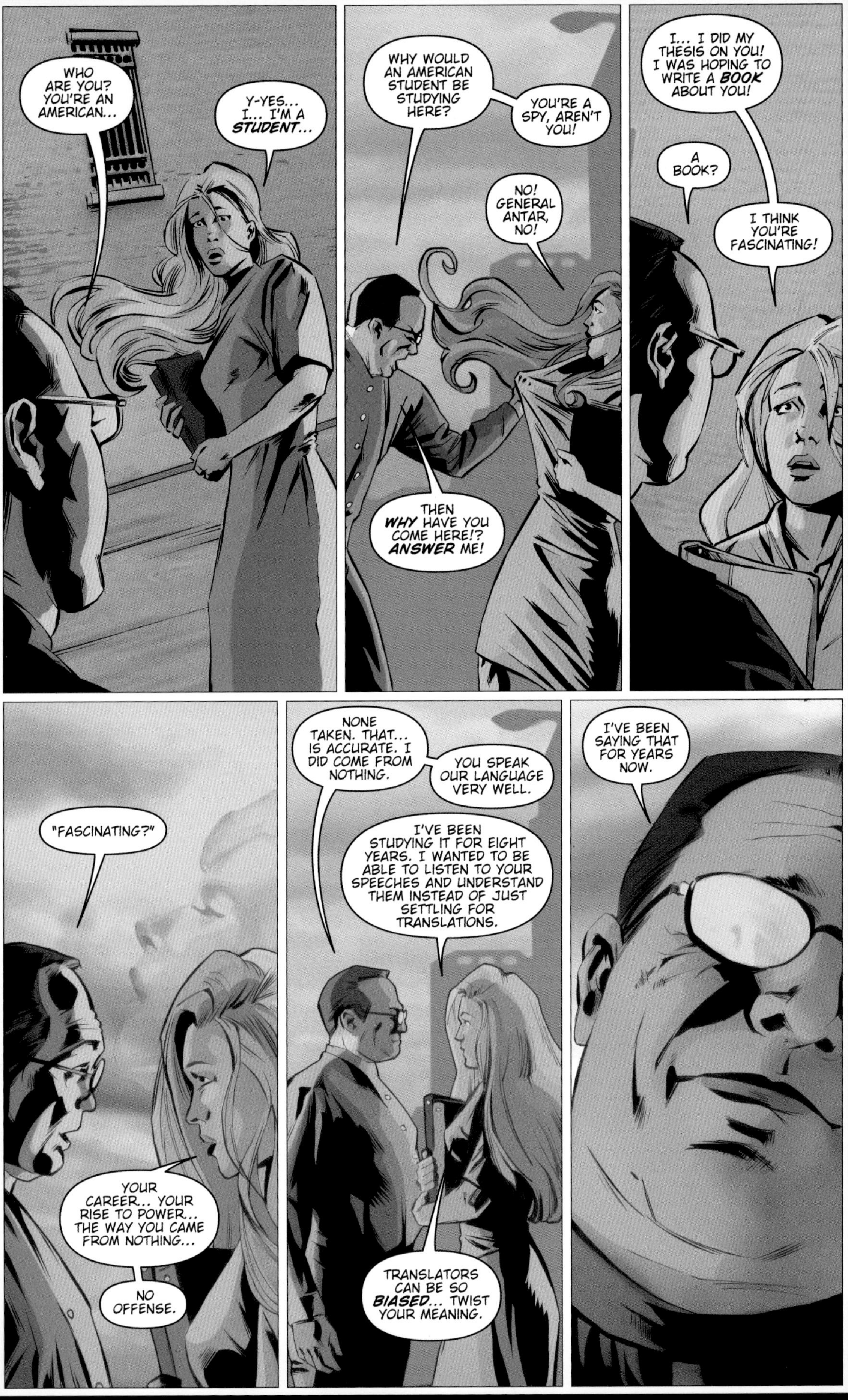
WHO ARE YOU? YOU'RE AN AMERICAN...
Y-YES... I... I'M A **STUDENT**...
WHY WOULD AN AMERICAN STUDENT BE STUDYING HERE?
YOU'RE A SPY, AREN'T YOU!
NO! GENERAL ANTAR, NO!
THEN **WHY** HAVE YOU COME HERE!? **ANSWER** ME!
I... I DID MY THESIS ON YOU! I WAS HOPING TO WRITE A **BOOK** ABOUT YOU!
A BOOK?
I THINK YOU'RE FASCINATING!
"FASCINATING?"
YOUR CAREER... YOUR RISE TO POWER... THE WAY YOU CAME FROM NOTHING...
NO OFFENSE.
NONE TAKEN. THAT... IS ACCURATE. I DID COME FROM NOTHING.
YOU SPEAK OUR LANGUAGE VERY WELL.
I'VE BEEN STUDYING IT FOR EIGHT YEARS. I WANTED TO BE ABLE TO LISTEN TO YOUR SPEECHES AND UNDERSTAND THEM INSTEAD OF JUST SETTLING FOR TRANSLATIONS.
TRANSLATORS CAN BE SO **BIASED**... TWIST YOUR MEANING.
I'VE BEEN SAYING THAT FOR YEARS NOW.

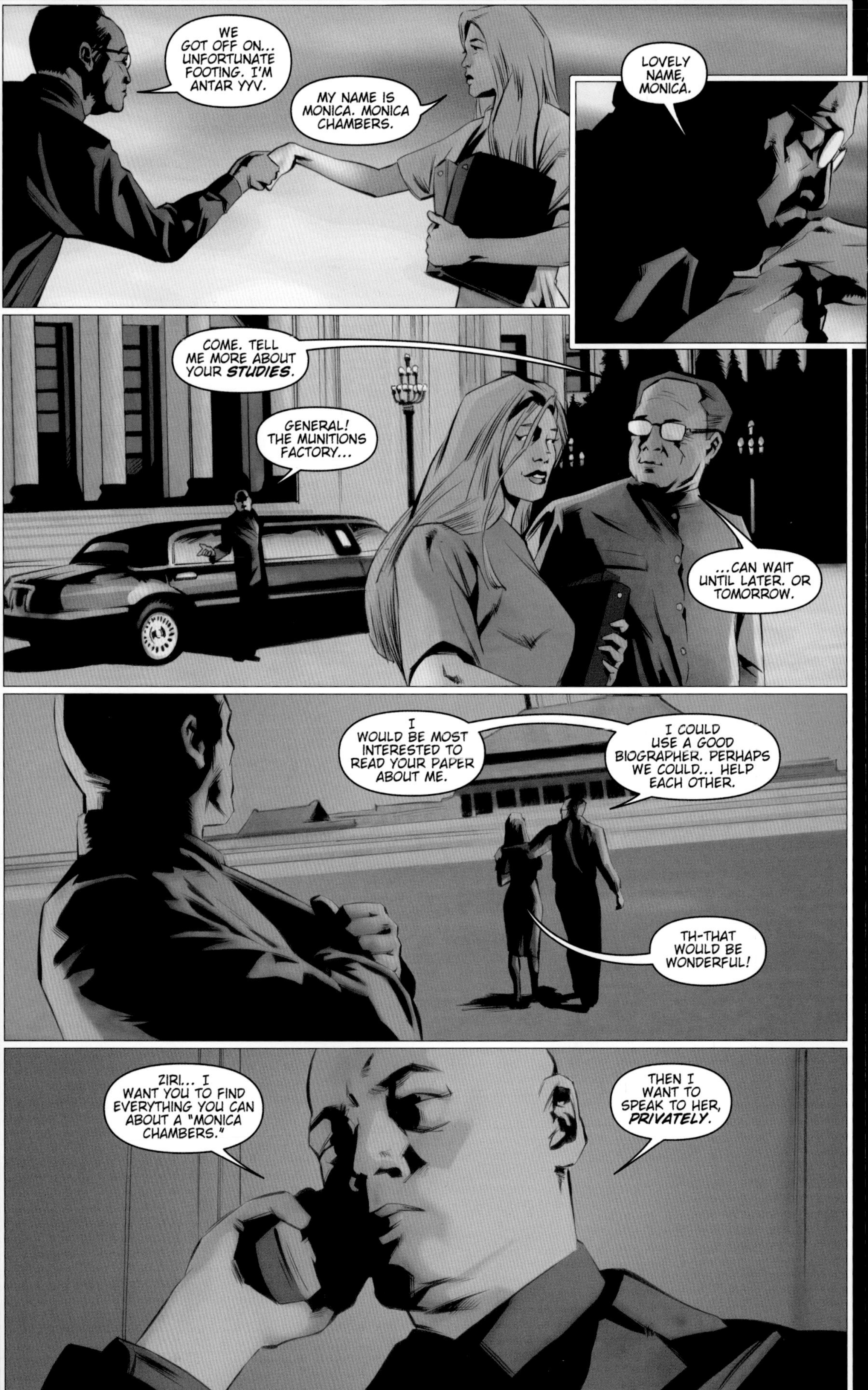

WE GOT OFF ON... UNFORTUNATE FOOTING. I'M ANTAR YYV.
MY NAME IS MONICA. MONICA CHAMBERS.
LOVELY NAME, MONICA.
COME. TELL ME MORE ABOUT YOUR *STUDIES*.
GENERAL! THE MUNITIONS FACTORY...
...CAN WAIT UNTIL LATER. OR TOMORROW.
I WOULD BE MOST INTERESTED TO READ YOUR PAPER ABOUT ME.
I COULD USE A GOOD BIOGRAPHER. PERHAPS WE COULD... HELP EACH OTHER.
TH-THAT WOULD BE WONDERFUL!
ZIRI... I WANT YOU TO FIND EVERYTHING YOU CAN ABOUT A "MONICA CHAMBERS."
THEN I WANT TO SPEAK TO HER, *PRIVATELY*.

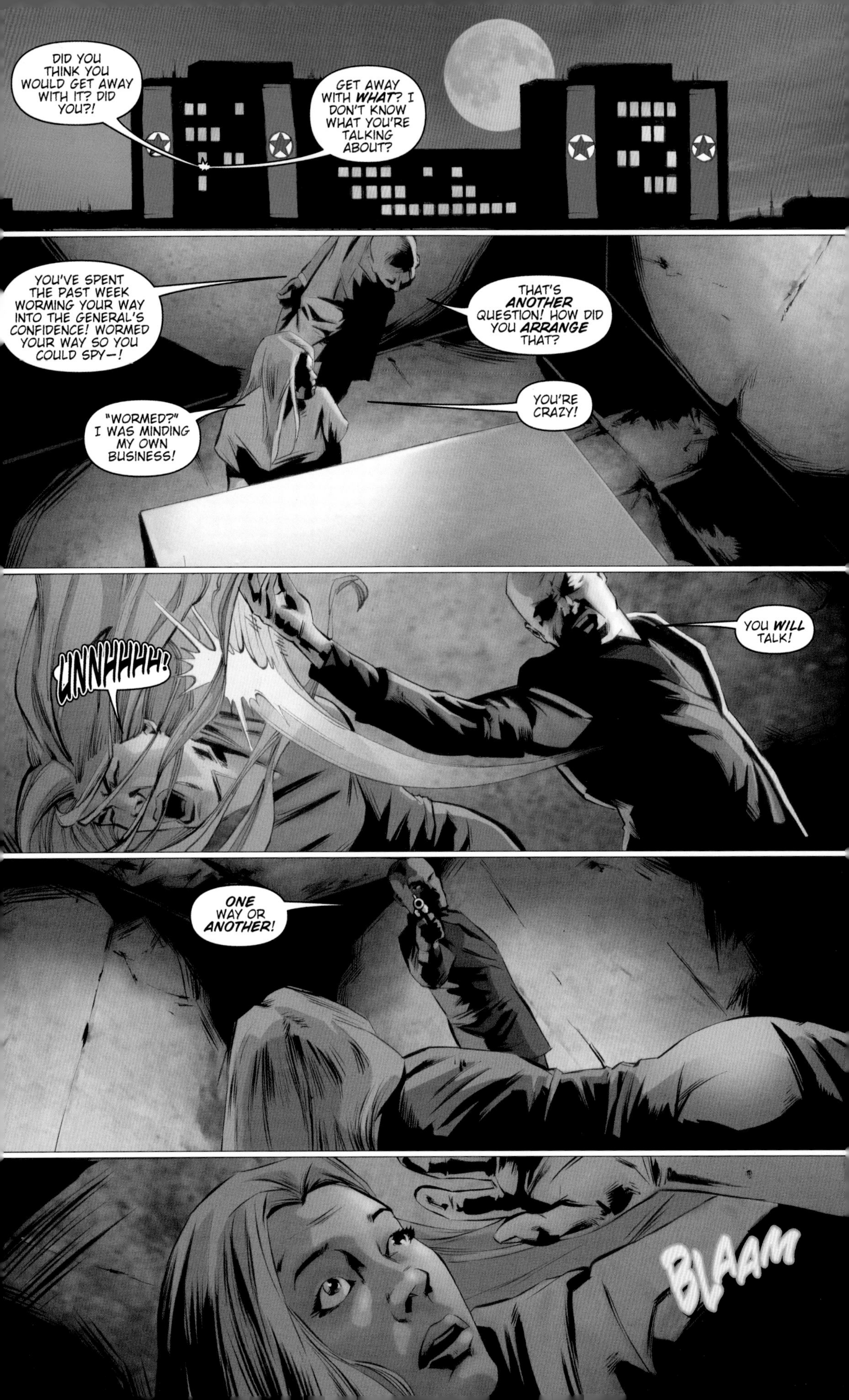
DID YOU THINK YOU WOULD GET AWAY WITH IT? DID YOU?!
GET AWAY WITH WHAT? I DON'T KNOW WHAT YOU'RE TALKING ABOUT?
YOU'VE SPENT THE PAST WEEK WORMING YOUR WAY INTO THE GENERAL'S CONFIDENCE! WORMED YOUR WAY SO YOU COULD SPY--!
"WORMED?" I WAS MINDING MY OWN BUSINESS!
THAT'S ANOTHER QUESTION! HOW DID YOU ARRANGE THAT?
YOU'RE CRAZY!
UNNHHHH!
YOU WILL TALK!
ONE WAY OR ANOTHER!
BLAAM

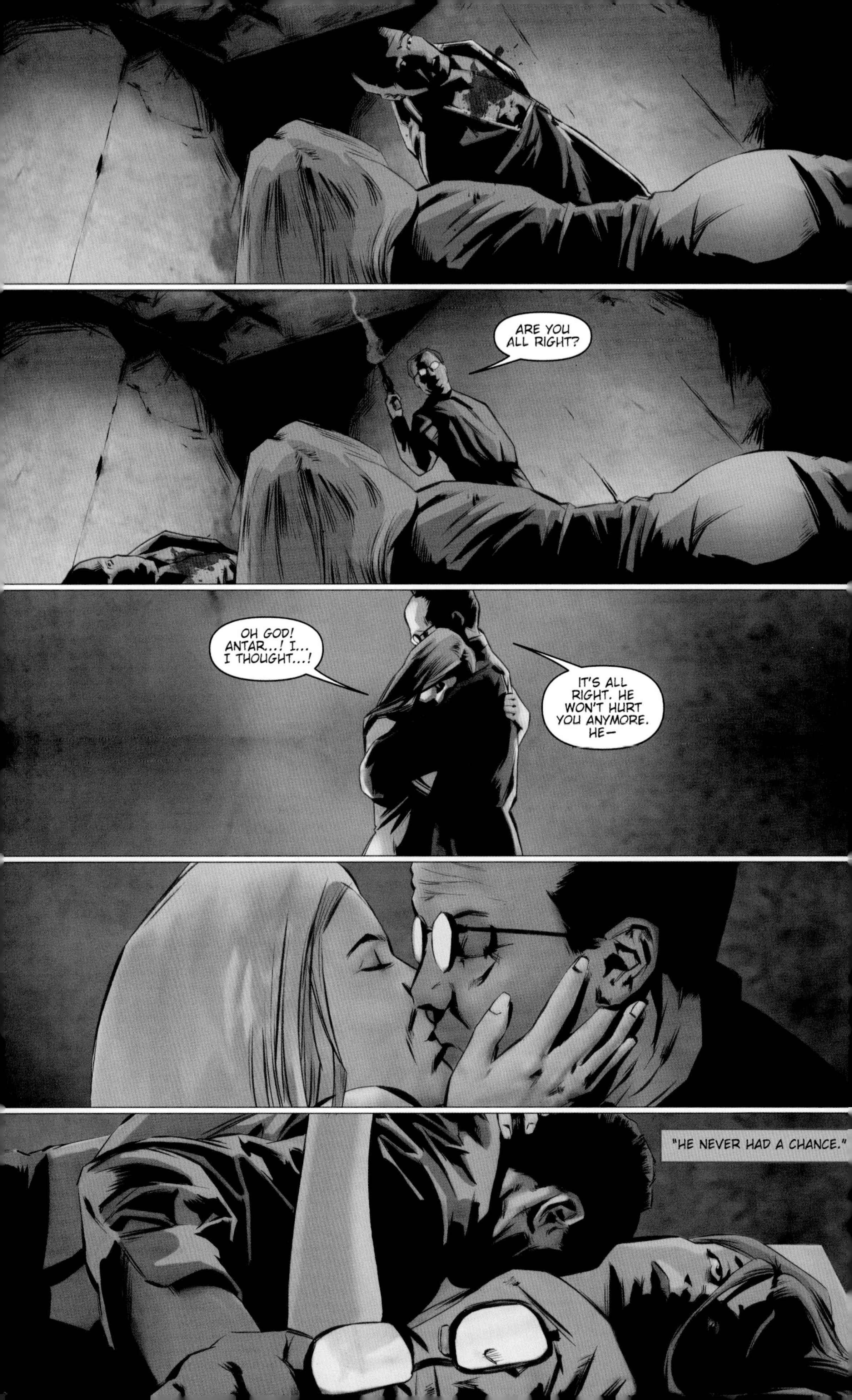
ARE YOU ALL RIGHT?
OH GOD! ANTAR...! I... I THOUGHT...!
IT'S ALL RIGHT. HE WON'T HURT YOU ANYMORE. HE—
"HE NEVER HAD A CHANCE."

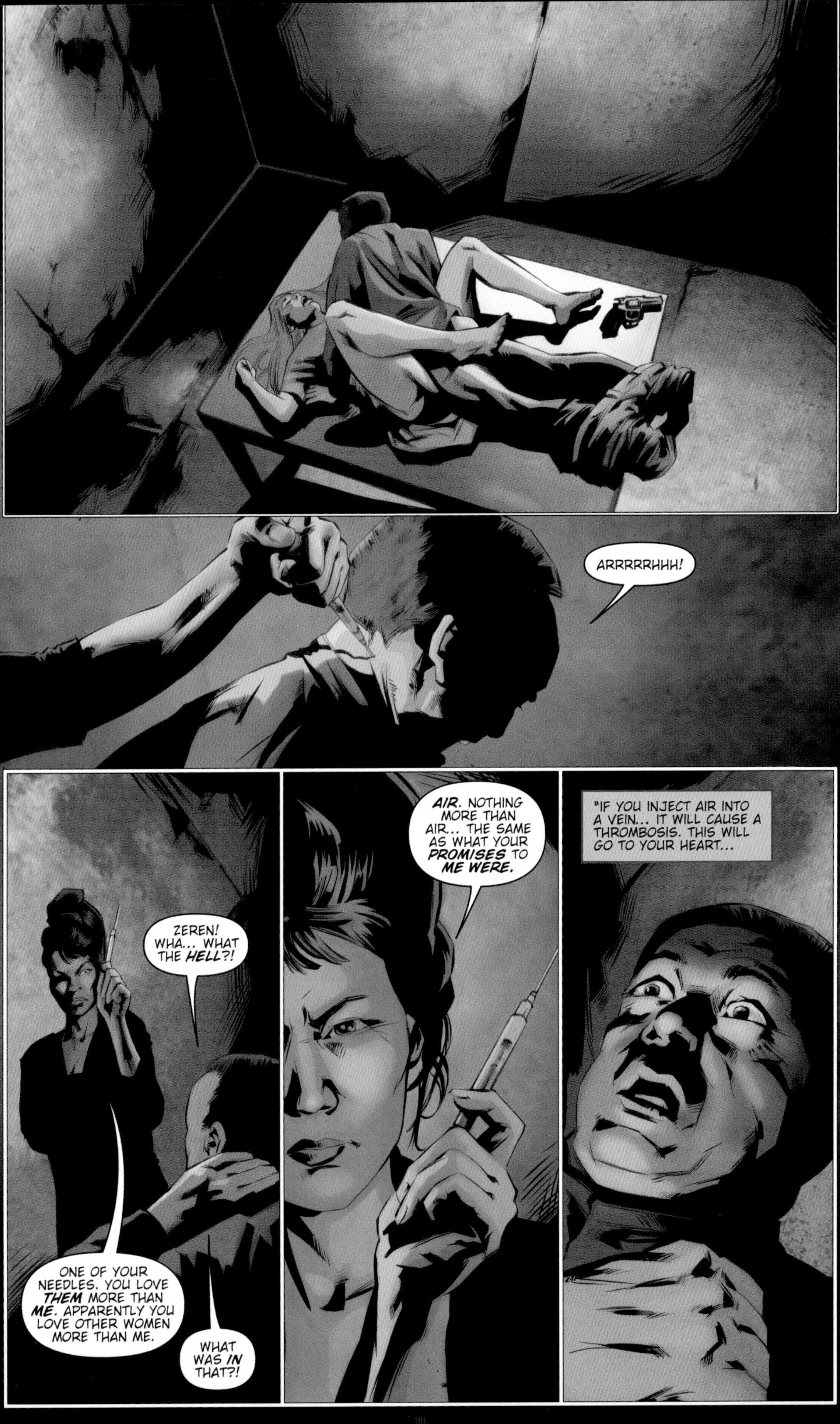
ARRRRRHHH!
ZEREN! WHA... WHAT THE HELL?!
ONE OF YOUR NEEDLES. YOU LOVE THEM MORE THAN ME. APPARENTLY YOU LOVE OTHER WOMEN MORE THAN ME.
WHAT WAS IN THAT?!
AIR. NOTHING MORE THAN AIR... THE SAME AS WHAT YOUR PROMISES TO ME WERE.
"IF YOU INJECT AIR INTO A VEIN... IT WILL CAUSE A THROMBOSIS. THIS WILL GO TO YOUR HEART...

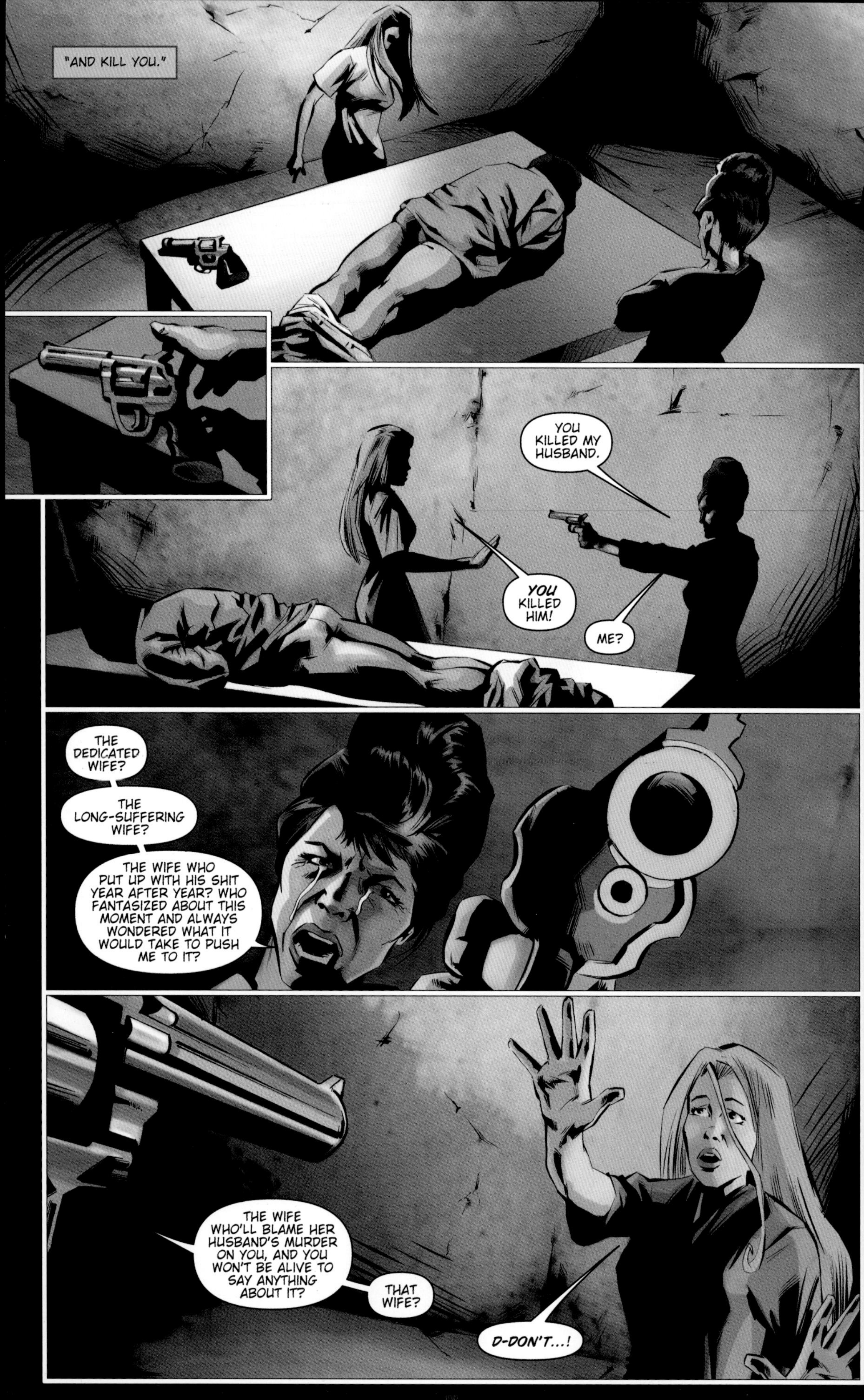
"AND KILL YOU."
YOU KILLED MY HUSBAND.
YOU KILLED HIM!
ME?
THE DEDICATED WIFE?
THE LONG-SUFFERING WIFE?
THE WIFE WHO PUT UP WITH HIS SHIT YEAR AFTER YEAR? WHO FANTASIZED ABOUT THIS MOMENT AND ALWAYS WONDERED WHAT IT WOULD TAKE TO PUSH ME TO IT?
THE WIFE WHO'LL BLAME HER HUSBAND'S MURDER ON YOU, AND YOU WON'T BE ALIVE TO SAY ANYTHING ABOUT IT?
THAT WIFE?
D-DON'T...!

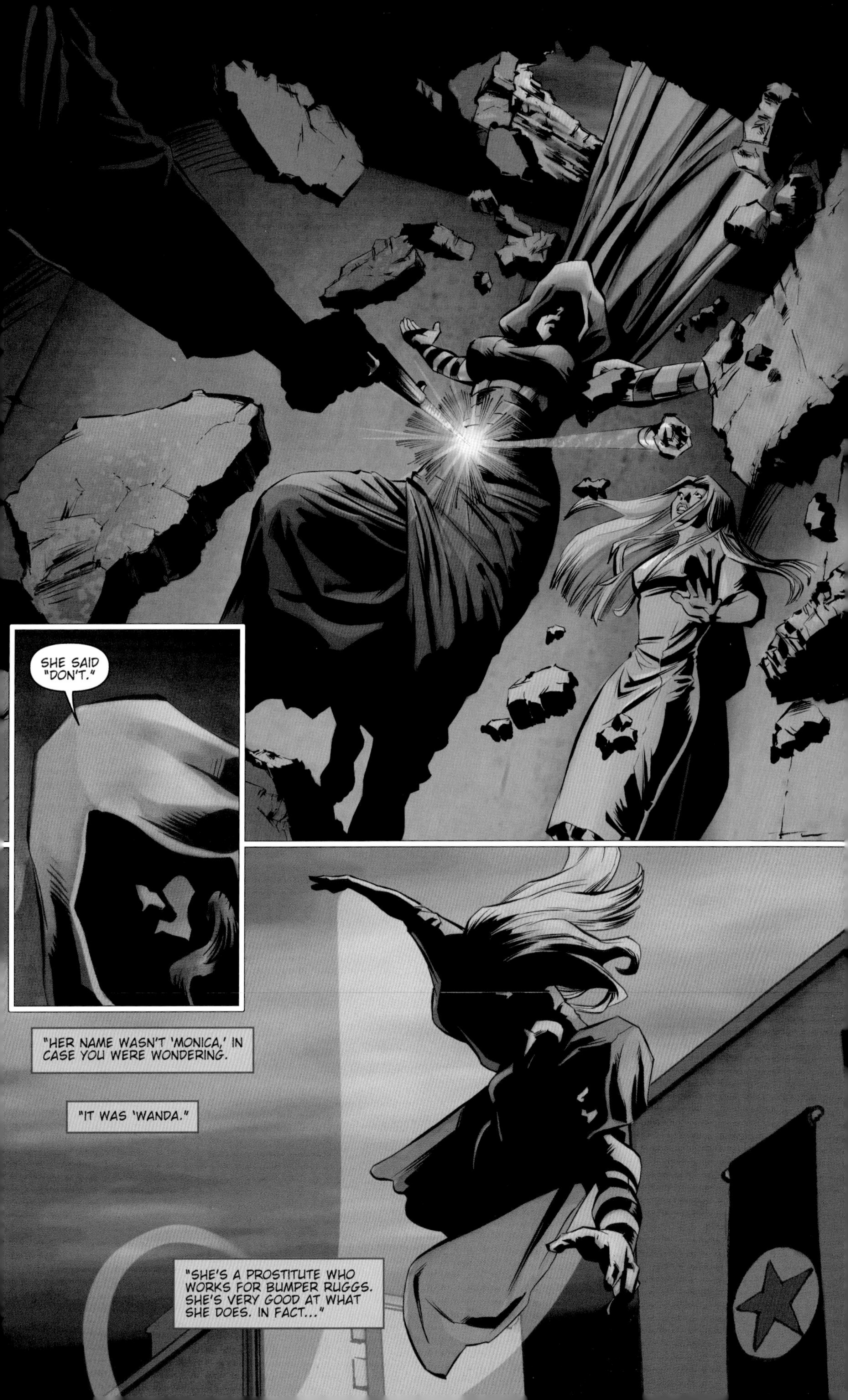
SHE SAID "DON'T."
"HER NAME WASN'T 'MONICA,' IN CASE YOU WERE WONDERING.
"IT WAS 'WANDA."
"SHE'S A PROSTITUTE WHO WORKS FOR BUMPER RUGGS. SHE'S VERY GOOD AT WHAT SHE DOES. IN FACT..."

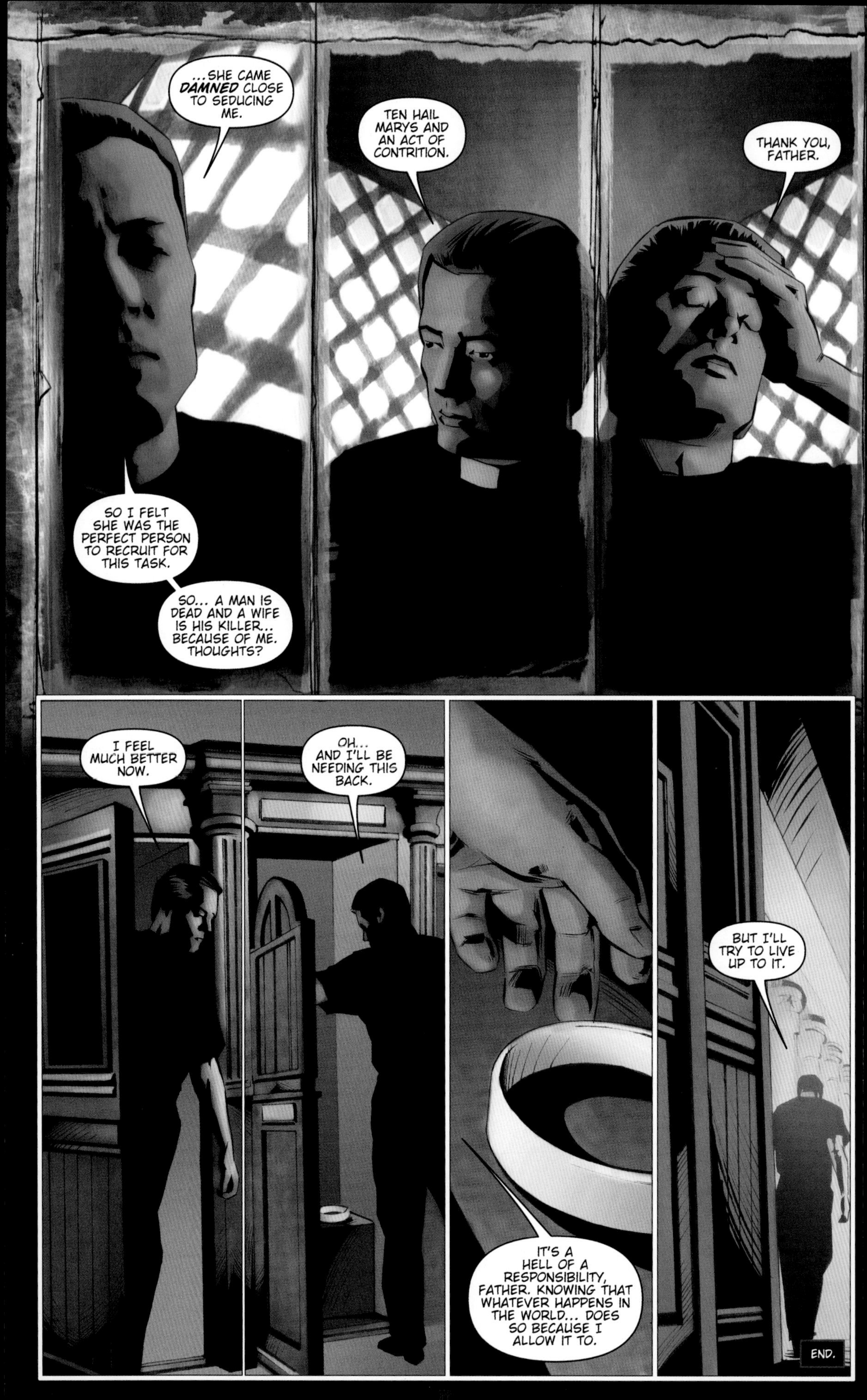
...SHE CAME DAMNED CLOSE TO SEDUCING ME.
SO I FELT SHE WAS THE PERFECT PERSON TO RECRUIT FOR THIS TASK.
SO... A MAN IS DEAD AND A WIFE IS HIS KILLER... BECAUSE OF ME. THOUGHTS?
TEN HAIL MARYS AND AN ACT OF CONTRITION.
THANK YOU, FATHER.
I FEEL MUCH BETTER NOW.
OH... AND I'LL BE NEEDING THIS BACK.
IT'S A HELL OF A RESPONSIBILITY, FATHER. KNOWING THAT WHATEVER HAPPENS IN THE WORLD... DOES SO BECAUSE I ALLOW IT TO.
BUT I'LL TRY TO LIVE UP TO IT.
END.

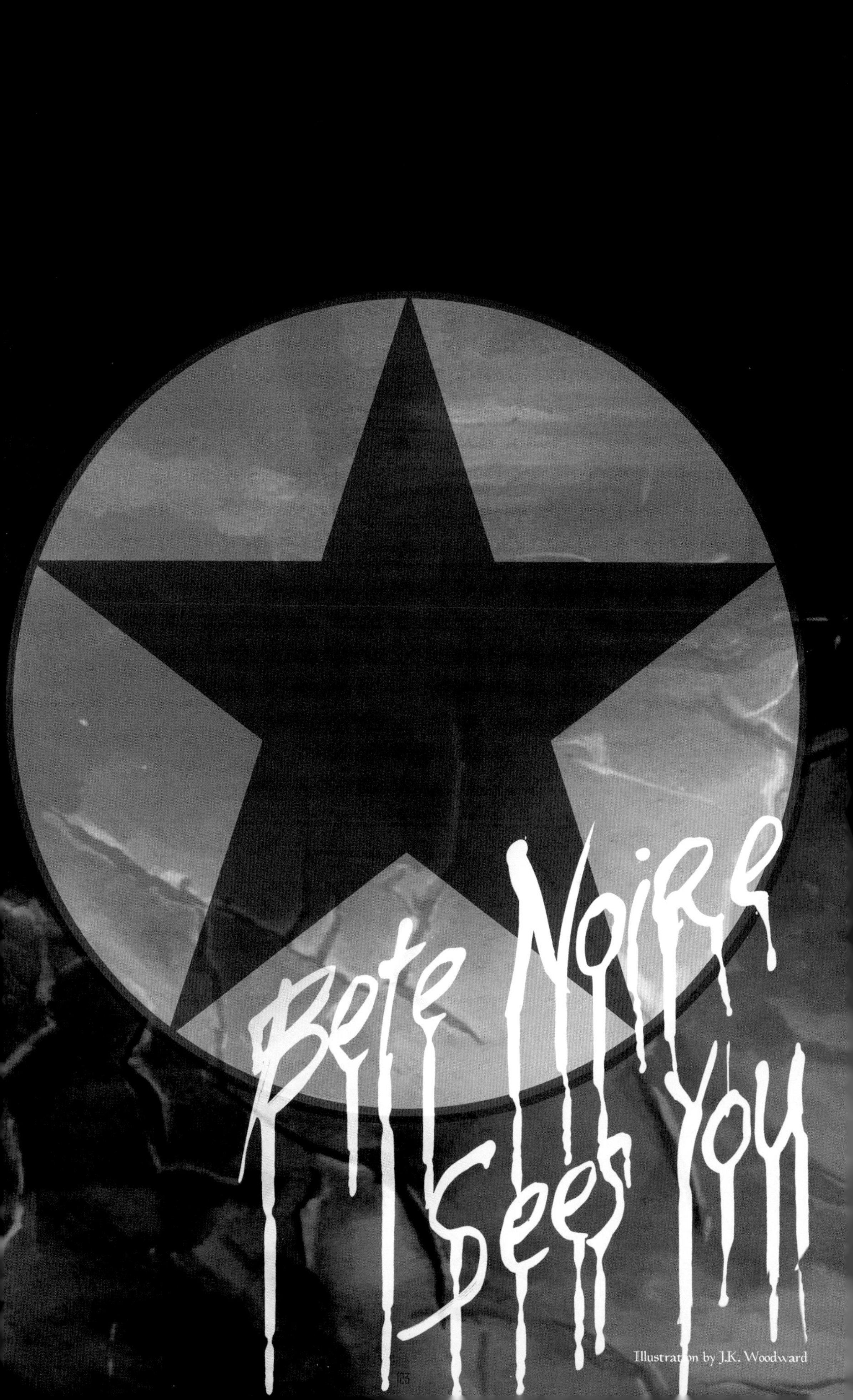
Bete Noire Sees You

Illustration by J.K. Woodward

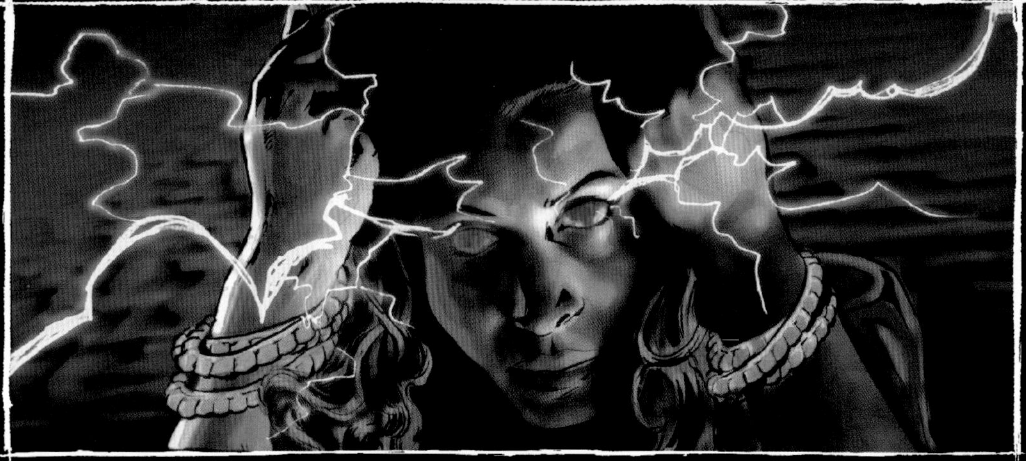

Art Gallery

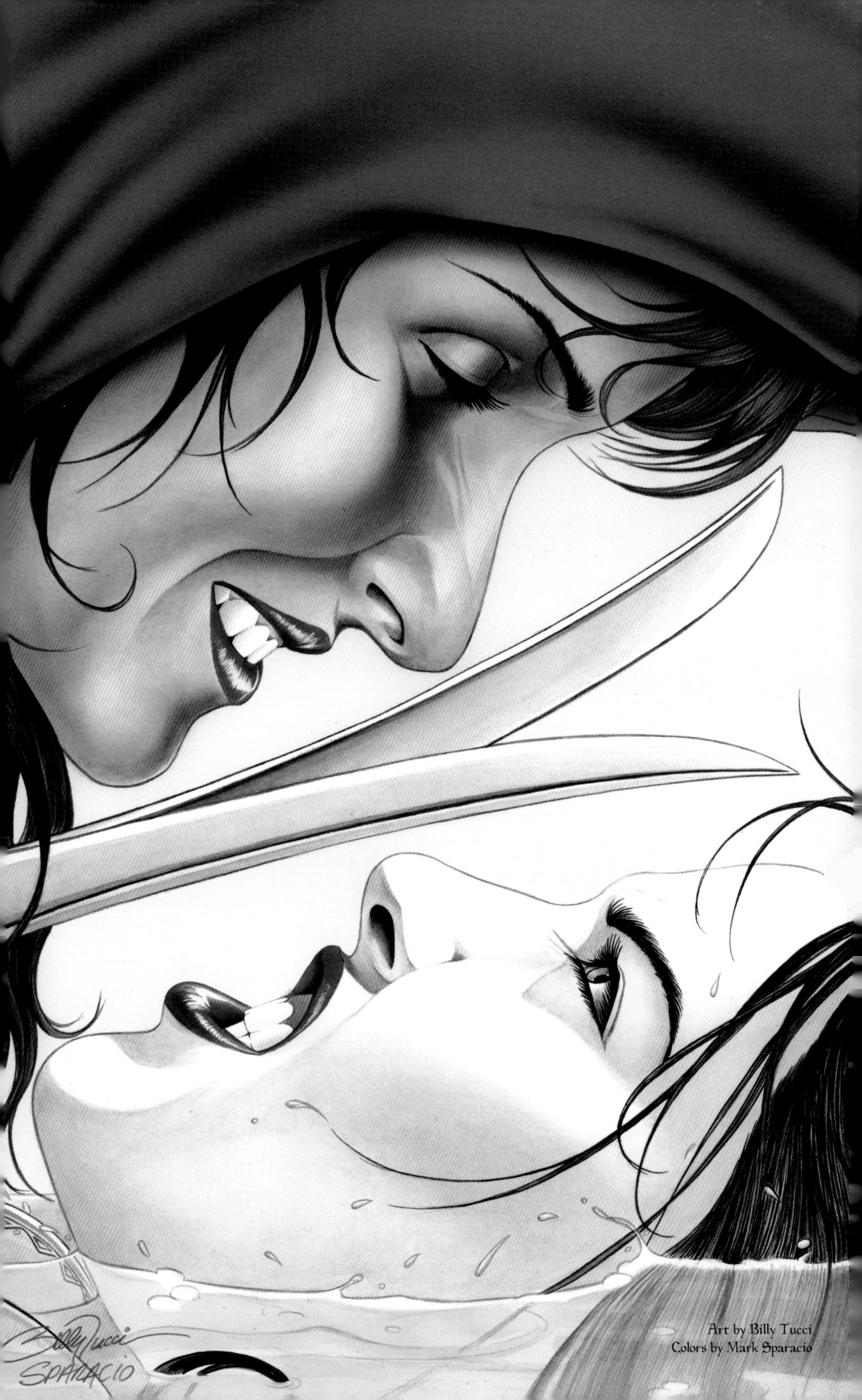

Art by Billy Tucci
Colors by Mark Sparacio

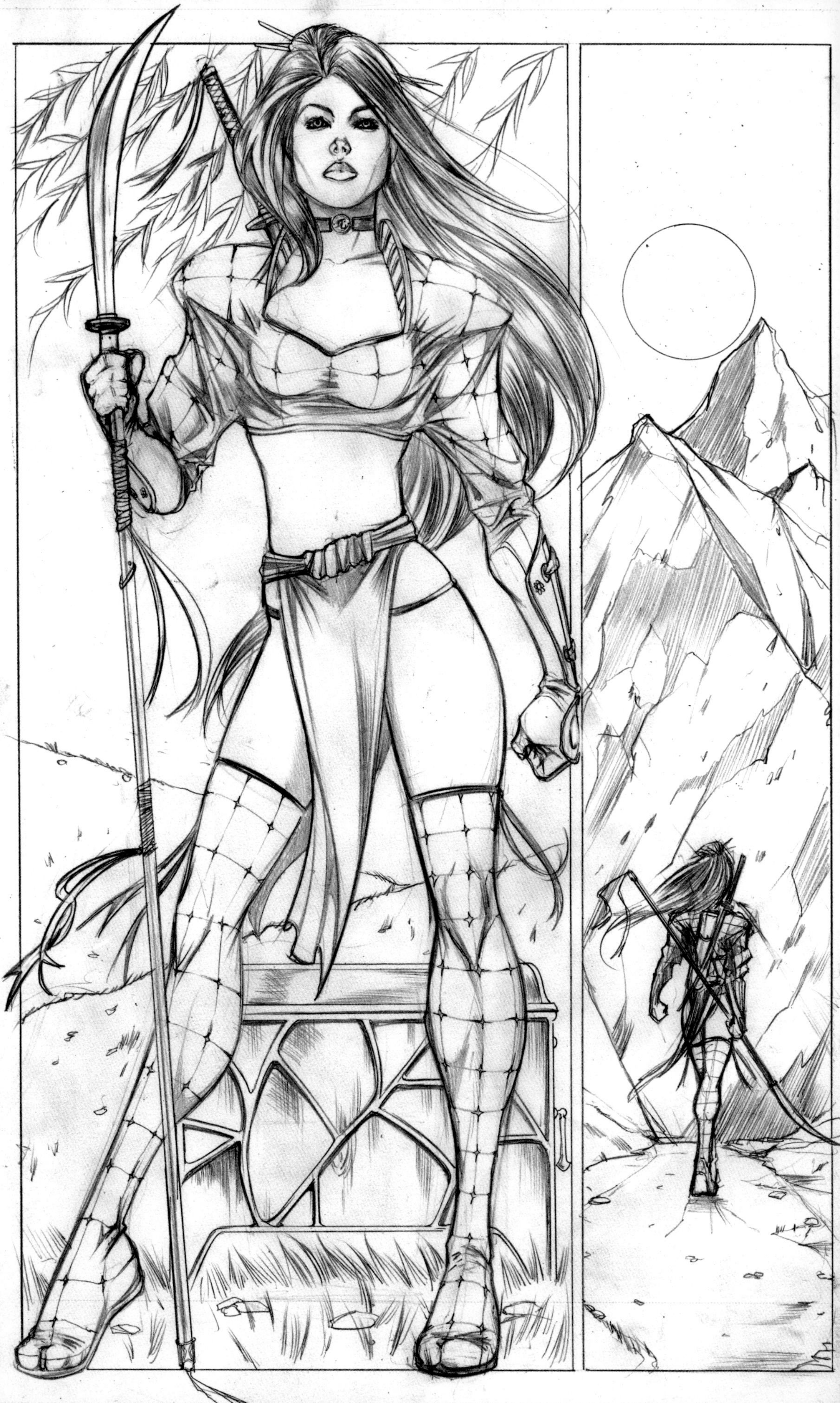

Art by Billy Tucci

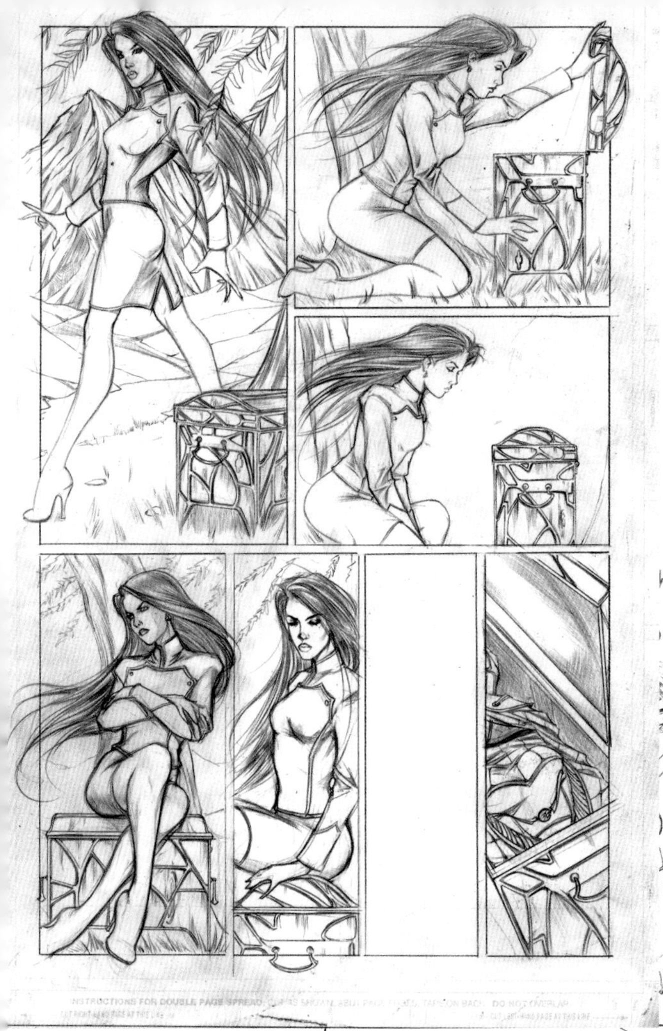

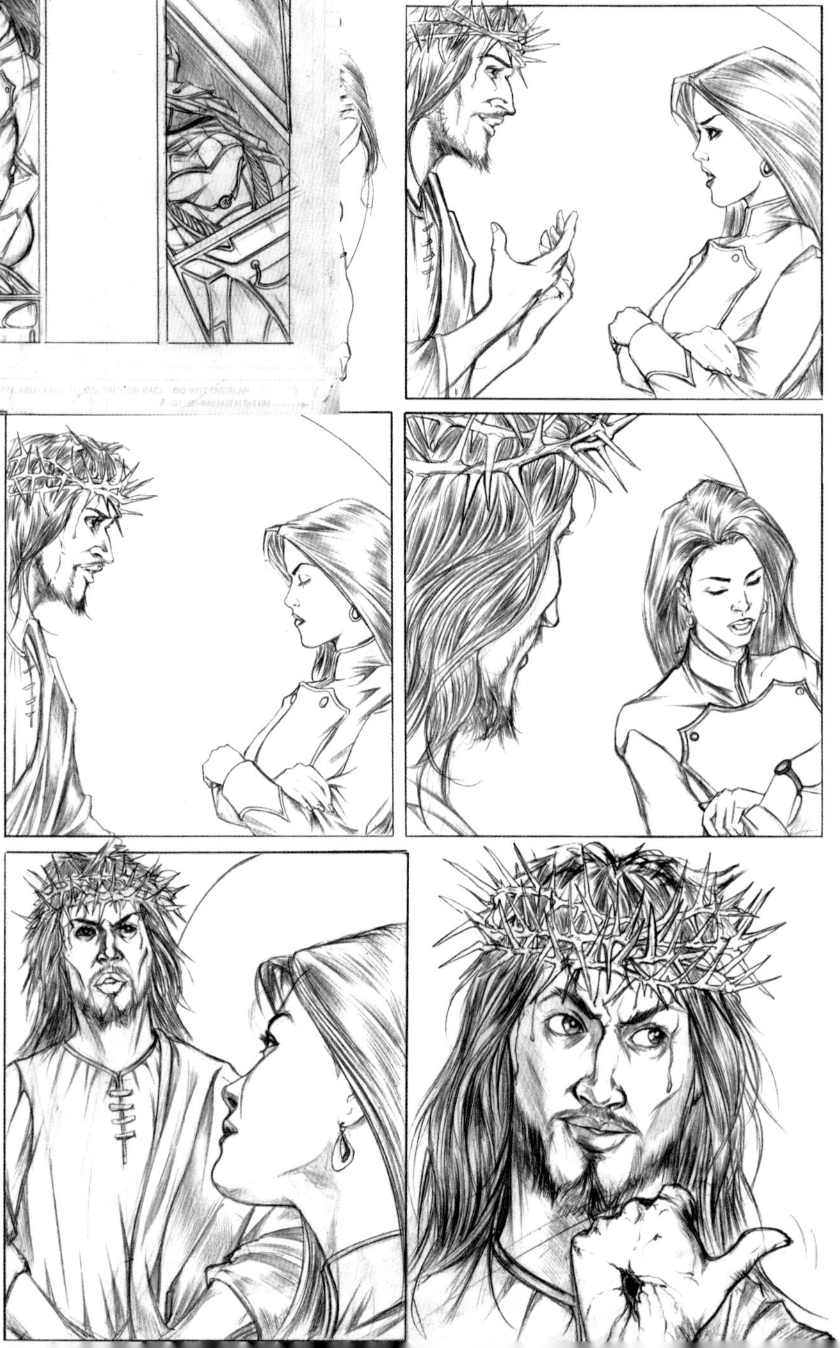

Art by Dennis Calero

9